The Diversity
of Hunter-Gatherer Pasts

The Diversity
of Hunter-Gatherer Pasts

edited by
Bill Finlayson and Graeme Warren

OXBOW | books
Oxford & Philadelphia

Published in the United Kingdom in 2017 by
OXBOW BOOKS
The Old Music Hall, 106–108 Cowley Road, Oxford OX4 1JE

and in the United States by
OXBOW BOOKS
1950 Lawrence Road, Havertown, PA 19083

© Oxbow Books and the individual contributors 2017

Paperback Edition: ISBN 978-1-78570-588-5
Digital Edition: ISBN 978-1-78570-589-2 (epub)

A CIP record for this book is available from the British Library and the Library of Congress

Printed in the United Kingdom by Hobbs the Printers Ltd

For a complete list of Oxbow titles, please contact:

UNITED KINGDOM
Oxbow Books
Telephone (01865) 241249, Fax (01865) 794449
Email: oxbow@oxbowbooks.com
www.oxbowbooks.com

UNITED STATES OF AMERICA
Oxbow Books
Telephone (800) 791-9354, Fax (610) 853-9146
Email: queries@casemateacademic.com
www.casemateacademic.com/oxbow

Oxbow Books is part of the Casemate Group

Front cover: Pillar 43, a monumental decorated t-shaped pillar from the early Neolithic site of Göbekli Tepe in Turkey. Photo: Klaus Schmidt, DAI.
Back cover: A young Raute woman (Highland Nepal) grinds spices using the butt of an axe (goro) as a pestle.
© Jana Fortier

Contents

Contributors

REINHARD BLUMAUER
Vienna. reinhard.blumauer@hotmail.com

ROBERT CARRACEDO-RECASENS
Department of Prehistory, Autonomous
University of Barcelona (UAB),
Bellaterra (Cerdanyola del Vallès).
AGREST Research Group, Barcelona, Spain.
robert.carracedo@uab.cat

JORDI ESTÉVEZ
Dept. of Prehistory. Universitat Autònoma de
Barcelona, 08193 Bellaterra, Catalonia.
email: jordi.estevez@uab.es

BILL FINLAYSON
Council for British Research in the Levant,
10 Carlton House Terrace, London SW1Y 5AH
billfinlayson@cbrl.org.uk

JANA FORTIER
University of California, San Diego (UCSD),
United States of America
jxfortier@gmail.com

ALBERT GARCÍA-PIQUER
Department of Prehistory, Autonomous
University of Barcelona (UAB), Bellaterra
(Cerdanyola del Vallès). AGREST Research Group,
Barcelona, Spain.
alberto.garcia.piquer@uab.cat

PAUL S. GOLDSTEIN
University of California, San Diego (UCSD),
United States of America
psgoldstein@ucsd.edu

COLIN GRIER
Department of Anthropology, Washington State
University, PO Box 644910, Pullman, Washington,
USA 99164-4910. cgrier@wsu.edu

GAIL HITCHENS
Department of Archaeology, University of York,
King's Manor, York, YO1 7EP

MARK J. HUDSON
Mt. Fuji World Heritage Centre for Mountain
Research, Shizuoka, Japan
mark1_hudson@pref.shizuoka.lg.jp

PAUL J. LANE
Department of Archaeology & Ancient History,
Uppsala University, Box 626, 751 26 Uppsala,
Sweden & Honorary Research Fellow, School
of Geography, Archaeology and Environmental
Studies, University of the Witwatersrand, PO Wits
2050, Johannesburg, South Africa.
paul.lane@arkeologi.uu.se

KATHRYN M. DE LUNA
Department of History, Georgetown University
deluna@georgetown.edu

ANDY NEEDHAM
Department of Archaeology, University of York,
King's Manor, York, YO1 7EP

ALFREDO PRIETO
Universidad de Magallanes, Centro Universitario,
Casilla 87 CP. 6160000. Puerto Natales, Chile.
alfredo.prieto@umag.cl

PENNY SPIKINS
Department of Archaeology, University of York,
King's Manor, York, YO1 7EP
penny.spikins@york.ac.uk

GRAEME WARREN
School of Archaeology, University College Dublin,
Newman Building, Belfield, Dublin 4, Ireland.
graeme.warren@ucd.ie

Acknowledgements

This volume derives from a session of the Eleventh Conference on Hunting and Gathering Societies (CHaGS 11), which was held in Vienna in September 2015. We would like to thank the organisers of the conference for the opportunity to run our session and our hosts in Vienna for their excellent hospitality. We are very grateful to all of the participants in the session including those who for varied reasons were not able to contribute to this volume. We would also like to thank the audience for their lively questions.

This volume would not have been possible without the support of Julie Gardiner at Oxbow Books and we are very grateful for her patience. We would also like to thank the referee who reviewed the entire volume and made very helpful comments on many of the papers. Our thanks also to our contributors for their prompt submission of papers and attention to editorial suggestions where required.

Chapter 1

The diversity of hunter-gatherer pasts: an introduction

Bill Finlayson and Graeme Warren

Introduction

This volume has developed from a session of the Eleventh Conference on Hunting and Gathering Societies (CHaGS11) held in Vienna, 9 September 2015. This session explored variation amongst hunting and gathering peoples past and present and the analytical challenges this diversity raises. Given the customary archaeological reliance on analogy, it is important to ask whether conceptions of hunter-gatherers based on recent or contemporary societies (the source- or subject-side of our comparisons) restrict our comprehension of past diversity and of how this changes over the long term (the target- or object-side). This problem is especially important in archaeology, where increasing empirical evidence illustrates ways of life that are not easily encompassed in the range of variation recognised in the contemporary world of hunter-gatherers. Put simply, how do past hunter-gatherers fit into our understandings of hunter-gatherers and the analytical categories we have constructed for these peoples? Such questions have been asked before, in this volume we attempt to go beyond this level of uncertainty, to move beyond archaeology simply being a consumer of modern hunter-gatherer data and consider how to use past diversity to contribute to our wider understanding of hunter-gatherers. This introduction provides a background to the session, highlights key issues in our approaches to diversity and analogy and outlines the structure of the volume as a whole.

Background

Viewed in retrospect, the origins of this volume clearly lie in conversations we had whilst writing *Changing Natures* (Finlayson & Warren 2010). That short book focused on the ways in which many accounts of the transition from hunter-gatherers to agricultural communities in Southwest Asia and Europe were based on simplistic approaches using problematic oppositions between hunter and farmer, mobile and sedentary, wild and domestic. Through a selection of often informal analogies and comparisons, hunter-gatherers had been defined as being radically different from farmers, and farming communities as being very similar to us, regardless of their antiquity. These approaches created analytical distance and difference between groups, and established the perceived significance of the so-called 'Neolithic Revolution' as a movement across a clear boundary. Surprisingly this is not a relict of 19th century models of progress, nor even an example of the overuse of academic shorthands – developments within archaeology, especially in cognitive approaches, were actually sharpening the perceived divide between hunter-gatherer and farmer (Cauvin 2000; Renfrew 2007; Watkins 2005). To our minds, it was clear that modern day analytical concepts, especially commonplace ones, restricted our understanding of past diversity.

This volume returns to these themes in more detail and with expanded geographic and temporal range. Contributors include anthropologists, archaeologists and linguists, and we present material from five continents and from *c.* 250,000 years ago to the present. By bringing in this range of contributors we have been able to enormously expand the scope of this study, which has substantially increased the range of diversity, past and present, which is illustrated.

The study of hunter-gatherer diversity is, of course, nothing new. Robert Kelly's seminal *The Foraging Spectrum: Diversity in Hunting & Gathering Lifeways* was published over 20 years ago (Kelly 1995) and argued that diversity was being downplayed:

> ... for many years the objective of hunter-gatherer research has been to seek out the essential core of the hunter-gatherer lifeway and consequently to ignore or explain away variability as the product of extraordinary natural environments or particular historical circumstance. (Kelly 1995, 2; see also Kelly 2013)

Recent years have seen increased emphasis on the historical agency of hunting and gathering communities (Cannon 2011) and the role of contingency in the historical development of hunting and gathering societies (Sassaman & Holly 2011). These and related studies clearly demonstrate the difficulty of universalising models and large-scale generalisations. Yet it is our belief that, at times, many archaeological approaches involve little more than lip service to the idea of diversity, whilst falling rapidly back on generalisations and so-called established truths about human behaviour. This is especially true of our approaches to hunter-gatherer communities, who are still perceived as forming some kind of base-line from which historical developments take place (see discussion in Finlayson & Warren 2010). Against this background, this volume has two main aims, which we will outline in turn: firstly, to foreground diversity across time and space and secondly, to consider how diversity affects our use of analogy and comparative analysis.

The diversity of hunter-gatherers

Hunter-gatherer is a very broad-brush term that has been invented, defined and redefined many times since the 17th century (Barnard 2004; 2014; Pluciennik 2004).

Different categorisations have been employed in other parts of the world, for example Russia and India, that do not have a one to one correspondence with the European term. The Russian term *pervobytnoe obshchestvo* refers to primordial or primitive society, based on the absence of class distinctions, not the subsistence base (Schweitzer 2001). That hunter-gatherer is a created concept is routinely forgotten in discussions that assume hunter-gatherers are the original society, or that hunter-gatherers represent the only way of life before the development or introduction of farming. Even the reliance on wild foods is a surprisingly weak component of the definition, with debates on modern hunter-gatherer definitions veering from discussion of the percentage of reliance on wild food, to a shift away from a basis on subsistence economy (Panter-Brick *et al.* 2001; Bird-David 1990; Smith 2001). The definition of what is wild or domestic, or the relationship between domesticates and agriculture (Zeder 2015) creates additional problems in the identification of past hunter-gatherers. This definitional struggle illustrates very clearly that hunter-gatherers are not a simple category, but a collection of societies perhaps only held together by the development and flexibility of definition. The strict classification by subsistence that was at its peak in the 1960s (Lee & DeVore 1968) went through the so-called revisionist debate on the existence of pure hunter gatherers (Schrire 1984; Wilmsen *et al.* 1990), and has now been replaced by arguments for unifying concepts of world view (Bird-David 1990; 1992), mode of thought (Barnard 2002; 2007) or, more recently, situation (Widlok 2016).

None of this debate over the definition of hunter-gatherers really succeeded in describing the diversity found both ethnographically and archaeologically. An additional category, a hunter-gatherer subset, was created, and the concept of the 'complex hunter-gatherer' was deployed to describe those societies that did not farm, were largely dependent on highly abundant wild resources, typically marine, and expressed some form of non-egalitarian social organisation (Price & Brown 1985; Arnold 1996; Sassaman 2004; Finlayson 2009). This enabled the idea of the hunter-gatherer, measured from an economic perspective, to continue. The cover photograph on this volume, one of the monumental carved stone 't-shaped' pillars from the early Holocene site of Göbekli Tepe in southern Turkey is part of a massive ceremonial site built by people who clearly did not farm. Their excavator, the late Klaus Schmidt, was adamant that the builders were hunter-gatherers (Schmidt 2006), but this very literal economic definition is an example of the extension of the use of hunter-gatherer beyond its normal meaning. The 'complex hunter-gatherer', introduced in part to rationalise the classification of societies that often shared little apart from their dependence on wild food resources, has a poor fit with the more recent social or ontological definitions. Equally, as discussed by Smith, it failed to deal with societies that are in between definitions of hunter-gatherers and farmers, and simply moved the boundaries to include them within a hunter-gatherer world (Smith 2001).

Such a background to the categorisation of hunter-gatherers should make it immediately apparent that their societies would be highly diverse. Inevitably a significant dependence on wild resources means that relationships with the world, or at least the local environment, will be different from societies who invest more heavily in control over that environment by the production of food. The diversity of environment may therefore be assumed to have a different impact on people, and major axes of variation, such as the degree of dependence on marine, faunal and plant foods have been identified – together with suggested correlated impacts on the construction of society (Binford 2001). This is not to argue that hunter-gatherers do not modify their environments – ironically niche construction theory is far more prevalent in prehistoric hunter-gatherer studies than for prehistoric farmers (Smith 2011; Rowley-Conwy & Layton 2011).

As Kelly observes:

> (w)hatever is commonly associated with ethnographically known hunter-gatherer economies cannot be causally linked with hunting and gathering because hunter-gatherer is a category we impose on human diversity – it is not itself a causal variable. (Kelly 1995, 3)

Precisely because the category of hunter-gatherer is a constructed one, not a natural classification, there has been great analytical emphasis on trying to find meaningful ways to keep its unity. This, in turn, has been essential for archaeological analogy, which works best if universals can be identified in the present and then applied to the past.

Implications of diversity for the use of analogy

Most archaeological analysis involves using things we understand to make sense of things we do not understand. Therefore, analogy is essential to archaeological interpretation and most archaeological statements are analogies (Wylie 1985). However, the inevitably analogical nature of archaeological practice is not always recognised, which can lead to problems in the use of analogy, and in particular in understanding the ways in which analogical reasoning influences our understanding of diversity. In this brief introduction it is not our intention to provide a historical review of the development and use of analogies (Jordan 2006) or ethno-archaeological perspectives (Lane 2014), but simply to highlight some important challenges and themes.

The first challenge in reconciling hunter-gatherer diversity and the use of analogy is the oft-stated risk of turning the past into the mirror of the present. A comparatively small number of ethnographically observed societies are the basis for many formal analogies and informal comparative interpretations of archaeological material (Lane 2014) with obvious implications for our understanding of diversity. In recent years, for example, scholars have recognised that one result of the use of Melanesian and New Guinean analogies in constructing accounts of the Neolithic of Northwestern Europe has been a 'Pacification' of the Neolithic (Roscoe 2009; Spriggs 2008) and it is clear that similar dangers exist in our understanding of hunter-gatherer societies (see Warren this volume).

There are also important issues surrounding access to, and selection of, source side information in constructing analogies. As noted above, there is a geographical limitation to the provision of source side information, and these societies are often located in marginal environments and have been significantly influenced by historical processes operating at global scale, such as the spread of colonial powers. The difficulties this raises in the justification of analogy are well recognised and need not detain us here. More importantly, the existence of a distinction between the analytical perspectives of archaeology and ethnography has long been observed. In 1978, for example, Wobst argued strongly that '(i)f we want to build a truly anthropological theory, capable of predicting behavior (*sic*) whether archaeological or ethnographic, we have to liberate our theories from the biases imposed upon them by the ethnographic record' (Wobst 1978, 303). Wobst's primary concern in his 1978 paper was on the geographical scale of analysis characteristic of archaeological and ethnographic approaches, but very similar concerns have been addressed about the temporal basis of observed behaviour. Grouped under the broad heading of 'time perspectivism' (Bailey 2007; Holdaway & Wandsnider 2008) a number of observers have stressed that observations of behaviour based on the ethnographic instant may not be pertinent for the longer time scales over which archaeological data has formed (Bailey 2007, 200). One of the underlying problems in ethnoarchaeology has always been that while it describes moments in time, it has been unable to contribute to the central archaeological concerns with change, given the inevitably different temporal perspectives of the observations (Bailey 2007). In our terms, the character and expression of diversity in ethnographically recorded societies may not easily be observed in archaeological examples, and the nature of diversity manifest in material remains may not easily map to the life experience of individual agents.

It is also important to note that although ethnoarchaeological research is an explicit attempt to bridge the analytical gaps between different disciplinary perspectives (Politis 2007; Binford 1978) in practice the geographical and thematic diversity of ethnoarchaeological research is conscribed (Lane 2014, 109ff). David and Kramer argue that:

> (a)s archaeologists turned to study cultural evolution and to the reconstruction of human behaviour and past environments, they realized that common-sense reflection on their own experiences and on the wealth of historical and ethnographic information on the world's peoples could no longer be held to constitute an adequate basis for analogical inference. Why? Because the cultural range of Us was too limited for plausible analogical extrapolation to peoples living in distant times, places and contexts. (David and Kramer 2001, 1)

It would appear that we have not sufficiently expanded our sense of possible diversity.

The definition of appropriate 'boundary conditions', or the justification for the selection of a particular comparison, is a particularly vexed subject. Many scholars work within a broadly evolutionary framework: that is to say that they tend to compare hunter-gatherers with hunter-gatherers, even if they may not be explicit about why they think these are the most useful comparisons. This has clear implications for understanding large scale changes in the nature of societies. Alongside this, an ability to provide some kind of historical link between source and target is often seen as significant. This raises important distinctions between regional research traditions. In some parts of the world, such as North America, archaeologists are working on the pasts of indigenous communities. In these situations indigenous perspectives on the nature of society combine with the observations of ethnographers to provide local source side information for archaeological analysis: at the risk of simplifying very crudely, there is a local historical justification for the examination of specific archaeological questions and trajectories. (It is in this sense of the 'direct historical approach' that Philip Phillips famously stated that 'New World archaeology is anthropology or it is nothing' (Phillips 1955, 246–247).) In places like southern Europe no such historical link exists with hunter-gatherer societies and the basis for the selection of analogies is more tenuous.

Finally in considering overarching issues in reconciling diversity and analogies it is important to note that increasingly we recognise societies in the archaeological record that don't seem to have any comparison amongst those observed ethnographically. Often, but not always, these are communities that lie somewhere in Smith's spectrum of low-level food-producers (Smith 2001), perhaps better understood as 'resource' producers (Crawford 2011, 331–332). One of us has already argued (and will discuss below) that the late Pleistocene and early Holocene societies of SW Asia were '... unlike any that exist today or in the ethnographic present' (Finlayson 2013, 134). Such situations raise considerable challenges, given the inevitable use of comparative, analogical reasoning, and highlight the potential danger of mis-using analogy as an end point in interpretation. As Binford argued many years ago, the aim of analogical reasoning is not simply to provide an explanation of the form of the archaeological data, but to seek out new questions about the relationships between social processes and material remains. In his terms, analogy is 'a means for provoking new types of investigation into the order observable in archaeological data' (Binford 1967, 1). Put simply, used carefully and imaginatively, analogy should allow us to consider the social order of non-analogue communities: indeed it may be the only way in which we can construct our knowledge of such societies and expand our appreciation of the nature and causes of diversity.

The structure of this volume

Most of the papers contained in this volume have their roots in presentations given at the seminar in Vienna, with a small number added to address particular themes. We have divided this volume into two thematic sections, the first 'Patterns of Diversity and Change' and the second 'Diversity, comparisons and analogies'. All papers address both themes to greater or lesser extents. For consistency and clarity all dates are presented in calibrated years before present unless stated otherwise.

Our first section, *Patterns of Diversity and Change*, is concerned with illustrating the diversity of hunter-gatherers in the past and present. Importantly, we have tried to observe diversity not as a fixed attribute of specific societies, but as part of a fluid process of change. As argued strongly by Grier (below) although identifying and describing diversity is important, it is not sufficient: analysis should attempt to explain the *causes* of diversity. The papers in this section of our volume all contain a significant diachronic dimension. The time depth that this represents is underlain, more or less explicitly through the various papers, by the role of historical contingency. The very specific examples, and their historic contexts, provide a strong counterbalance to the universals that underpin much analogical argument. Many of the previous debates about the nature of hunting and gathering societies were conducted in part to underwrite the notion of progress, from Morgan's typology of savage, barbarian and civilised, to the means of removing such savage peoples living in a colonial context by denying them any ownership of land due to their lack of fences, enclosures, or agriculture, by denying their humanity, or differentiating them from ourselves by the principles of social evolution (Pluciennik 2014). Hunter-gatherers are therefore contained by a framework made of the checklist of achievements that formed the Neolithic package (agriculture, pastoralism, pottery, sedentism, etc) and fitted the law-like generalisations of the New Archaeology. The historical context that constrains the nature of developments is a good counter to such generalisation, and the problem of an equifinality that sees all farmers as part of the modern world.

The role of historical contingency might be seen as the target of a recent polemical paper that argued strongly against what it describes as historical particularism in research on agricultural origins (Gremillion *et al.* 2014). While Gremillion and colleagues welcome recent enhancements to the empirical record, and the recognition of variable routes to emergent food production, they argue that there has been a consequent loss of enthusiasm for general explanations (especially those based in human behavioural ecology and in particular optimal foraging theory) for the transition to agriculture. However, general models have not been thrown out, indeed historically specific analyses have shown various forms of optimal foraging theory, such as diet breadth models, to be innappropriate in all the major regions of agricultural innovation, and the early stages of food production seem far better suited to cultural niche construction models (Zeder 2012; 2015; Smith 2015). There are other flaws in the attack on historical approaches, such as confusion between concepts of the rational actor in optimisation models, and the role of agency, where 'decision makers have complete information about the long-term consequences of their actions' (Gremillion *et al.* 2014, 6173). Agency theory, in contrast to the optimising rational actor, recognises that the unintended consequences of agency are often the most important. This is particularly relevant to the developments of both domestication and agriculture, where the long-term consequences of actions clearly could not be conceived in advance.

The focus of Gremillion *et al.* is almost exclusively on economic behaviour, and that is perhaps at the heart of the problem of their critique of historical analysis.

Although the gulf between the study of hunter-gatherers and farmers, characterised by research on subsistence as opposed to society, may have narrowed in recent years, there is still a shift in archaeological focus over this transition. We need not be as extreme as Cauvin, who saw the Neolithic as the start of history (Cauvin 2000), to recognise that the Neolithic transformation is as much characterised by social, as economic, change. Equally, evolutionary theory is not denied when we note that, in contrast to most optimal foraging models, the social changes associated with the Neolithic often appear to drive the economic ones.

The diversity amongst hunter-gatherers and low-level food producers that is presented in this volume illustrates the weaknesses of general theory based on subsistence based generalisation, and arguments that propose that diversity is about a trajectory of development to a particular goal. In reality, the degree of diversity from place and time to place and time means that we are simply not comparing like with like, and the historic pathways taken do not start or end in the same places.

Grier's paper focuses on the Coast Salish of the Northwest Coast of North America. Hunter-gatherer societies of this region have long been associated with the origins and rise of 'complexity'. Grier demonstrates that significant diversity exists within this broad classification and, most importantly, that this diversity is explicable by reference to the playing out of organisational principles over time. Combining archaeological and ethnographic data he demonstrates how historical trajectories involving the 'the physical and long-term construction of place, ownership and the maintenance of economic diversity, proprietorship, and local autonomy' generate specific forms of social organisation in the present.

Kathryn De Luna uses historical linguistic perspectives to examine changing ideas of 'bushcraft' or food collection in food producing societies in Central Africa. Comparing and contrasting western ideas about subsistence with a historic approach to the concept of bushcraft expressed in the Boatwe languages shows that many of the distinctions we hold between forms of subsistence practice are not meaningful in a Central African context. This also shows a diverse range of social and political changes that can be associated with subsistence change, providing some contrast to simplistic notions of farming being linked to particular forms of organisation.

In 'The end of hunting and gathering' Bill Finlayson examines the remarkable societies who lived in the Levant at the end of the Pleistocene and start of the Holocene. These societies are typically conceived as (complex) hunter-gatherers who change into farmers through a revolutionary process of transformation. Finlayson demonstrates that these are societies unlike any known ethnographically, and shows how the use of simplistic ethnographic analogies reduces our understanding of hunter-gatherer diversity.

Hudson provides a proto-historical analysis of diversity amongst hunter-gatherers in northern Japan. A combination of archaeological and historical analysis allows him to introduce a number of unusual concepts into hunter-gatherer studies, not only the idea of Iron Age hunter-gatherers, but also 'trade-based' hunter-gatherers. The historical accounts that he uses serve to remind that there is considerable antiquity to the marginalisation of hunter-gatherers, as various groups collectively described as 'Emishi' included farmers and hunter-gatherers, unified by their opposition to political control. Archaeological diversity was not always matched by historical classifications.

Jordi Estévez and Alfredo Prieto present a comparative long-term analysis of the development of hunting and gathering societies at opposite ends of the Pacific Coast of America in Tierra del Fuego and in the Northwest coast. Using a historically materialist perspective, they examine how the ways in which hunting and gathering societies control social production and reproduction as ways of managing demographic trends influences their long term development. In particular they highlight how resource intensification in the Northwest example contrasts with the imposition of demographic controls in Tierra del Fuego. As with Grier's analysis, the result is an explanation of diverse forms of social practice, not simply a description of the existence of diversity.

Our second thematic section, *Diversity, Comparisons and Analogies*, develops the theme of diversity and considers what the implications of this diversity may be for archaeology and analogy. This includes a focus on the nature of claimed equivalences in analogical reasoning, comparisons between archaeological, ethnographic and (in one instance) linguistic perspectives, and an explicit concern about the application of analogies to the comparatively deep past. All of these papers accept that the study of hunter-gatherers is inevitably comparative, and that this carries implications for our analytical practice.

Fittingly, for a volume based on a conference that took place in Vienna, Reinhard Blumauer's contribution re-visits the Viennese School of Ethnology of the early 20th century. This culture-historical approach to human variation across space and time 'developed a scheme of a universal world history that combined, at least theoretically, cultural anthropology and archaeology with a special focus ... on hunter-gatherer societies'. Many aspects of these approaches are now discredited, especially the idea of some modern hunter-gatherers representing an original culture, or *Urkultur*. However, Blumauer demonstrates that there is still value in considering how these scholars understood difference and similarity and the ways in which overarching theoretical frameworks allow researchers from different disciplines to collaborate in understanding human diversity.

Robert Carracedo-Recasens and Albert García-Piquer return our focus to Tierra del Fuego and outline an 'experimental ethnoarchaeological approach' which combines ethnographic observations with archaeological data, examining how our understanding of a hunting and gathering society differs depending on which source of evidence is used. They develop a quantitative approach to examine whether ethnographically observed inequality in hunter-gatherer societies is present at archaeological time scales and conclude that discrimination against females was important in Tierra del Fuego.

It is an oft-made claim that humans have lived as hunter-gatherers for 90% or 99% of the existence of our species, with the exact time period being determined by when we define the appearance of the first humans to have been. Barker, for example, argues that 'humans have occupied our planet for several millions years, but for almost all of that period that have lived as foragers, by various combinations of gathering, collecting, scavenging, fishing and hunting' (Barker 2006, 1). Archaeologists often focus on the points at which people stop being hunter-gatherers and become farmers. We have spent much less time asking when did we start to live in the kinds of hunter-gatherer societies observed ethnographically. This is especially important in the long term of human evolution which may include different species of humans: beyond the platitude that they hunted and gathered wild foods, were *Homo neanderthalensis*, or *Homo floresiensis* hunter-gatherers in the sense that we often use this term? These critical questions frame Penny Spikins' discussion of the use of ethnographic analogies to understand Neanderthal lives. Spikins argues that many aspects of the material records from Neanderthal Europe suggest that their social organisation was different from the models of hunter-gatherer models that are sometimes imposed on them.

Graeme Warren's chapter examines how analogy has been used in constructing narratives about Mesolithic Europe. He argues that analogies have become common place and that a small number of generalisations are dominating our approaches to the period, making the past seem very familiar. Against this background he highlights aspects of Mesolithic behaviour that speak to different forms of hunter-gatherer practice, and different approaches to the past.

The final paper in Part 2, by Jana Fortier and Paul S. Goldstein, focuses on Highland Nepal, and examines the potential use of ethnographic analogies to make sense of the archaeological record from this region. Fortier and Goldstein compare ethnographic observations of the Raute, supported by evidence of linguistic continuity where possible, with aspects of the archaeological record. They argue that combinations of environmental, linguistic and historical links help to create the most robust forms of analogy.

The volume concludes with a review of the papers by Paul Lane. Lane argues that the papers 'destabilise' common archaeological useages of terms such as hunter-gatherer and forager, and that they highlight the importance of historicising hunter-gatherer practices. He identifies four 'contexts' that shape the discussions of diversity in the different chapters: the contexts within which hunter-gatherer lives were and are lived; the context of our research traditions; the context of change and continuity over time; and finally the relationship of context and analogy. Lane's conclusion is that what 'the chapters in this volume accomplish is to highlight just how diverse and how complex the concept of HFG (*hunter-fisher-gatherers*) diversity really is, and hence also just how necessary it is to deconstruct the concept and the taken-for-granted assumptions concerning HFGs on which it is based'.

This is much in keeping with our own assessment of the volume, which we believes adds to the wider debate on what hunter-gatherers are, and illustrates how archaeology now makes an important contribution to this study.

References

Arnold, J. E. (1996) The archaeology of complex hunter-gatherers. *Journal of Archaeological Method and Theory* 3, 77–126.

Bailey, G. (2007) Time perspectives, palimpsests and the archaeology of time. *Journal of Anthropological Archaeology* 26, 198–223.

Barker, G. (2006) *The Agricultural Revolution in Prehistory: Why did Foragers become Farmers?* Oxford, Oxford University Press.

Barnard, A. (2002) The foraging mode of thought. In H. Stewart, A. Barnard & K. Omura (eds) *Self- and Other Images of Hunter-gatherers*, 5–24. Senri Ethnological Studies 60. Osaka, National Museum of Ethnology.

Barnard, A. (2004) Hunting-and-gathering society: an eighteenth century Scottish invention. In A. Barnard (ed.), *Hunter-Gatherers in History, Archaeology and Anthropology*, 31–43. Oxford, Berg.

Barnard, A. (2007) From Mesolithic to Neolithic modes of thought. In A. Whittle & V. Cummings (eds), *Going Over: the Mesolithic–Neolithic Transition in North-West Europe*, Proceedings of the British Academy 144, 5–19. London, British Academy.

Barnard, A. (2014) Defining Hunter-Gatherers: Enlightenment, Romantic and Social Evolutionary Perspectives. In V. Cummings, P. Jordan & M. Zvelebil (eds) *The Oxford Handbook of the Archaeology and Anthropology of Hunter-gatherers*, 43–54. Oxford, Oxford University Press.

Binford, L. R. (1967) Smudge pits and hide smoking: the use of analogy in archaeological reasoning. *American Antiquity* 32, 1–12.

Binford, L. R. (1978) *Nunamiut Ethnoarchaeology*. London, Academic Press.

Binford, L. R. (2001) *Constructing Frames of Reference: an Analytical Method for Archaeological Theory Building Using Ethnographic Data Sets*. Berkley, University of California Press.

Bird-David, N. (1990) The giving environment: another perspective on the economic system of hunter-gatherers. *Current Anthropology* 31, 183–196.

Bird-David, N. (1992) Beyond 'The hunting and gathering mode of subsistence': culture-sensitive observations on the Nyaka and other modern hunter-gatherers. *Man* 27, 19–44.

Cannon, A. (ed). (2011) *Structured Worlds: The Archaeology of Hunter-Gatherer Thought and Action*. Sheffield, Equinox Publishing.

Cauvin, J. (2000) *The Birth of the Gods and the Origins of Agriculture* (trans. T. Watkins). Cambridge, Cambridge University Press.

Crawford, G. W. (2011) Advances in understanding early agriculture in Japan. *Current Anthropology* 52, S331–S345.

David, N. & Kramer, C. (2001) *Ethnoarchaeology in Action*. Cambridge, Cambridge University Press.

Finlayson, B. (2009) The 'Complex Hunter-gatherer' and the transition to farming. In N. Finlay; S.McCartan . N. Milner & C Wickham-Jones (eds), *From Bann Flakes to Bushmills; Papers in Honour of Professor Peter Woodman*, 175–188. Prehistoric Society Research Papers 1. Oxford, Prehistoric Society and Oxbow Books.

Finlayson, B. (2013) Imposing the Neolithic on the past. *Levant* 45, 133–148.

Finlayson, B. & Warren, G. (2010) *Changing Natures: Hunter-Gatherers, First Farmers and the Modern World*. London, Duckworths.

Gremillion, K. J., Barton, L. & Piperno, D. R. (2014) Particularism and the retreat from theory in the archaeology of agricultural origins. *Proceedings of the National Academy of Sciences* 111, 6171–6177.

Holdaway, S. & Wandsnider, L. (eds) (2008) *Time in Archaeology: Time Perspectivism Revisited*. Salt Lake City, University of Utah Press.

Jordan, P. (2006) Analogy. In C. Conneller & G. M. Warren (eds), *Mesolithic Britain and Ireland: New Approaches*, 83–100. Stroud, Tempus.

Kelly, R. L. (1995) *The Foraging Spectrum: Diversity in Hunter-gatherer Lifeways*. London, Smithsonian Institute Press.

Kelly R. L. (2013) *The lifeways of Hunter-Gatherers: The Foraging Spectrum*. Cambridge, Cambridge University Press.

Lane, P. J. (2014) Hunter-gatherer-fishers, ethnoarchaeology and analogical reasoning. In V. Cummings, P. Jordan & M. Zvelebil (eds), *The Oxford Handbook of the Archaeology and Anthropology of Hunter-gatherers*, 104–150. Oxford, Oxford University Press.

Lee, R. & DeVore, I. (eds) (1968) *Man the Hunter*. Chicago, Alidine.

Panter-Brick, C., Layton, R. H. & Rowley-Conwy, P. (2001) Lines of enquiry. In C. Panter-Brick, R. Layton & P. Rowley-Conwy (eds), *Hunter-gatherers: an Interdisciplinary Perspective*, 1–11. Cambridge, Cambridge University Press.

Phillips, P. (1955) American archaeology and general anthropological theory. *Southwestern Journal of Anthropology* 11, 246–250.

Pluciennik, M. (2004) The meaning of 'hunter-gatherers' and modes of subsistence: a comparative historical perspective. In A. Barnard (ed.), *Hunter-Gatherers in History, Archaeology and Anthropology*, 17–29. Oxford, Berg.

Politis, G. G. (2007) *Nukak: Ethnoarchaeology of an Amzonian People*. Walnut Creek, Left Coast Press.

Price, D. T., Brown, J. A. (1985) Aspects of hunter-gatherer complexity. In D. T. Price & J. A. Brown (eds), *Prehistorc Hunter-Gatherers: the Emergence of Complexity*, 3–20. Orlando, Academic Press.

Renfrew, C. (2007) *Prehistory: the Making of the Human Mind*. London, Weidenfeld & Nicolson.

Roscoe, P. (2009) On the 'pacification' of the European Neolithic: ethnographic analogy and the neglect of history. *World Archaeology* 41, 578–588.

Rowley-Conwy, P. & Layton, R. (2011) Foraging and farming as niche construction: stable and unstable adaptations. *Philosophical Transactions of the Royal Society B: Biological Sciences* 366, 849–862.

Sassaman, K. E. (2004) Complex hunter–gatherers in evolution and history: a North American perspective. *Journal of Archaeological Research* 12, 227–280.

Sassaman, K. E. & Holly, D. H. (eds) (2011) *Hunter-Gatherer Archaeology as Historical Process*. Tucson, University of Arizona Press.

Schrire, C. (1984) Wild surmises on savage thoughts. In C. Schrire (ed.), *Past and Present in Hunter Gatherer Studies*, 1–25. Orlando, Academic Press.

Schmidt, K. (2006) *Sie bauten die ersten Tempel*. Munich, C.H. Beck.

Schweitzer, P. (2001) Silence and other misunderstandings: Russian anthropology, Western Hunter-gatherer debates, and Siberian peoples. In P. Schweitzer, M. Biesele & R. Hitchcock (eds), *Hunters & Gatherers in the Modern World: Conflict, Resistance, and Self-Determination*, 29–51. Oxford, Berghahn.

Smith, B. (2011) A cultural niche construction theory of initial domestication. *Biological Theory* 6, 260–271.

Smith, B. (2015) A comparison of niche construction theory and diet breadth models as explanatory frameworks for the initial domestication of plants and animals. *Journal of Archaeological Research* 23, 215–262.

Smith, B. D. (2001) Low-Level Food Production. *Journal of Archaeological Research* 9, 1–43.

Spriggs, M. (2008) Ethnographic parallels and the denial of history. *World Archaeology* 40, 538–552.

Watkins, T. (2005) The Neolithic Revolution and the emergence of humanity: a cognitive approach to the first comprehensive world view. In J. Clake (ed.), *Archaeological Perspectives on the Transmission and Transformation of Culture in the Eastern Mediterranean*, 84–88. Levant Supplementary Series 2. Oxford, Oxbow Books and Council for British Research in the Levant.

Widlok, T. (2016) Hunter-gatherer situations. *Hunter Gatherer Research* 2, 127–143.

Wilmsen, E. N., Denbow, J. R., Bicchieri, M. G., Binford, L. R., Gordon, R., Guenther, M., Lee, R. B., Ross, R., Solway, J. S., Tanaka, J., Vansina, J. and Yellen, J. E. (1990) Paradigmatic history of San-Speaking peoples and current attempts at revision [and comments and replies]. *Current Anthropology* 31, 489–524.

Wobst, H. M. (1978) The archaeo-ethnology of hunter-gatherers or the tyranny of the ethnographic record in archaeology. *American Antiquity* 43, 303–309.

Wylie, A. (1985) The reaction against analogy. *Advances in Archaeological Method and Theory* 8, 63–111.

Zeder, M. A. (2012) The broad spectrum revolution at 40: resource diversity, intensification, and an alternative to optimal foraging explanations. *Journal of Anthropological Archaeology* 31, 241–264.

Zeder, M. A. (2015) Core questions in domestication research. *Proceedings of the National Academy of Sciences* 112, 3191–3198.

Part 1: Patterns of diversity and change

Chapter 2

Expanding notions of hunter-gatherer diversity: identifying core organisational principles and practices in Coast Salish societies of the northwest Coast of North America

Colin Grier

Introduction

The diversity of hunter-gatherer lifeways has been significantly narrowed by western colonial expansion over the last 500 years. While new forms of hunter-gatherer organisation emerged as a result of contact with states (Martindale 2003; Wilmsen 1983), many examples disappeared as a result of contact, or even in advance of it (Pluciennik 2004; Murdock 1968, 13). An unknown number went incompletely or perhaps entirely undocumented (Burch 1994; Layton 2001). As a result, our understanding of hunter-gatherer diversity is incomplete when read from ethnographic and historical records. By extension, anthropological models generated from those datasets inadequately account for the organisational breadth of small-scale human societies (Ames 2004).

Since its inception, the term 'hunter-gatherer' has served to identify a distinct category of societies that existed without agriculture, centralised governments and structural inequalities (Rowley-Conwy 2001). While this distinction has expanded our view of the human organisational strategies that are possible, reification of the hunter-gatherer/agricultural divide has emphasised differences while cloaking many aspects of diversity within hunter-gatherers themselves (Feit 1994; Rowley-Conwy 2001). The development of the complex hunter-gatherer (CHG) concept some three decades ago has helped address this problem (e.g., Arnold 1993; Price & Brown 1985; Koyama & Thomas 1981; Woodburn 1982). Recognition of CHGs has focused our attention on hunter-gatherers that existed in productive rather than marginal environments, and which seemingly had more complicated and specialised economic, social and political arrangements. Affluent foragers (Koyama & Thomas 1981; Kim & Grier 2006), delayed return systems (Woodburn 1982), and transegalitarian societies

(Hayden 1995) are just a few of the anthropological and archaeological terms advanced to capture this complexity.

But CHGs are themselves an incredibly diverse set of societies, and are not best characterised by general or essentialist anthropological models or trait lists. Northwest Coast societies as they have been described ethnographically, and, to a lesser extent, reconstructed through archaeology are often invoked as the archetype of CHGs. Yet, the Northwest Coast also contains diversity that goes unrecognised outside of, and even sometimes within, anthropological and archaeological research on the coast (e.g., Sassaman 2004; Estevez & Vila 2010).

My objective in this paper is to highlight the organisational principles of the Coast Salish peoples of the central Northwest Coast of North America. Coast Salish traditional territory includes most of coastal southwestern British Columbia and northwestern Washington State – an area known as the Salish Sea (Fig. 2.1). A developing thread of

Figure 2.1. Location of the Coast Salish region within the Northwestern Coast of North America.

research in this region focuses on the need to move beyond traditional anthropological models and typologies, instead drawing critically on ethnography, revamping the role of analogy, and utilising some novel theoretical perspectives (e.g., Angelbeck 2009; Angelbeck & Grier 2012; Grier & Angelbeck 2017; Schaepe 2009; Thom 2005; 2010). The objective of this scholarship is to adequately characterise how Coast Salish peoples have organised themselves economically, socially and politically for the last three millennia. This research considers Coast Salish societies on their own terms rather than with reference to generalised models.

In this paper, I draw together several threads of this recent research, and carry the project forward by outlining what I see as the core elements of Coast Salish practices over their long-term history. Drawing on ethnographic and archaeological data, I argue that four principles have been and continue to be key to the organisation of Coast Salish societies. These include (1) the physical and long-term construction of place, (2) ownership and the maintenance of economic diversity, (3) proprietorship and (4) local autonomy. I take these up individually below, with the objective of illustrating these overarching organisational principles and practices so as to add significantly to our conception of how non-agricultural, small scale societies can be organised. In the final section I address why this diversity matters in the bigger picture, considering some examples of how recognition of this diversity expands our possibilities for action in the world both in the present and for the future.

Facing up to diversity: the Northwest Coast and complex hunter-gatherers

The Northwest Coast has long been viewed as an exception to overarching trajectories of social evolution, in that these societies do not fall neatly in a linear view of social evolution from simple to complex, from small to large scale, and from egalitarian to centralised and hierarchical forms of sociopolitical organisation (Cannon 2001; Moss 2011). Ostensibly, this is because Northwest Coast societies have elements of agricultural-based, hierarchical societies but retained an economy that relied on food acquisition rather than food production (Deur & Turner 2005; Smith 2001). As such, they have been situated as a bridge between foraging hunter-gatherers and agricultural systems (e.g., Johnson & Earle 2000; Hayden 1995). Alternatively, they have been described as essentially unrecognised chiefdoms, which allows them to be comfortably fitted back into the classic band-tribe-chiefdoms-states typology (Arnold *et al.* 2015; Miller & Boxberger 1994).

But both solutions to the Northwest Coast 'problem' have been critiqued within Northwest Coast scholarship (Angelbeck & Grier 2012; Cannon 2001; Grier 2007; Miller & Boxberger 1994; Moss 2011) and as a more general proposition outside the region (Rowley-Conwy 2001; Sassaman 2004). Much of this critique is a rejection of efforts to shoehorn variability into narrow categories, typologies and trajectories in order to preserve inadequate models of diversity and culture change. This critique also attempts to appropriately recognise the dynamic rather than unilinear histories of small-scale societies in many regions the world (Moss 2011; Pauketat 2007).

I do not intend to revisit these arguments in detail here, but wish to emphasise that the way forward must involve approaching societies on their own terms, and analyses must proceed with the objective of accounting for diversity rather than simply categorising it. Clearly, ordering diversity is a necessary step in confronting the complexity of the archaeological and ethnographic records, but is not an end in itself.

Analogy on the Northwest Coast: some considerations

Recognising diversity is intimately connected to where we get our ideas to evaluate and make sense of our data. In North American archaeology, the ethnographic record has provided a deep well of possibilities to account for patterns seen in the archaeological record (Grier 2007). But the ethnographic record documents a time of profound change, and so its relationship to deep time is not unproblematic. Also, many aspects of the ethnographic record may be capricious, situational or incomplete observations rather than reflective of core structural elements or patterns (Miller 2004).

Nonetheless, on the Northwest Coast ethnographic descriptions have been employed quite straightforwardly in archaeological reconstructions of the past. Ethnographic insights should not be rejected outright, of course, since these illuminate practices that might not be gleaned otherwise. To cite a couple of specific examples, we might have little knowledge of the possibility for slavery or stratified social classes in hunter-gatherer societies without the benefit of the ethnographic record. Also, despite changes associated with contact and colonisation over the last two centuries, the Northwest Coast ethnographic record undoubtedly reveals elements of long-standing practices that reflect deeply entrenched historical structures. Systems under stress, as they clearly were in the historic period, can reveal their inner workings with unusual clarity. But, because of its potential perils, the ethnographic record should be thought of as a source of testable hypotheses concerning the past rather than 'off-the-shelf' explanations for our observations (Grier 2007; Moss 2011).

At a higher theoretical level, the problem, as outlined in Grier (2007) and Moss (2011), has been a fixation with explaining ethnographic expressions of Northwest Coast societies as straightforward culminations of deep evolutionary trajectories (Cannon 2001). This produces an accounting for long-term history that is teleological, in that the end product appears as an inevitable unfolding of a relatively scripted process. In recent years, Northwest Coast archaeology has moved away from such unilinear, evolutionary-driven histories (Grier 2014a). But in that shift we must be cautious to avoid veering towards an ahistorical recounting of diversity for diversity's sake. The critical element, as I advocate here, is not only to promote recognition of diversity, but to reconstruct dynamic histories and long-term trajectories of change that produced that diversity, and that these derive from principles and practices that have temporal persistence. This offers an opportunity to have historical processes front and centre in explanations. For this, ethnography is useful (when handled properly) but is not enough. If our overarching objective is to confirm ethnographic observations with archaeological data, we limit the possibility to learn anything new and recognise organisational forms that are not described in ethnographies (Grier 2007).

Core principles

In a 2012 paper, Bill Angelbeck and I attempted to explicate Coast Salish economic, social and political organisation over the latter half of the Holocene. Coast Salish practices – primarily ethnographic but as hinted at archaeologically – were simply not effectively captured through current approaches based in progressive complexity and standard typologies (Angelbeck & Grier 2012). We drew on the theory of anarchism as a basis for contextualising Coast Salish practices because the principles of anarchism, including autonomy, justified authority, and resistance to centralisation, seemed to mirror the fundamentals of Coast Salish organisation (Thom 2010).

The point, however, was not to label Salish peoples as anarchists, nor was it to place Salish societies into some new category of anarchic societies with certain properties. The objective was to identify foundational principles that accounted for the dynamic practices in Coast Salish history. The tensions in operationalising and maintaining these principles played out in novel ways over long stretches of time. We therefore approached the problem as a form of historical analysis, revealing the consistent tension between autonomy and centralisation as a dynamic in structuring Coast Salish history. We also argued that Coast Salish history illustrates the emergence of institutionalised inequalities and other aspects of complexity in a decentralised rather than hierarchical form.

While anarchism was a useful body of theory to structure such an analysis, the principles of anarchism are somewhat abstract, and, as presented in academic contexts, specific to late 19th century European political history. It is therefore important to contextualise these general principles in terms of Coast Salish specifics. This is the objective of the remainder of this paper. Below, I identify and discuss four elements of Coast Salish society past and present that can productively be described as core principles: (1) physical and long-term construction of place, (2) ownership and the maintenance of resource diversity, (3) proprietorship and (4) local autonomy.

The physical and long-term construction of place

Hunter-gatherers, including those of the Northwest Coast, have typically been viewed as having limited impacts on their environments, rarely modifying their landscapes in intentional or planned ways (Deur & Turner 2005; Grier 2014b). This view has been slowly eroding through the study of complex hunter-gatherers around the world. For example, work on the Archaic period of the US southeast and Florida has revealed a long tradition of construction of monumental earthworks by hunter-gatherers over much of the Holocene (Gibson & Carr 2004; Randall 2015; Sassaman 2004; Schwadron 2010).

Recent archaeological data and ethnographic analyses from the Northwest Coast also point to significant physical modifications of places both unintentionally and intentionally, in two respects. First, large-scale production features that can be legitimately described as monumental (that is, involving substantial inputs of labour) have been documented, including features such as clam gardens (Grier 2014b; Lepofsky *et al.* 2015), fish traps and weirs (Caldwell *et al.* 2012; Greene *et al.* 2015; Monks 1987) and plant gardens (Deur 2000).

Second, along with these resource production features, substantial landscape terraforming and constriction is evident. My recent fieldwork has focused on a series of long-standing settlement locations in the southern Gulf Islands of the Strait of Georgia. Known as coastal spit locations, these low-lying landforms developed as long-term settlements initially in the mid-Holocene. Their form is primarily anthropogenic, having been constructed and maintained through the intentional deposition of shell midden and other material for various purposes, including the creation of freshwater bogs and to protect low-lying land from sea inundation (Grier *et al.* 2009). The large-scale terraforming of undulating and sloped natural locations to accommodate cedar plankhouses (Grier 2003; 2014b) and the construction of fortified earthworks for defensive purposes (Angelbeck 2009) were similarly monumental undertakings.

Beyond the physical construction of places, ethnographic literature in the Coast Salish region and across the greater Pacific Northwest reveals patterns of landscape burning and management, suggesting spatially-extensive modification of landscape ecologies over significant periods of time (Derr 2014; Lepofsky & Lertzman 2008). Archaeological indicators of such practices remain subtle, but work on forest fire reconstruction has been illuminating the time depth of burning as a landscape management tool (Ames 2005; Derr 2014). This research stems from larger efforts to consider ecologies as human-influenced over deep time, which has implications for modelling ecosystem variability and restoration targets (Higgs *et al.* 2014).

Along with these physical modifications that have primarily practical outcomes, landscape modifications have included the construction of large cemeteries that contain mound and cairn burials over the last 2000 years. Sometimes containing up to hundreds of burial features, monumental mortuary landscapes were part of the symbolic construction of place in the Coast Salish region (Lepofsky *et al.* 2000; Mathews 2014; Thom 1995).

These lines of data point to substantial and enduring connections with place both physically and conceptually over much of the Holocene. Continuity in habitation of specific places on the Northwest Coast has long been recognised, with sites such as Namu on the central British Columbia coast having been occupied as village locations for perhaps 9000 years (Cannon 2003; Cannon *et al.* 2011; McLaren *et al.* 2015). The notion of continuity and time depth in the use of places has been a dominant theme in Northwest Coast archaeology and in indigenous oral history (Martindale

& Marsden 2003; McLaren *et al.* 2015). However, the more recent archaeological recognition of the degree to which place was physically and intentionally constructed adds a new dimension to this profound connection with place. The implication of this transformation of the physical, social and symbolic worlds has been addressed for the transition to farming. For example, Hodder's (1990) discussion of the tensions between the *domus* (home sphere) and *agrios* (wild sphere) that accompanied the spread of farming in Europe suggests conceptual reconfigurations as the relationship to land shifts with the construction of place. Wilson (1991) discusses a more general domestication process over a much longer span of human history, in which relationships of people to their environments and to each other change as they increasingly exist in built environments, effectively domesticating themselves.

The domestication metaphor, and the idea that building places transforms social and symbolic relations, has been applied on the Northwest Coast as well. Marshall (2006) argues that the large Northwest Coast cedar plankhouse is a critical element of the built environment, and thus the domestication of people. Perhaps the most cogent statement of the relationship of Coast Salish peoples to place comes in Brian Thom's PhD dissertation (2005), where, drawing upon the Basso (1996) concept that 'wisdom sits in places', Thom develops 'a phenomenology of dwelling which takes profound attachments to home places as shaping and being shaped by ontological orientation and social organization' (Thom 2005, i).

The overarching theme is that there are deep, historical connections to place that structure Coast Salish symbolic and social action. Archaeological data illustrating both built environments and anthropogenically-altered landscape heighten this connection. This continuity of place, and the relations that the construction of place reifies, do not imply stability or static relationships, however. In the US southeast, monumental features have been interpreted as actors in the symbolic production of new world views, and in contesting histories and representations of the world (e.g., Martin 2005; Randall 2015; Wallis 2008). Similarly, in the Coast Salish region, significant changes are evident over the last two millennia in the nature of elite power and both elite and non-elite resistance to that power (Angelbeck & Grier 2012). Monumental constructions and connections to place play into this historical process. The physical and symbolic aspects of anthropogenic landscapes are a critical element of shaping histories and, from the vantage point of the present, reconstructing and studying these histories (Grier 2014b).

Ownership and the maintenance of economic diversity

Places produce resources that are the foundation of enduring economies. In this respect, economics in the Coast Salish region connects directly with place. As discussed in the previous section, large-scale resource production features were a significant element of the physical construction of places, grounding the economy in specific locations on the landscape. The social element of the economy – how relationships between people serve to mobilise and distribute resources (Halperin 1989) – knits together the material and the social. Connecting the material and the social element of an economy in the Coast Salish region requires considering ownership, which was a significant organising principle of the economy (Grier 2014b; Matson 1985; Richardson 1982). The institution of ownership, with which individuals and corporate entities control access to resources, played a central role in ensuring resource productivity, maintaining resource diversity and avoiding overexploitation of resources.

Diversity is a central concept in Coast Salish economic practices, but has received only limited consideration. Past models for social change on the Northwest Coast have emphasised unilinear and coast-wide transformations towards complexity and intensive resource production (Croes & Hackenberger 1988; Matson 1992). Explicit in the models has been a singular economic focus in various culture historical periods (Croes & Hackenberger 1988; Matson & Coupland 1995), with an ultimate shift over the last three millennia to a focus on mass-harvested, abundant and seemingly inexhaustible salmon resources. As outlined in Moss (2011) and Grier (2014b), and reinforced by studies of the representation of salmon remains in Northwest Coast assemblages (e.g., Butler & Campbell 2004; Coupland *et al.* 2010), Northwest Coast economies emphasised local diversity and diet breadth in conjunction with mass-harvested resources such as salmon (Bilton 2014; McKechnie 2014; Monks 1987).

The debate between resource specialisation and diversity may seem like a diet breadth/optimal foraging problem of the kind typically addressed in hunter-gatherer studies with faunal data. However, the issues and implications are much broader in the Coast Salish region. Why was diversity of diet maintained despite the possibility of intensive production and storage available with salmon? Risk buffering may have played into the equation. Suttles (1968) has been among those who highlight variability in salmon productivity and their potential for failure in any given year as a rationale for maintaining a diversity of alternative resource access options. But rather than just a 'back up plan', diversity may be interpreted as a strategy for pursuing the longer term objectives of sustainability and resource management. This requires treating economies more broadly, and examining more closely how ownership facilitated economic productivity over the long term.

Ownership is typically associated with complex societies where land itself is owned, as with agricultural systems that require predictable land tenure. However, ownership of places as an organising principle is not confined to agricultural societies, though it is rare in hunter-gatherer societies. For the Coast Salish, where plant tending and horticulture rather than full intensive cereals-based agriculture prevailed (Deur & Turner 2005), the general principle of ownership may have emerged from the physical construction of places, the argument being that the anthropogenic construction of large-scale production features creates ownable places on the landscape (Grier 2014b).

While this view is akin to the theory of property initially offered by Locke (Widerquist 2010), the principle plays out in novel and enduring ways in the Coast Salish context. Most past efforts to account for ownership have viewed ownership systems within a behavioural ecology framework, essentially developing out of the defense of territory (e.g., Chabot-Hanowell & Smith 2013; Dyson-Hudson & Smith 1978; Matson 1985; Richardson 1982). But many hunter-gatherer groups have long-standing connections to territories and places, yet do not have ownership systems. Long-term connections provide for preferential claims of access to resources, but do not themselves generate the ownership of places. Alternatively, the construction of place from the efforts of many individuals requires the (re)negotiation of rights of access to those places, creating the social arena for the development of restrictions on access, and that ultimately can be formalised into systems of ownership (Grier 2014b).

Clam gardens provide an important example of this approach to explaining ownership. Clam gardens are lines of boulders piled in the lower intertidal zone. The objective is to trap sediment to create improved microhabitat for many types of bivalves (Groesbeck *et al.* 2014; Lepofsky *et al.* 2015). These rock lines are often substantial, and measure as long as 1 km. They represent large-scale labour investments in modifying the landscape for elevated and sustainable resource production (Lepofsky *et al.* 2015). These features are usually in proximity to settlement locations, as with the large clam garden near the Shingle Point site on Valdes Island in the Strait of Georgia (Fig. 2.2). Other features such as large-scale fish traps or the construction of freshwater bogs

Figure 2.2. Clam garden at Shingle Point, Valdes Island, exposed at an extreme low summer tide in 2009. Photograph: Colin Grier.

to enhance plant productivity represent similar efforts at maintaining and enhancing a range of resources (Grier 2014b).

The construction and use of these features sets up some complex social problems to resolve in terms of resource access. Who has access to the features and the resources produced if these features were constructed through collaborative efforts? Who controls the cycle of harvesting? The features may have been managed communally in some respect, but there is clear evidence for dramatic material inequalities in Coast Salish societies over the last two millennia (Angelbeck & Grier 2012). As such, it is clear the benefits of ramped up production were not equitably distributed. Indeed, it is over the range of time (the last 2000 years) that we see large-scale production features that dramatic material and social inequalities become evident. I see the investment in large-scale production features across a diversity of resources as intimately connected to the construction of social inequalities through establishing systems of control over resource access, institutionalised as ownership. It is therefore useful to see ownership and the maintenance of resource diversity as interconnected principles that simultaneously fostered sustainability but also inequality (Grier & Angelbeck 2017).

Proprietorship

In the previous section, I focused on the institution of ownership and its relationship to maintaining resource productivity and diversity. However, using the term ownership to describe the regulation of resource access in Coast Salish societies has some limitations. First, it connotes a very western, capitalist way of relating to property, where private property rights are absolute and protected in jurisprudence. Second, resource control (ownership) was embedded in a broader principle in Coast Salish societies – proprietorship. Developed primarily in the work of Trosper (2002; 2009), proprietorship is a much broader construct than ownership, since it prescribes action and responsibilities rather than consisting of a static set of rights and prerogatives (Trosper 2002).

Proprietorship involves obligations to manage resources and social relationships in ways that benefit more than the individual. Under specific conditions, typically those that maintain the viability and sustainability of the resource, access to controlled resources is to be provided for others. Exclusion of others from access is conditional, being justified, for example, in situations where failure to limit access might harm the resource itself. Proprietors may dictate when harvesting should be undertaken and what strategy and intensity of production is appropriate (Richardson 1982; Trosper 2009). Self-serving, arbitrary exclusion was often sanctioned.

An important element of proprietorship is therefore the maintenance of the resource through active management that promotes sustainable use. This theme is recurrent in Coast Salish societies and reflects a strong notion of stewardship. But importantly, proprietorship does not involve equal access, since proprietors of resources have preferential access and control access to the resource. Proprietorship rights could also be passed on, as they were the corporate property of individuals, households or lineages (Richardson 1982; Trooper 2009).

Overall then, proprietorship has been described as a strategy for effectively managing a set of diverse resources sustainably in coastal environments (Trosper 2009). Many of these resources (invertebrates, fish and limited terrestrial ungulates) can be easily overexploited by large, sedentary populations. At the core of the system is a set of resource location-owning individuals or entities, who act as a network of resource managers (Grier & Angelbeck 2017). While they benefit from this position, their benefits are limited by social obligations to others and to maintaining the integrity of the resource. The significance of this organisational approach is that the control of resources remains in the hands of individuals and groups that have an intimate understanding of the local ecology, promoting sustainable use.

Though covered only briefly here, the expansive concept of proprietorship provides a foundational framework for understanding the broader relationship between resource and people, and the social obligations and prerogatives surrounding resource access. This system of resource management appears to have significant time depth in Coast Salish societies (Thom 2005; 2010) though archaeological data provide only indirect indications of its antiquity and process of development (Grier 2014b).

Local autonomy

A fourth foundational principle of Coast Salish society I consider is that of autonomy. A central element of Coast Salish social action now and in the past has been an emphasis on local autonomy. Despite increasing regional interactions over the last three millennia, political units existed no greater in scale than the large extended family household that inhabited a single cedar plankhouse. As evident both ethnographically and archaeologically, households had a set of titled, property-owning elite individuals and families, as well as other commoner individuals and families with more limited rights and access to household corporate property (Ames 1995; Suttles 1960; Grier 2006).

Households operated as coherent political units under house chiefs (Ames 1995; Suttles 1960). House chiefs operated regionally in horizontal, peer-to-peer relationships, primarily through affinal ties (Suttles 1960). These affinal ties connected households over a landscape, facilitating access to distant resources. The most significant economic, social and political relationships for households were with other households in other communities. These connections facilitated access to distant resources without the need for centralised, community-level coordinating authorities (Miller & Boxberger 1994; Suttles 1960).

This decentralised network of households and the emphasis on local autonomy and control can be considered a core organising principle that had economic, social and political expressions. From an economic perspective, decentralisation reinforced local control over access to resources. Socially and politically, the maintenance of local autonomy through the active resistance to centralising efforts of elites structured the historical development of social inequalities and power (Angelbeck & Grier 2012). For example, periods of greater elite power are evident in the restriction of symbols of authority and prestige, as with the use of prominent burial mounds and cairns for primarily elite burial between 1600 and 1000 years ago (Mathews 2014; Thom 1995). Resistance to this increasing social power and difference can be seen subsequently through the more widespread distribution of cranial deformation – a trait previously restricted to elites. Resistance to centralisation is also evident in the prevalence of warfare after 1400 BP, which Angelbeck (2009) interprets as the intensified use of conflict as a political levelling mechanism.

These historical dynamics both sustained and reinforced local autonomy while facilitating complex decentralised forms of regional interaction. Hunter-gatherers have many forms of regional interactions, but these tend to remain relatively fluid and predominantly non-hierarchical in nature. Complex, more formalised and hierarchical networks can exist in CHG societies, but these have usually been attributed to emergent regional centralisation under unusual circumstances, such as contact with state systems or extreme ecological events (e.g., Arnold *et al.* 2015; Martindale 2003).

The Coast Salish case in hunter-gatherer perspective

The four foundational principles of Coast Salish societies outlined above played out in ecological, social and political arenas in complex ways over the past several millennia. In combination, they point to a novel set of Coast Salish and, to a certain extent, pan-Northwest Coast practices that significantly expands our view of hunter-gatherer (and human) organisational possibilities. Decentralised, flexible forms of organisation that nonetheless involve regionally structured interactions provide an alternative model to the standard view that increasing scale requires increasing centralisation.

Importantly, the Coast Salish case represents not a society that somehow bridges the gulf between hunter-gatherers and agricultural societies, nor one that should be construed as some form of hunter-gatherer chiefdom. Chiefdoms, including those advanced as hunter-gatherer examples of chiefdoms (e.g., Arnold 1993; Arnold *et al.* 2015) imply a regionally centralised control of resources and authority not seen in the Coast Salish case. As such, Coast Salish societies illuminate how the horizontal elaboration of increasingly complex but decentralised relationships can operate at a regional scale. Past debates about whether chiefdoms in any form have existed on the Northwest Coast have largely been settled with the recognition that centralised regional control was almost certainly a product of historic-period processes related to contact with nation states (Martindale 2003; Miller & Boxberger 1994). Attempts to stretch and bend the chiefdom concept to accommodate Northwest Coast and Coast Salish decentralised organisation provides little analytical benefit, and ultimately detracts from considering these societies on their own terms.

The time depth over which these principles of Coast Salish organisation have existed will need to be better stipulated if we hope to understand the way in which such organisational strategies emerge and are maintained. Ascertaining how such a system developed is the charge of archaeology, though such an effort will not be a straightforward process using archaeological data alone. The historical dynamics are themselves quite complex and the data available to reconstruct them are at times frustratingly indirect.

Back to the future: why does diversity matter?

Having made the argument that the Coast Salish case expands our notion of hunter-gatherer diversity, the question can be posed: what does this effort accomplish outside of the discipline of hunter-gatherer studies? In short, why does hunter-gatherer diversity matter?

One way in which we might draw some useful and broader observations is to appreciate how small-scale organisations can manage resources without recourse to centralised decision-making. Decentralisation, where stakeholders with local and intimate knowledge of the status of resources take the lead in decision-making concerning resource exploitation, presents a viable alternative and template for managing resources in larger-scale systems. Such an approach can potentially be applied at more local scales within modern, hierarchical nation states to promote sustainability. The significance of appreciating and properly characterising hunter-gatherer diversity therefore lies in the recognition and potential implementation of organisational principles to better manage resources today and in the future. Nation states typically employ highly centralised bureaucracies in their management institutions, which poorly mobilise the knowledge of local stakeholders in their centralised decision-making.

One concrete way in which this approach is being operationalised is in the implementation and analysis of community-based observing networks (CBONs) (Alessa *et al.* 2016). Programmes in Alaska are actively collecting and assembling knowledge from those who live off the land. As it turns out, these individuals are recognising with high fidelity the kinds of ecological changes that are being recorded more 'objectively' through scientific observations. For example, recent climate change and its effect on sea ice conditions in arctic locales have been recognised by indigenous peoples of Alaska as outside the parameters of historic norms. This suggests that local resource monitoring has been a highly effective tool prior to modern science, and can be today (Alessa *et al.* 2016). These 'on-the-ground' observations provide valuable information that can be mobilised in larger-scale efforts to sustain northern resource viability.

CBONs are but one example of the organisations that hunter-gatherers have used to negotiate and adapt to their environment socially and economically over the millennia. Recognising the diversity of approaches and strategies that have been successful in the past can illuminate new, decentralised and locally-based strategies for resource sustainability.

Beyond this, the profound and enduring connection to place that exists in Coast Salish societies has been only weakly recognised in both historic-period and modern legal contexts. More fully explicating these connections provides a basis for effective restorative justice for colonial infringements on indigenous territories and livelihoods. An inability (and unwillingness) on the part of colonial governments to recognise these connections led to the disenfranchisement of ingenious people from their traditional livelihood and lands (Deur & Turner 2005). With a much stronger appreciation for how diverse human connections to place can be, we open the door to more fully recognise indigenous rights and title and provide indigenous communities with a more just and viable future (Thom 2005).

Acknowledgements

This paper owes a profound debt to the Penelakut First Nation and many other Coast Salish Nations who have opened up their communities and their ancestral places for study, and who have shared knowledge of their long-standing practices with myself and many other anthropologists over the last two centuries. I am also grateful to Graeme Warren and Bill Finlayson for extending the opportunity to participate in this volume. Bill Angelbeck provided important and insightful comments on this manuscript and offered many insights that improved its quality and coherence.

References

Alessa, L., Kliskey, A., Gamble, J., Fidel, M., Beaujean, G. & Gosz, J. (2016). The role of Indigenous science and local knowledge in integrated observing systems: Moving toward adaptive capacity indices and early warning systems. *Sustainability Science* 11, 91–102.

Ames, K. M. (1995) Chiefly power and household production on the Northwest Coast. In T. D. Price & G. M. Feinman (eds), *Foundations of Social Inequality*, 155–187. New York, Plenum Press.

Ames, K. M. (2004) Supposing hunter-gatherer variability. *American Antiquity* 69, 364–374.

Ames, K. M. (2005) Intensification of food production on the Northwest Coast. In D. Deur & N. J. Turner (eds), *Keeping It Living: Traditions of Plant Use and Cultivation on the Northwest Coast of North America*, 67–100. Vancouver, UBC Press.

Angelbeck, B. (2009) 'They Recognize No Superior Chief': Power, Practice Anarchism and Warfare in the Coast Salish Past. Unpublished PhD Dissertation, University of British Columbia.

Angelbeck, B. and Grier, C. (2012) Anarchism and the archaeology of anarchic societies: resistance to centralization in the Coast Salish region of the Pacific Northwest Coast. *Current Anthropology* 53(5), 547–587.

Arnold, J. E. (1993) Labor and the Rise of Complex Hunter-Gatherers. *Journal of Anthropological Archaeology* 12, 75–119.

Arnold, J. E., Sunell, S., Nigra, B. T., Bishop, K. J., Jones, T. & Bongers, J. (2015) Entrenched disbelief: complex hunter-gatherers and the case for inclusive cultural evolutionary thinking. *Journal of Archaeological Method and Theory* 23(2), 1–52.

Basso, K. (1996) *Wisdom Sits in Places: Landscape and Language Among the Western Apache*. Albuquerque, University of New Mexico Press.

Bilton, D. (2014) Northern, Central, Diversified, Specialized: The Archaeology of Fishing Adaptations in the Gulf of Georgia (Salish Sea), British Columbia. Unpublished PhD Dissertation, University of Toronto.

Burch, E. S. (1994) The future of gunter-gatherers. In E. S. Burch, Jr & L. J. Ellanna (eds), *Key Issues in Hunter-Gatherer Research*, 441–455. Oxford, Berg.

Butler, V. L. & Campbell, S. K. (2004) Resource intensification and resource depression in the Pacific Northwest of North America: a zooarchaeological review. *Journal of World Prehistory* 18, 327–405.

Caldwell, M. E., Lepofsky, D., Combes, G., Washington, M., Welch, J. R. & Harper, J. R. (2012) A bird's eye view of Northern Coast Salish intertidal resource management features, southern British Columbia, Canada. *The Journal of Island and Coastal Archaeology* 7(2), 219–233.

Cannon, A. (2001) Was salmon important in Northwest Coast prehistory? In S. C. Gerlach & M. S. Murray (eds), *People and Wildlife in Northern North America: Essays in Honor of R. Dale Guthrie*, 178–187. Oxford, British Archaeological Report S944.

Cannon, A. (2003) Long-term continuity in central Northwest Coast settlement patterns. In R. L. Carlson (ed.), *Archaeology of Coastal British Columbia: Essays in Honour of Philip M. Hobler*, 1–12. Burnaby, B.C., Archaeology Press, Simon Fraser University.

Cannon, A., Yang, D. & Speller, C. (2011) Site-specific salmon fisheries on the central coast of British Columbia. In M. Moss & A. Cannon (eds), *The Archaeology of North Pacific Fisheries*, 57–74. Fairbanks, University of Alaska Press.

Chabot-Hanowell, B. & Alden Smith, E. (2013) Territorial and nonterritorial routes to power: reconciling evolutionary ecological, social agency, and historicist approaches. *Archaeological Papers of the American Anthropological Association* 22, 72–86.

Coupland, G., Stewart, K. & Patton, K. (2010) Do you ever get tired of salmon? Evidence for Extreme salmon specialization at Prince Rupert Harbour, British Columbia. *Journal of Anthropological Archaeology* 29, 189–207.

Croes, D. R. & Hackenberger, S. (1988) Hoko River archaeological complex: modeling prehistoric Northwest Coast economic evolution. In B. L. Isaac (ed.), *Prehistoric Economies of the Pacific Northwest Coast*, 19–85. Research In Economic Anthropology Supplement 3. Greenwich, JAI Press.

Derr, K. M. (2014) Anthropogenic fire and landscape management on Valdes Island, southwestern BC. *Canadian Journal of Archaeology* 38(1), 250–279.

Deur, D. (2000) *A Domesticated Landscape: Native American Plant Cultivation on the Northwest Coast of North America*. Unpublished PhD Dissertation, Louisiana State University.

Deur, D. & Turner, N. (2005) Introduction: reassessing indigenous resource management, reassessing the history of an Idea. In D. Deur & N. J. Turner, (eds), *Keeping It Living: Traditions of Plant Use and Cultivation on the Northwest Coast of North America*, 3–34. Vancouver, UBC Press.

Dyson-Hudson, R. & Smith, E. B. (1978) Human territoriality: an ecological reassessment. *American Anthropologist* 80, 21–41.

Estévez, J. & Vila, A. (2010) Introduction: el porque de este libro y de nuestra ida a la Costa Noroeste. In A. Vila & J. Estévez (eds), *La excepción y la norma: las sociedades indígenas de la Costa Noroeste de Norteamérica desde la arqueología*, 6–62. Treballs d'Etnoarqueologia 8. Madrid, CSIC.

Feit, H. A. (1994) The enduring pursuit: land, time and social relationships in anthropological models of hunter-gatherers and in the Subarctic hunters' images. In E. S. Burch, Jr & L. J. Ellanna (eds), *Key Issues in Hunter-Gatherer Research*, 421–440. Oxford, Berg.

Gibson, J. L. & Carr, P. J. (2004) Big mounds, big rings, big power. In J. L. Gibson & P. J. Carr (eds), *Signs of Power: The Rise of Cultural Complexity in the Southeast*, 1–9. Tuscaloosa, University of Alabama Press.

Greene, N. A., McGee, D. C. & Heitzmann, R. J. (2015) The Comox Harbour fish trap complex: a large-scale, technologically sophisticated intertidal fishery from British Columbia. *Canadian Journal of Archaeology* 39(2), 161–212.

Grier, C. (2003) Dimensions of regional interaction in the Prehistoric Gulf of Georgia. In R. G. Matson, G. Coupland & Q. Mackie (eds), *Emerging from the Mist: Studies in Northwest Coast Culture History*, 170–187. Vancouver UBC Press.

Grier, C. (2006) Temporality in Northwest Coast households. In E. A. Sobel, D. A. Trieu Gahr & K. M. Ames (eds), *Household Archaeology on the Northwest Coast*, 97–119. Ann Arbor, International Monographs in Prehistory.

Grier, C. (2007) Consuming the recent for constructing the ancient: the role of ethnography in Coast Salish archaeological interpretations. In B. G. Miller (ed.), *Be Of Good Mind: Essays on the Coast Salish*, 284–307. Vancouver, UBC Press.

Grier, C. (2014a) Which way forward? *Canadian Journal of Archaeology* 38(1), 135–139.

Grier, C. (2014b) Landscape construction, ownership and social change in the southern Gulf Islands of British Columbia. *Canadian Journal of Archaeology* 38(1), 211–249.

Grier, C. & Angelbeck, B. (2017) Tradeoffs in Coast Salish Social Action: Balancing Autonomy, Inequality and Sustainability. In M. Hegmon (ed), *The Give and Take of Sustainability: Archaeological and Anthropological Perspectives on Tradeoffs*, in press. Cambridge, Cambridge University Press.

Grier, C., Dolan, P., Derr, K. & McLay, E. (2009) Assessing sea level changes in the southern Gulf Islands of British Columbia using archaeological data from coastal spit locations. *Canadian Journal of Archaeology* 33, 254–280.

Groesbeck, A. S., Rowell, K., Lepofsky, D. and A. K. Salomon (2014) Ancient clam gardens increased shellfish production: adaptive strategies from the past can inform food security today. *PLoS One* 9(3): e91235. DOI: 10.1371/journal.pone.0091235

Halperin, R. (1989) Ecological versus economic anthropology: changing 'place' versus changing 'hands'. *Research in Economic Anthropology* 11, 15–41.

Hayden, B. (1995) Pathways to power: principles for creating socioeconomic inequalities. In T. D. Price & G. M. Feinman (eds), *Foundations of Social Inequality*, 15–86. New York, Plenum Press.

Higgs, E., Falk, D. A., Guerrini, A., Hall, M., Harris, J., Hobbs, R. J., Jackson, S. T., Rhemtulla, J. M. & Throop, W. (2014) The changing role of history in restoration ecology. *Frontiers in Ecology and the Environment* 12(9), 499–506.

Hodder, I. (1990) *The Domestication of Europe*. Oxford, Blackwell.

Johnson, A. & Earle, T. (2000) *The Evolution of Human Societies*. Palo Alto, Stanford University Press.

Kim, J. & Grier, C. (2006) Beyond affluent foragers. In C. Grier, J. Kim & J. Uchiyama (eds), *Beyond Affluent Foragers: Rethinking Hunter-Gatherer Complexity*, 192–200. Oxford, Oxbow Books.

Koyama, S. & Thomas, D. H. (1981) *Affluent Foragers: Pacific Coasts East and West*. Senri Ethnological Studies 9. Osaka, National Museum of Ethnology.

Layton, R. H. (2001) Hunter-gatherers, their neighbours, and the Nation State. In C. Panter-Brick, R. H. Layton & P. Rowley-Conwy (eds), *Hunters and Gatherers: An Interdisciplinary Perspective*, 292–321. Cambridge, Cambridge University Press.

Lepofsky, D., Blake, M., Brown, D., Morrison, S., Oakes, N. & Lyons, N. (2000) The archaeology of the Scowlitz site, SW British Columbia. *Journal of Field Archaeology* 27, 391–416.

Lepofsky, D. & Lertzman, K. (2008) Documenting ancient plant management in the northwest of North America. *Botany* 86, 129–145.

Lepofsky, D., Smith, N., Cardinal, N., Harper, J., Morris, M., Gitla (Elroy White), Bouchard, R., Kennedy, D., Salomon, A., Puckett, M., Michelle & Rowell, K. (2015) Ancient shellfish mariculture on the Northwest Coast of North America. *American Antiquity* 80, 236–259.

Marshall, Y. (2006) Houses and domestication on the Northwest Coast. In E. A. Sobel, D. A. Trieu Gahr & K. M. Ames (eds), *Household Archaeology on the Northwest Coast*, 37–56. International Monographs in Prehistory. Ann Arbor.

Martin, A. (2005) Agents in inter-action: Bruno Latour and agency. *Journal of Archaeological Method and Theory* 12(4), 283–311.

Martindale, A. (2003) A Hunter-gatherer paramount chiefdom: Tsimshian developments through the contact period. In R. G. Matson, G. Coupland & Q. Mackie (eds), *Emerging from the Mist: Studies in Northwest Coast Culture History*, 12–50. Vancouver, UBC Press.

Martindale, A. & Marsden, S. (2003). Defining the Middle Period (3500 BP to 1500 BP) in Tsimshian history through a comparison of archaeological and oral records. *BC Studies* 138, 13–50.

Matson, R. G. (1985) The relationship between sedentism and status inequalities among hunter-gatherers. In M. Thompson, M. T. Garcia & F. J. Kense (eds), *Status, Structure, and Stratification: Current Archaeological Reconstructions*, 245–252. Calgary, University of Calgary Archaeological Association.

Matson, R. G. (1992) The evolution of Northwest Coast subsistence. In D. R. Croes, R. A. Hawkins & B. L. Isaac (eds), *Long-Term Subsistence Change in Prehistoric North America, Research In Economic Anthropology Supplement*, 6, 367–428.

Matson, R. G. & Coupland, G. (1995) *The Prehistory of the Northwest Coast*. New York, Academic Press.

Mathews, D. (2014) Funerary Ritual, Ancestral Presence, and the Rocky Point Ways of Death. Unpublished PhD Dissertation, University of Victoria.

McKechnie, I., Lepofsky, D., Moss, M. L., Butler, V. L., Orchard, T. J., Coupland, G., Foster, F., Caldwell, M. & Lertzman, K. (2014) Archaeological data provide alternative hypotheses on Pacific Herring (*Clupea pallasii*) distribution, abundance, and variability. *Proceedings of the National Academy of Sciences* 111(9), E807–E816.

McLaren, D, Rahemtulla, F., Gitla (Elroy White) & Fedje, D. (2015) Prerogatives, sea level, and the strength of persistent places: archaeological evidence for long-term occupation of the central Coast of British Columbia. *BC Studies* 187, 155–191.

Miller, B. G. (2004) Rereading the ethnographic record: the problem of justice in the Coast Salish World. In M. Mauze, M. E. Harkin and S. Kan (eds), *Coming to Shore: Northwest Coast Ethnology, Traditions, and Visions*, 305–322. Lincoln, University of Nebraska Press.

Miller, B. G. & Boxberger, D. L. (1994) Creating chiefdoms: the Puget Sound case. *Ethnohistory* 41, 267–293.

Monks, G. G. (1987) Prey as bait: The Deep Bay example. *Canadian Journal of Archaeology* 11, 119–142.

Moss, M. L. (2011) *Northwest Coast: Archaeology as Deep History*. Washington DC, SAA Press.

Murdock, G. P. (1968) The current statius of the World's hunting and gathering peoples. In R. B. Lee & I. DeVore (eds), *Man the Hunter*, 13–20. New York, Aldine.

Pauketat, T. R. (2007) *Chiefdoms and Other Archaeological Delusions*. New York, Altamira Press.

Pluciennik, M. (2004) The meaning of "hunter-gatherers' and modes of subsistence: a comparative historical perspective. In A. Barnard (ed.), *Hunter-Gatherers in History, Archaeology and Anthropology*, 17–30. Oxford, Berg.

Price, T. D. & Brown, J. A. (1985) Aspects of hunter-gatherer complexity. In T. D. Price & J. A. Brown (eds), *Prehistoric Hunter-Gatherers: The Emergence of Cultural Complexity*, 3–20. New York, Academic Press.

Randall, A. R. (2015) *Constructing Histories: Archaic Freshwater Shell Mounds and Social Landscapes of the St. Johns River, Florida*. Gainsville, University Press of Florida.

Richardson, A. (1982) The control of productive resources on the Northwest Coast of North America. In N. W. Hunn & E. Hunn (eds), *Resource Managers: North American and Australian Hunter-Gatherers*, 93–112. Boulder, Westview Press.

Rowley-Conwy, P. (2001) Time, change, and the archaeology of hunter-gatherers: how original is the original affluent society? In C. Panter-Brick, R. H. Layton & P. Rowley-Conwy (eds), *Hunters and Gatherers: An Interdisciplinary Perspective* 39–72. Cambridge, Cambridge University Press.

Sassaman, K. E. (2004) Complex hunter–gatherers in evolution and history: a North American perspective. *Journal of Archaeological Research* 12, 227–280.

Schaepe, D. (2009) Pre-Colonial Sto:Lo-Coast Salish Community Organization: An Archaeological Study. Unpublished PhD Dissertation, University of British Columbia.

Schwadron, M. (2010) Landscapes of Maritime Complexity: Prehistoric Shell Work Sites in the Ten Thousand Islands, Florida. Unpublished PhD Dissertation, University of Leicester.

Smith, B. (2001) Low-level food production. *Journal of Archaeological Research* 9, 1–43.

Suttles, W. (1960) Affinal ties, subsistence, and prestige among the Coast Salish. *American Anthropologist* 62(2), 296–305.

Suttles, W. (1968) Coping with abundance: subsistence on the Northwest Coast. In R. B. Lee & I. DeVore (eds), *Man the Hunter*, 56–68. New York, Aldine.

Thom, B. (1995) The Dead and the Living: Burial Mounds and Cairns and the Development of Social Classes in the Gulf of Georgia Region. Unpublished MA Thesis, University of British Columbia.

Thom, B. (2005) Coast Salish Senses of Place: Dwelling, Meaning, Power, Property and Territory in the Coast Salish World. Unpublished PhD Dissertation, McGill University.

Thom, B. (2010) The anathema of aggregation: toward 21st century self-government in the Coast Salish World. *Anthropologica* 52(1), 33–48.

Trosper, R.L. (2002) Northwest Coast indigenous institutions that supported resilience and sustainability, *Ecological Economics* 41(2), 329–344.

Trosper, R. R. (2009) *Resilience, Reciprocity and Ecological Economics: Northwest Coast Sustainability*. New York, Taylor & Francis.

Wallis, N. J. (2008) Networks of history and memory: creating a nexus of social identities in Woodland Period mounds on the Lower St Johns River, Florida. *Journal of Social Archaeology* 8, 236–271.

Widerquist, K. (2010) Lockean theories of property: justifications for unilateral appropriation. *Public Reason* 2(1), 3–26.

Wilmsen, E. N. (1983) The ecology of illusion: anthropological foraging in the Kalahari. *Reviews in Anthropology* 10, 9–20.

Wilson, P. (1991) *The Domestication of the Human Species*. New Haven, Yale University Press.

Woodburn, J. (1982) Egalitarian societies. *Man* ns 17, 431–451.

Chapter 3

Conceptualising subsistence in central Africa and the West over the *longue durée*

Kathryn M. de Luna

The transition from hunting and gathering to farming dominates histories of early Africa and other world regions. The association between political complexity and the development of farming, sedentism and food surplus has been a particularly productive model of historical change, but it assumes a complete distinction between the activities of farmers and those of hunter-gatherers. Histories of subsistence demonstrate that, in practice, the ways people fed themselves muddy the waters of our tidy classifications: farmers have long collected famine foods after poor harvests or in the hungry season, hunter-gatherers tended small stock, pastoralists and farmers hunted, and, as studies of domestication reveal, ancient hunter-gatherers must have weeded, cultivated and selectively harvested stands of ancient grains, eventually domesticating them. Yet, *intellectual* histories of subsistence have followed the categories of its classification. These studies painstakingly reconstruct from Antiquity to the 20th century the political significance of cultural ideas about a particular kind of subsistence, such as the transition to agriculture, or specific kinds of practitioners, such as hunter-gatherers or pastoralists. Historians and anthropologists usually do not explore how these categories are coproduced within an ideology of subsistence that separates food collection from food production (but see Finlayson & Warren 2010).[1]

The study of subsistence encompasses the tools, organisation of labour and differing values assigned to the products used to provision the community, connecting them to a range of social practices and beliefs that exist beyond the domain of food but, like food, are bound up with existential concerns in the broadest sense. For this reason, the invocation of distinct subsistence strategies like 'pastoralist' or 'hunter-gatherer' has been a powerful tool for articulating cultural difference within many societies. Even the idea that some societies are 'beyond' a subsistence lifestyle is a way to articulate a set of values about how labour, food procurement and exchange should be organised in a 'modern' society. This chapter traces two intellectual histories of subsistence over the *longue durée*, one focused on central Africa and one focused on Western Europe, in order to demonstrate the impact of western ideologies of subsistence on our understanding of subsistence in other societies and to bring to light novel categories of subsistence practice. In each narrative, subsistence served as a tool for the conceptualisation and political mobilisation of difference.

We can best understand what was original about the history of subsistence in central African communities by setting this story side-by-side with some of the strands of intellectual thought surrounding categories of subsistence in the Western cultural tradition. This story of the role of subsistence in some strands of Western political, economic and moral thought is important because terms like 'farmer' and 'hunter-gatherer' were applied as universal, naturalised categories to describe and explain African ethnicities, social organisation, political culture and economies. The result was a paradigm in which there could be no intellectual history of indigenous subsistence categories and their social and political powers (e.g. Klieman 2003), exactly the kind of story presented in the second half of the chapter.

Chapters in this volume contribute to a wider interest in foregrounding processes of change, rather than 'start points' and 'end points' of transformations from one to another form of subsistence. As a way to problematise the very categories of subsistence through which societies are thought to transition, I will go a bit further and trace out a history of practices of food collection among communities usually identified as 'food producers' *after* the transition to cereal agriculture in south central Africa (see Fig. 3.1, below). This chapter traces the history of bushcraft – hunting, fishing and foraging – among farming communities who spoke languages of the Botatwe language group (see Table 3.1, below). Approaching the food collection-production divide from the opposite direction of studies of the diversity of hunter-gatherer subsistence practices, the project from which this paper stems (de Luna 2016) reunites the activities of hunters, fishers and foragers with those of farmers to better understand wild resource use in farming communities.

Ideals of subsistence in strands of Western intellectual thought[2]

The rich scholarship on the variety of hunter-gatherer lifestyles has also inspired research on the history of the concept 'hunter-gatherer' in the Western intellectual tradition. Other scholars, particularly historians of political philosophy, have similarly traced the history of the conceptual category 'farmer' in the intellectual tradition of the West, revealing the many ways in which categories like 'farmer', 'hunter-gatherer', 'non-farmers' and 'barbarians' were put to political use in particular historical circumstances from Antiquity through the Enlightenment. Although Finlayson and Warren's volume (2010) stands as an exception, this scholarship tends to study subsistence categories in isolation, tracing the origins of the concept 'hunter-gatherer', for example, divorced from the history of the concept 'farmer'. As a body of research, these studies reveal a common thread: since Antiquity, subsistence categories have functioned much like other categories of identity, such as race, gender or ethnicity – and have often been implicated in their construction. This assumption has graver implications for our understanding of subsistence in other historical contexts than we might expect from its simplicity.

Subsistence and antique ideals of civilisation

The intellectual foundations for the distinction between food production and food collection reach deep into classical Antiquity and appear in the writings of Thucydides, Aristotle, Siculus, Lucretius, Tacitus, Strabo and others. In some classical texts, the subsistence-based classification was a dichotomy of farmers against non-farmers, a dichotomy that hinged on the importance of sedentism, the affiliated trappings of civilisation, and the ideal of the agrarian life as superior for its self-sufficiency (Baloglou 2012). Through this binary, explanations for the origins of society converged with explanations for the origins of agriculture and progress from a state of nature to a state of culture, in which property ownership was fundamental to both society and agriculture (Rudebeck 2000). Other classical thinkers articulated the value of the agricultural lifestyle and its distinction from other subsistence strategies through stadial schemes meant to explain change in human history (Pluciennik 2002; Rudebeck 2000, 37–46; Vencl 1988). Of course, the juxtaposition of nomadic, barbaric hunter-gatherers and civilised, sedentary farmers developed in particular historical contexts, such as the expansion of the early Roman Empire under Augustus (consider Strabo's comparison of Celts and Britons described in Zvelebil 2002, 129; see also Cartmill 1993). These ideas performed political work in periods of conquest and colonisation, much as similar ideas did in the seventeenth and eighteenth centuries in Europe, often consciously drawing on classical models. The Antique practice of recognising and explaining difference through subsistence practices has proven to be a persistent, if not an unchanging, root metaphor in which food production stands in for qualities like 'progressive' and 'civilised' and invokes values like sedentism and property ownership (Ferguson 1992; Janko 1997; Kuper 1988; Pluciennik 2002; Rudebeck 2000; Vencl 1988).

Subsistence and Christian morality

Although ideas about the superiority of farming persisted to some degree into the Middle Ages, the medieval period marks a break between classical and early modern uses of subsistence-based classifications, a point best seen in ideas about hunting and woodlands. For early Christians, subsistence connected mobility, environment and spiritual well-being. The wandering life of the hunter was undesirable for St Augustine because the wilderness was a reflection of man's fall from grace. Agriculture, however, was a gift from God and represented man's dominion over nature. A few centuries later, Christian understandings of forests and hunting shifted as holy men sanctified the wilderness, using it as a symbol of the state of nature before the fall of man. This shift from the savage wilderness to the sylvan forest was connected to the redistribution of forestland to elites in the 10th century. Peasants and serfs who farmed, tended livestock and gathered wild fruits resented the loss of the forests to the sporting hunt of the European aristocracy. By the 13th century, the hunt was a path to status and Godliness for nobles; it symbolised the quest for love and Christ and was an important venue to practice the martial arts of God-sanctioned violence. But hunting also invoked the agency and spite of the poor, who deliberately hunted in forests, even though it was often illegal to do so (Cartmill 1993; Klieman 2003; Rudebeck 2000).

Subsistence and the ideals of progress

The ascendency of ideas developed during the Renaissance and Enlightenment about the linear, progressive nature of time and man's place in the biological world converged in the study of subsistence activities during the 17th and into the 18th centuries. By the mid-17th century, centuries-old scepticism of man's dominion over animals transformed hunting from a leisurely pastime analogous to the quest for Christ into a base and cruel activity (Cartmill 1993, 76–91). While this transformation was surely rooted in the erosion of the landed aristocracy, peasant demands for access to meat, a rejection by the middle class of elite frippery, as well as the influence of newly popular classical texts demonstrating the Roman disdain for hunting, it was also tied to the scientific study of man's relationship to other beings (Cartmill 1993; Klieman 2003). The morality of hunting was suddenly in question in light of the possibility that animals, in their likeness to man, also held rights. Importantly, questions about the morality of hunting emerged at the same time that the first 'scientific' ethnographic observations of societies in the New World circulated among European intellectuals. It was a small step from the observation that 'primitives' encountered in the colonial enterprise relied on hunting and foraging to describing them as a 'natural' state of man and their hunting as the 'primordial human enterprise', one so 'morally objectionable' that it was identified by James Burnett (Lord Monboddo) at the end of the 18th century as the root of human depravity (Cartmill 1993, 25–26). The complicated articulation of particular subsistence practices, morality and progressive stages of human development would continue to have profound effects on popular and scholarly understandings of non-Western societies.

This was also a period of bold thinking about the relationship between subsistence and politics. Working under the assumption that social progress was a law of nature, Enlightenment thinkers explored the relationships between land tenure, labour, subsistence and socio-political organisation, eventually leading to the invention of the subsistence category hunter-gatherer (Barnard 1999; 2004; Meek 1976; Pluciennik 2001; 2004; Rudebeck 2000). Popular antiquarian texts associating farming and the civilised life were combined with new ideas about the relationship between man and animals, allowing intellectuals to attach a particular moral value to farming. As worked land came to be understood as an 'improvement', progress was understood to be directly associated with cultivation and private property, both essential to the work of building a moral society. Such ideas justified both the colonisation of distant lands and, by implying that the labour of societies relying on subsistence other than agriculture could not be understood as productive labour, the forced removal of native peoples, especially hunter-gatherers.

In the 18th century, in the context of the rapid growth of agrarian and mercantile capitalism, subsistence practice became a short-hand for political organisation and a key factor in understanding differences between societies both historically and in the contemporary world. Earlier 17th century intellectuals like Hobbes and Locke understood hunter-gatherers to precede other means of subsistence because they represented man's 'natural' state. From the 18th century, Scottish Enlightenment thinkers assumed that subsistence practices determined property rights and social inequality, which then shaped the form of social organisation and government of a particular society. Subsistence became the key to understanding inequality, class, the accumulation of capital, social and political organisation, the division of labour and many other problems that came to be foundational to the social sciences (Barnard 1992; Trigger 2006). Ultimately, the distinction between hunting and gathering, pastoralism and farming, and the discrete political and social capacities associated with each, proved an enduring Rubicon whose course shaped generations of scholarship, including, paradoxically, later work challenging the very distinctions between hunter-gatherers, herders and farmers.

Subsistence and evolutionary paradigms

Nineteenth century thinkers replaced their predecessors' emphasis on the economy and the development of property rights as well as the static categories of earlier stadial schemes with the paradigm of evolutionary adaption, in which adaptations were the engines of change and differentiation. Drawing on the idea that subsistence strategies developed as evolutionary adaptions, researchers in the emerging field of hunter-gatherer studies argued in the late 19th and early 20th centuries that hunter-gatherers represented a primordial state of humanity. For this reason, the study of contemporary human populations could answer questions about early human history (e.g. Sollas 1911). Even those who did not subscribe to the idea that humanity was evolving for the better saved an important place for hunter-gatherers in their understandings of difference and historical change. Some celebrated the 'Noble Savage', building on older narratives of degeneration and new ideas about conservation to critique the societies at the apex of the social Darwinist hierarchy (Kuper 1988; compare to Ellingson 2001). Whether you subscribed to or critiqued social evolution, the evolutionary paradigm was merely another way to articulate the political value of the distinction between hunter-gatherers and farmers.

The notion that subsistence technologies were, themselves, human adaptations became a central problem for early 20th century scholars who pondered the origins and significance of modes of subsistence. V. Gordon Childe's masterful reformulation of the nationalist archaeologies of Europe purposefully equated all the transformations to human lifestyles that had resulted from techno-economic innovation: the Neolithic represented the introduction of farming; the Bronze Age marked the establishment of regular trade and craft specialisation; and the Iron Age drastically altered the demography of Europe facilitating land clearance and population expansion (1936). To Childe, these adaptations marked moments of punctuated development in early human history that were as transformative as the more recent Industrial Revolution. For Childe and his contemporaries, agriculture and sedentism not only facilitated but inevitably created the accumulation of property and surplus production (Rudebeck 2000, 154–160). Childe's earliest musings on the significance of the advent of farming were contemporary with a parallel, related interest among physical anthropologists in the significance of the advent of hunting. The Killer Ape theory suggested that the invention of hunting was an adaptation that allowed humans to evolve into a new branch of the primate tree and that human depravity was rooted in a primate propensity for predation (Dart 1925; see also Cartmill 1993).

Both the Killer Ape theory and the Neolithic Revolution followed the long-established idea that subsistence could explain difference. Although each had far earlier roots, these ideas became particularly significant in both scholarly and popular thought in the aftermath of World War II. Shifts from one subsistence strategy to another seemed to show remarkable similarity across cultures and periods and, therefore, underscored the importance of adaptation, rather than race, in explanations of human variability. The study of transformations in subsistence practices in the early 20th century played an important role in recovering social evolutionary theory from its 19th century racial trappings (Klieman 2003).

The idea that changes in subsistence practices were evolutionary adaptations with the power to produce new socio-political configurations – even new species! – continued to shape mid-20th century anthropology. For many, the transition from hunting and gathering to farming resulted in new sociopolitical organisation, whether from family to band to tribe to nation or from band to tribe to chiefdom to state (e.g. Service 1962; Steward 1955). Other scholars debated the relative productivity of different categories of subsistence. Marshall Sahlins famously claimed that hunter-gatherers were the 'original affluent society' if time and labour, rather than property, was placed at the centre of definitions of poverty (1968; 1972). That Sahlins' observation was remarkable in 1966 speaks to the persistence of Enlightenment ideas asserting private property and farming as essential to moral, productive labour. Mid-century scholars of hunter-gatherers also puzzled over why so many foragers became farmers if farming was neither a better way of life than the other, nor a certain evolutionary destination. Indeed, this question suggested that the Killer Ape theory had the hunting hypothesis backward. While humans may have evolved from apes because they developed hunting, this adaptation was not the source of human depravity but an achievement in the universal narrative of human history (Washburn & Lancaster 1968). This 'Man the Hunter' hypothesis inspired the 'Woman the Gatherer' thesis, which asserted the significant contributions of women to the prehistoric larder in part by conflating gender and subsistence, a conflation with a precedent in the 'Mother of Agriculture' thesis of James Frazer's *Golden Bough* (Dahlberg 1981; Rudebeck 2000, 129–135). Although 20th century scholars had developed more sophisticated categories of and meanings for subsistence than the dichotomised worldview of Antiquity, the terms of the debate had changed very little: subsistence defined societies and changes to subsistence were transformative to society.

Strands of social evolutionist research that had dominated scholarship through the mid-20th century were beginning to unravel by the 1970s. The hunting hypothesis was largely rejected after nearly two decades in textbooks (Binford 1981; Brain 1981; Oakley 1954; Washburn 1957; compare to Hard & Sussman 2005). The ennobling 'affluent society' theory was critiqued by work on 'complex' hunter-gatherers (Price & Brown 1985; see also Sassaman 2004). Indeed, the very categories of 'farmer' and 'hunter-gatherer' were vulnerable to attack as calls mounted for a better understanding of the broad spectrum of economic practice to which farming and foraging belonged (e.g. Kelly 1995; Kent 1996). However, hunting and gathering and farming remain reified heuristic categories precisely because they lay at the heart of anthropological theory on social evolution. The distinction between farmers and hunter-gatherers remains essential for formulating research questions across disciplines because the distinction provides the theoretical foundation for many forms of 'origins' research. For example, current research in the fields of economics and biology explore similarities between the gathering work and group organisation of primates and hunter-gatherers in the contemporary world, who, we must suppose, represent once again the very earliest, very first attempts of our more distant ancestors in becoming human, in distinguishing themselves (unsuccessfully, this research would suggest) from their beastly neighbours (Yengoyan 2004). In a new twist on the relationship between subsistence and human origins, some scholars are now claiming that it was the shift to agriculture that produced the first culturally modern humans, recalling the Antique juxtaposition of the civilised farmer and the barbaric non-farmer (Cauvin 2000; Hodder 1990; Renfrew 2008; Watkins 2005; see also Finlayson & Warren 2010). These ideas about the origins of our humanity range in quality from sophisticated to ridiculous, but they prove the power of the association between subsistence and difference, an association which continues to shape research on the early history of Africans and humanity more generally.

In sum, the methods by which communities feed themselves have long been used to articulate difference in many strands of Western intellectual thought, distinguishing the civilised from the barbarians, modern societies from those who lag behind, and even humans from animals. The durability of the notion that subsistence marks difference relies on assumptions embedded in the very terms we use to conceptualise and talk about subsistence. Our folk conceptualisation of subsistence requires us to identify people and communities by one, single, main method of subsistence. We can clearly see this in our language. People are farmers or herders. Or, they might be hunter-gatherers. When their subsistence regime is more diversified, we are forced to privilege one form of subsistence over others and qualify it: 'mixed farmer' or the 'foraging spectrum' are two examples of thinking with blurred categories. We also invent complicated, hyphenated neologisms. From my region of study, consider recent scholarship on Nguni 'agro-pastoralists', Herero, Ju/'hoansi and other 'pastro-foragers' in southwest Africa, and even 'agro-pastroforagers' (Bollig & Gewald 2000; Homewood 2008; Perry 2006). Although we have terms to generalise about how folks get food – terms like 'subsistence', that can encompass almost any strategy or combinations thereof – when we shift our discussion to labelling *people*, we are, quite literally, left speechless. Our vocabulary reflects the unique, long-standing cultural ideal that every society (or practitioner) should rely on one primary means of securing food, with which they can be identified and, thereby, rendered politically, economically and culturally legible. We are severely constrained in our conceptualisation of subsistence by what we can say. We still struggle with the legacy of how this ideal was universalised in the political philosophy of Enlightenment thinkers and the evolutionary models of the 19th, 20th and even 21st centuries. Yet, 'Western' societies were not the only communities to recruit subsistence practices into identity politics.

Toward an intellectual history of subsistence in central Africa
Methodology
Central Africans similarly invented and politicised novel categories of subsistence. And, similarly, these conceptualisations were embedded in their vocabulary over the course of centuries of speech and practice. The communities of this central African case study were oral societies. The evidence that undergirds the *longue durée* intellectual history of subsistence categories in central Africa – the histories of reconstructed words – requires a cursory knowledge of the methodology of comparative historical linguistics.

Words used today by speakers of central African Bantu languages – in this case study, Botatwe languages (Fig. 3.1) – carry astonishing information about the interconnected histories of subsistence and politics in their etymologies and morphological markers. In the absence of the historian's customary documentary archive, I use comparative historical linguistics to reconstruct the history of subsistence. Briefly, comparative historical linguistics uses a word's phonological shape and distribution in extant languages to determine its place in particular 'branches' of a language family tree (Table 3.1). Its phonological shape and distribution also tell us which of three historical processes is responsible for its presence in that branch: inheritance, internal innovation or borrowing from other languages. A historical linguist determines when a word was produced and by what process, and then uses that information to tell a story with broad geographical and chronological scope. The historical actors of these stories are the speakers of the ancestral languages (protolanguages) to which particular words can be reconstructed. Reconstructed histories of words' invention and changing meanings reveal generalised patterns of change because they illuminate

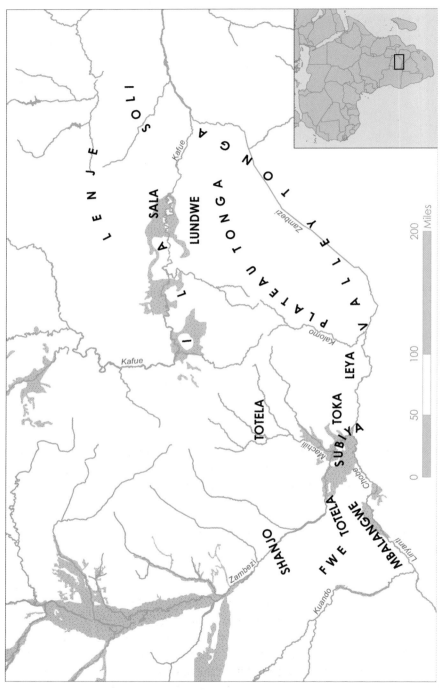

Figure 3.1. Location of Botatwe languages c. 1900.

Table 3.1. Outline classification of Botatwe languages

Botatwe (57–71% [100–900]; 64% median [500])

I. *Greater Eastern Botatwe* (63–74% [500–1000]; 68.5% median [750])

    a. *Central Eastern Botatwe* (70–77% [800–1100]; 73/5% median [950]

        i. *Kafue* (78–81% [1200–1300]; 79.5% median [1250])

            1. *Ila*

            2. *Tonga*

            3. *Sala*

            4. *Lenje*

        ii. *Falls* (91% [1700])

            1. *Toka*

            2. *Leya*

        iii. *Lundwe*

    b. *Soli*

II. *Western Botatwe* (76–81% [1100–1300]; 78.5% median [1200])

    a. *Zambezi Hook* (83% [1400])

        i. *Shanjo*

        ii. *Fwe*

    b. *Machili* (84–85% [1400–1450]; 84.5% median [1425])

        i. *Mbalangwe*

        ii. *Subiya*

        iii. *Totela*

Note: Extant languages are italicised. Cognation rates, both the range of the normal distribution curve and its median, are provided in parentheses. Calendar years for the ranges and medians are provided in brackets (adapted from de Luna 2010).

the cumulative trends embedded in the utterances of generations of speakers, who, together, constitute the speech community of a protolanguage. In this way, I am able to write *longue durée* histories of the oral societies of central Africa using speakers' own words.

The history of Botatwe subsistence vocabulary in central Africa, 1000 BCE to 1250 CE[3]

The binary between food production and food collection has been integral to Western intellectual history. But this binary only serves to obscure vernacular subsistence categories and their politicisation in central Africa during the very centuries and millennia during which the paradigmatic binary was crafted in Europe. The intellectual history of subsistence developed by generations of speakers of Botatwe languages in central Africa reveals a parallel process by which subsistence was grafted onto politics. But Botatwe speakers used a different set of mechanisms to tie the activities of food procurement to the politics of identity and the practice of power.

Throughout the last millennium BCE, the distinction between producing yams and collecting food was not entirely clear among Botatwe peoples, who planted traps among cultivars and harvested both the wild and domesticated plants that grew in tended fields. As cereal agriculture and pastoralism spread into the area in the early 1st millennium, central Africans committed to more sedentary lifestyles and food production. By the 6th century CE, linguistic and archaeological evidence suggest a more substantial commitment to cereal agriculture, some cattle-keeping and a greater degree of sedentism.

Counter-intuitively, Botatwe societies' commitment to a subsistence economy dominated by cereals sustained innovation in those domains of subsistence that agriculture is usually thought to replace. From the middle of the 8th century through the middle of the 13th century, Central Eastern Botatwe communities and their linguistic descendants, speakers of proto-Kafue, participated in a regional revolution in the technologies of spear hunting, rapid current fishing and metallurgy (Fig. 3.2). They invented a new category of landscape, the bush, which allowed them to cultivate a distinction between work undertaken in the fields nearer the village and work undertaken in the bush. Celebrated spearmen, rapid-current fishers and famous smelters sought to distinguish their activities from forms of related labour, such as trapping, basket fishing and smithing, which were undertaken in or near the village and were more closely associated with agriculture. Therefore, bushcraft emerged out of and was not prior to the creation of a cereal-based savanna agricultural system.

The invention of a distinction between the labours of agriculture and the work of the bush was transformative. With it, Central Eastern Botatwe speakers created a novel path to singularity, fame, friendship and ancestor-hood based on knowledge of the bush. This politics of talent and technology recast local understandings of the landscape and resisted the centralisation of political and ritual authority around the agricultural economy. Significantly, we have no archaeological or linguistic evidence for specialisation in the new subsistence category of 'bushcraft'; its practitioners were farmers most of the time. Here I will share three reconstructed words that teach us what 'bushcraft' as a category of subsistence meant to the central Africans who first invented and, subsequently, modified it over the centuries.

As part of a regional revolution in the technology of spearcraft between the mid-8th and mid-13th centuries, Central Eastern Botatwe speakers re-conceptualised the social meaning of skill in the kinds of hunting and fishing undertaken with spears (de Luna 2012a; see also Derricourt 1985; Fagan 1967; Fagan *et al.* 1969). From an older word for a kind of long blade, the inhabitants of the southern savannas, from northeast Angola to the middle Kafue, developed a new noun, *-pàdó, to name a 'celebrated, skilled hunter/spearman' (de Luna 2012b; 2016, root 68; Ehret 1998, 113). Skill in hunting with spears was nothing new, but the category of person who might be celebrated for it was a novel contribution to the social landscape. The honorific ultimately derived from an ancient Bantu verb *-pá, 'to give', with the extensive verbal affix. The extensive affix has been reconstructed on Proto-Bantu verbs with

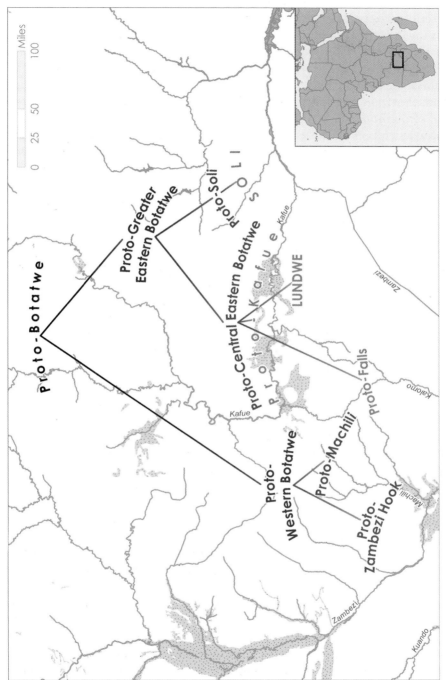

Figure 3.2. Approximate location of major Botatwe-language communities of south central Africa, c. 1000 BCE to 1200 CE.

the connotation 'to be in a spread-out position'. Thus, the verb literally meant 'to give or send across space' or 'to give widely'. In many southern Bantu languages, the extensive affix also connotes repetition of an action undertaken on a large scale: 'he who repetitively, intensively gives'. The morphology also reflected the social, discursive nature of ascription: the /–ú/ suffix indicates that the root was used as a verb of quality able to function as an adjective of quality, glossing inelegantly as 'hunt-ious'. Further derivation from the verb or adjective of quality produces both the noun of quality, *bwaalu* ('huntsmanship', noun class 14) and the noun denoting a person who embodied huntsmanship, *mwaalu* (noun class 1/2). If the repetitive, intensive connotation of the extensive affix dates to proto-Central Eastern Botatwe, *-pàdó was the consummate huntsman, both a 'good shot' and a 'generous giver'. The morphology of *-pàdó supported this polysemy because the verb's object – what the hunter 'gives' – could be both his weapon and the game he distributed. Thus, *-pàdó poetically captured in one word fleeting scenes of the *mwaalu*'s craft: his spear thrown across great distances, repeated stabbings of the close kill and followers' expectation of his expansive and repeated munificence in sharing meat.

To describe what was new about the kind of work undertaken by *-pàdó, Central Eastern Botatwe speakers invented a new verb, *-wèz-, to talk about hunting or fishing with spears, possibly throwing spears (de Luna 2016, root 63). In Ila, the best documented Botatwe language, *kuweza* also refers to the hunt for economic success and its use to launch and manage one's social position, precisely the process that could produce a status like *-pàdó (Fielder 1979, 624). Indeed, the most likely source root is *-gèd-, a widespread Bantu verb with a broad range of meanings. As a verb, the root glosses as 'to try', 'to think' or 'to measure', but in noun form, it commonly means 'wisdom' or even 'guile' in central African Bantu languages. When Central Eastern Botatwe speakers developed the verb *-wèz- in the last quarter of the 1st millennium to talk about a new form of hunting and fishing with spears, they sought to describe the social implications of such technological knowledge and skill (Fig. 3.3).

Central Eastern Botatwe speakers and their linguistic descendants distinguished work undertaken in the fields from labours in the bush by christening that landscape with a new name: *-sókwe (de Luna 2015; 2016, root 75). This word innovation elaborated on an older, more widespread verb, *-còk-, 'to incite', which, itself, derives from an ancient Bantu term that glosses as 'to poke in, put in, prick with a point, hide, ram in'. Contemporary attestations in the best documented Botatwe languages reveal a complicated network of meanings tying together ideas about 'provoking', 'inciting' and 'stabbing' with 'being first', 'establishing' or 'originating'. This semantic range suggests that speakers thought that acts of creation in the bush required provocation by poking or spearing. Modern attestations make explicit the link to hunting. When Central Eastern Botatwe, Kafue and neighbouring communities named the open bush around them with the passive tense of the verb *-còk- sometime between the mid-8th and mid-13th centuries, they imagined this landscape to be a place of potential creation, a place that was literally 'the poked,

Figure 3.3. Ila spearmen honing their skills in a throwing competition in the early 20th century. Photograph by E. W. Smith. Reprinted from Smith & Dale (1920, vol. 2, 242).

the prodded, the hidden, the entered' place, a setting for and ingredient in acts of origination incited by the plunging action of spears thrust into quarry stalked, netted or trapped in the bush.

Importantly, the centuries-old technology of iron smelting shifted from village centres to the bush between the 7th and 11th centuries throughout central and southern Africa (Bisson 1976; Fagan 1967, 88–91; Fagan *et al.* 1969, 43; Inskeep 1962, 152–156; 1978, 113–117; Killick 1990, 76–77; Robertson 2001, 262; Vogel 1971a, 39–41; 1971b, 39; 1975, 66). This shift occurred at just the moment when the landscape category of *isokwe* was invented. Speakers conceptualised the act of poking and prodding into action as a link between spearcraft and smelting, asserting this embodied experience as the quintessential action from which the bush was named. Each of the technologies practised in the bush – spearcraft and smelting – shared a further tie as the activities whose practitioners were named with terms that also glossed as 'celebrated, famous person'. With the invention of the bush, activities that had once been familiar to and practiced by many villagers were elevated from banal, quotidian tasks into a pathway to fame and notability. Together, these activities constituted the new subsistence category 'bushcraft'.

Spearmen and smelters worked only part of the time at their labours and theirs were activities open to and practiced by many other villagers. What was unique to Botatwe speakers' conceptualisation of these subsistence categories was their location in the bush, their common kinaesthetics, and the possibility that demonstrating skill in such domains might bring celebrity and, thereby, secure one's place in the future as a remembered and efficacious ancestor. The invention and celebration of practitioners of bushcraft had an important effect on Botatwe political history: it diffused political authority, contributing to the persistently decentralised character of politics across three millennia.

The mid-1st millennium transition in central Africa from a very diverse, even eclectic, subsistence system that integrated yam horticulture, small stock, fishing, gathering and hunting to a more sedentary subsistence economy focused on cereals and livestock actually resulted in great innovation in some of the technologies that would be labelled 'food collection' in the binary that so widely influences scholarly approaches to subsistence. But Botatwe speakers conceptualised this subsistence category as something more akin to spearcraft, for it did not encompass all forms of food collection. More specifically, it was a form of economic activity located in the bush and associated with other technologies – notably smelting – that are usually studied as something other than subsistence, however central the products are to food procurement. Much of the anthropological literature would suggest we approach the innovation of bushcraft as a specialisation that developed as a result of a local Neolithic transition. But the desire to apply the label 'specialisation' to the central African subsistence category of bushcraft is just another iteration of the ideal that people should be identified with one primary form of subsistence strategy. Botatwe speakers held no such view.

Conclusion

When told alongside the parallel intellectual history of subsistence categories in the West, the case study of Botatwe bushcraft exposes a number of social, political and economic changes assumed to be natural outcomes of innovations in subsistence practice. For Botatwe speakers, the work of procuring food was not necessarily separated from the production of tools related to food collection and food production. For that matter, food production and collection were not always seen as distinct. Differences and similarities between subsistence strategies were maintained using very different systems of categorisation relating to geographic location, ideas about how fame worked (de Luna 2015) and bodily actions. For Botatwe speakers, accumulation and control over agricultural surplus was not the foundation of political power; their politics emphasised the affective dimensions of some categories of subsistence. Because bushcraft was a not a professional or specialised endeavour, the celebrity it might bring afforded famous practitioners an ephemeral, sometimes even seasonal form of political and social influence (de Luna 2012b; 2016).

The binary that still shapes the Western conceptualisation of subsistence (and that inspired this volume) certainly deserves to be complicated on its own terms through the study of complex transitions to agriculture, food producers' many reversions to food collection, or even complex hunter-gatherers. To be sure, the inadequacy of our subsistence vocabulary begs the question: how did subsistence categories acquire their exclusionary quality and what purpose did it serve those who deployed them? But this binary should also be compared to the subsistence categories developed in other cultures and time periods. We may not escape inheriting the conceptual limits of our language, but we can certainly stretch those limits by borrowing novel ideas and words from the creative subsistence strategies of those who came before us. In other words, we can and should study histories of subsistence in others' terms.

Notes

1. This section on subsistence categories in Western thought draws on but also elaborates arguments in de Luna 2016, 4–12.
2. This section summarises and amplifies arguments in the introduction to de Luna 2016.
3. Unless indicated otherwise, the evidence and arguments in this section summarise those in de Luna 2016, chaps 2–4.

References

Baloglou, C. (2012) The tradition of economic thought in the Mediterranean World from the Ancient Classical times through the Hellenistic times until the Byzantine times and Arab-Islamic World. In J. G. Backhaus (ed.), *Handbook of the History of Economic Thought: Insights on the Founders of Modern Economics*, 7–91. New York, Springer.

Barnard, A. (1992) Through Radcliffe-Brown's spectacles: reflections on the history of anthropology. *History of the Human Sciences* 5, 1–20.

Barnard, A. (1999) Images of hunter-gatherers in European social thought. In R. Lee & R. Daly (eds), *The Cambridge Encyclopedia of Hunters and Gatherers*, 375–383. Cambridge, Cambridge University Press.

Barnard, A. (2004) Hunting-and-gathering society: an eighteenth century Scottish invention. In A. Barnard (ed.), *Hunter-Gatherers in History, Archaeology and Anthropology*, 31–43. New York, Berg.

Binford, L. (1981) *Bones: Ancient Man and Modern Myths*. New York, Academic Press.

Bisson, M. (1976) The Prehistoric Coppermines of Zambia. Unpublished Ph.D. thesis, University of California, Santa Barbara.

Bollig, M. & Gewald, J. B. (2000) *People, Cattle and Land-transformations of Pastoral Society: an Introduction*. Köln, Köppe.

Brain, C. (1981) *The Hunters or the Hunted? An Introduction to African Cave Taphonomy*. Chicago, University of Chicago Press.

Cartmill, M. (1993) *A View to a Death in the Morning: Hunting and Nature through History*. Cambridge MA, Harvard University Press.

Cauvin, J. (2000) *The Birth of the Gods and the Origins of Agriculture*. Cambridge, Cambridge University Press.

Childe, V. G. (1936) *Man Makes Himself*. London, Watts.

Dahlberg, F. (1981) Introduction. In F. Dahlberg (ed.), *Woman the Gatherer*, 1–33. New Haven, Yale University Press.

Dart, R. (1925) *Australopithecus Africanus*: The man-ape of South Africa. *Nature* 115, 195–199.

de Luna, K. M. (2010) Classifying Botatwe: M.60 and K.40 languages and the settlement chronology of south central Africa. *Africana Linguistica* 16, 65–96.

de Luna, K. M. (2012a) Surveying the boundaries of history and archaeology: early Botatwe settlement in south central Africa and the 'sibling Ddsciplines' debate. *African Archaeological Review* 29(2/3), 209–251.

de Luna, K. M. (2012b) Hunting Reputations: Talent, Individuals, and Community in Precolonial South Central Africa. *Journal of African History* 53, 3, 279–99.

de Luna, K. M. (2015) Marksmen and the bush: the affective micro-politics of landscape, sex, and technology in precolonial south central Africa. *Kronos: Southern African Histories* 41, 21–44.

de Luna, K. M. (2016) *Collecting Food, Cultivating People: Subsistence and Society in Central Africa, 1000 BC to AD 1900*. New Haven, Yale University Press.

Derricourt, R. (1985) *Man on the Kafue: the Archaeology and History of the Itezhitezhi area of Zambia*. New York, Lilian Berber.

Ehret, C. (1998) *An African Classical Age: Eastern and Southern Africa in World History, 1000 B.C. to A.D. 400*. Charlottesville, University of Virginia Press.

Ellingson, T. (2001) *The Myth of the Noble Savage*. Berkeley, University of California Press.

Fagan, B. (1967) *Iron Age Cultures in Zambia* 1. London, Chatto and Windus.

Fagan, B. Phillipson, D. & Daniels, S. (1969) *Iron Age Cultures in Zambia* 2. London, Chatto and Windus.

Ferguson, A. (1992) *Utter Antiquity: Perceptions of prehistory in Renaissance England*. Durham, Duke University Press.

Fielder, R. (1979) Economic spheres in Pre-Colonial Ila society. *African Social Research* 28, 617–641.

Finlayson, B. & Warren, G. (2010) *Changing Natures: Hunter-Gatherers, First Farmers and the Modern World*. London, Duckworth.

Hard, D. & Sussman, R. (2005) *Man the Hunted: Primates, Predators, and Human Evolution*. Boulder, Westview Press.

Hodder, I. (1990) *The Domestication of Europe: Structure and Contingency in Neolithic Societies*. Oxford, Blackwell.

Homewood, K. (2008) *Ecology of African Pastoralist Societies*. Athens, Ohio University Press.

Inskeep, R. (1962) Some Iron Age sites in Northern Rhodesia. *South African Archaeological Bulletin* 17, 91–96.

Inskeep, R. (1978) An iron-smelting furnace in southern Zambia. *South African Archaeological Bulletin* 33, 113–117.

Janko, J. (1997) Two Concepts of the World in Greek and Roman thought: cyclicity and degeneration. In M. Teich, R. Porter & B. Gustafsson (eds), *Nature and Society in Historical Context*, 18–36. Cambridge, Cambridge University Press.

Kelly, R. (1995) *The Foraging Spectrum: Diversity in Hunter-Gatherer Lifeways*. Washington, Smithsonian Institution Press.

Kent, S. (ed.) (1996) *Cultural Diversity among Twentieth Century Foragers: an African Perspective*. Cambridge, Cambridge University Press.

Killick, D. (1990) Technology in its Social Setting: Bloomery Iron-Smelting at Kasungu, Malawi, 1860–1940. Unpublished PhD thesis, Yale University.

Klieman, K. (2003) *The Pygmies were Our Compass: Bantu and Batwa in the History of West Central Africa, Early Times to c. 1900 C.E.* Portsmouth, Heinemann.

Kuper, A. (1988) *The Invention of Primitive Society: Transformations of an Illusion*. New York, Routledge.

Meek, R. (1976) *Social Science and the Ignoble Savage*. Cambridge, Cambridge University Press.

Oakely, K. (1954) The dating of Australopithecinae of Africa. *American Journal of Physical Anthropology* 12, 9–28.

Perry, W. R. (2006) *Landscape Transformations and the Archaeology of Impact: Social Disruption and State Formation in Southern Africa*. Dordrecht, Springer Science & Business Media E-book.

Pluciennik, M. (2001) Archaeology, Anthropology and Subsistence. *Journal of the Royal Anthropological Institute* 7(4), 741–758.

Pluciennik, M. (2002) The invention of hunter-gatherers in seventeenth-century Europe. *Archaeological Dialogues* 9(2), 98–151.

Pluciennik, M. (2004) The meaning of 'hunter-gatherers' and modes of subsistence: a comparative historical perspective. In A. Barnard (ed.), *Hunter-Gatherers in History, Archaeology and Anthropology*, 17–29. Oxford & New York, Berg.

Price, D. & Brown, J. (eds) (1985) *Prehistoric Hunter-Gatherers: The Emergence of Cultural Complexity*. New York, Academic Press.

Renfrew, C. (2008) *Prehistory: The Making of the Human Mind*. London, Weidenfeld and Nicolson.

Robertson, J. (2001) South African Early Iron Age in Zambia. In P. Peregrine & M. Ember (eds), *Encyclopedia of Prehistory, vol. 1, Africa*, 260–271. New York, Springer.

Rudebeck, E. (2000) *Tilling Nature, Harvesting Culture: Exploring Images of the Human Being in the Transition to Agriculture*. Stockhom, Almqvist & Wiksell International.

Sahlins, M. (1968) Notes on the Original Affluent Society. In R. Lee & I. DeVore (eds), *Man the Hunter*, 85–89. Chicago, Aldine.

Sahlins, M. (1972) *Stone Age Economics*. Chicago, Aldine.

Sassaman, K. (2004) Complex hunter-gatherers in evolution and history: a North American perspective. *Journal of Archaeological Research* 12(3), 227–280.

Service, E. (1962) *Primitive Social Organization*. New York, Random House.

Smith, E. & Dale, A. (1920) *The Ila-Speaking Peoples of Northern Rhodesia 2*. London: Macmillan.

Sollas, W. (1911) *Ancient Hunters and their Modern Representatives*. London, Macmillan.

Steward, J. (1955) *Theory of Culture Change: the Methodology of Multilinear Evolution*. Urbana, University of Illinois Press.

Trigger, B. (2006) *A History of Archaeological Thought* (2nd edn). Cambridge, Cambridge University Press.

Vencl, S. (1988) The problem of disappearance of hunter-gatherer societies in prehistory: archaeological evidence and testimonies of Classical authors. *Listy Filologické* 111, 129–143.

Vogel, J. (1971a) *Kumadzulo: An Early Iron Age Village Site in Southern Zambia*. Lusaka & London, Oxford University Press for the National Museums of Zambia.

Vogel, J. (1971b) *Kamangoza: An Introduction to the Iron Age Cultures of the Victoria Falls Region*. Nairobi & London, Oxford University Press for the National Museums of Zambia.

Vogel, J. (1975) *Simbusenga: the Archaeology of the Intermediate Period in Southern Zambia*. London, Oxford University Press for the National Museums of Zambia.

Washburn, S. (1957) Australopithecines: the hunters or the hunted? *American Anthropologist* 59, 612–614.

Washburn, S. & Lancaster, C. (1968) The evolution of hunting. In R. Lee & I. DeVore (eds), *Man the Hunter*, 293–303. Chicago: Aldine.

Watkins, T. (2005) The Neolithic Revolution and the emergence of humanity: a cognitive approach to the first comprehensive World view. In J. Clarke (ed.), *Archaeological Perspectives on the Transmission and Transformation of Culture in the Eastern Mediterranean*, 84–88. Oxford, Council for British Research in the Levant & Oxbow Books.

Yengoyan, A. (2004) Anthropological history and the study of hunters and gatherers: cultural and non-cultural. In A. Barnard (ed.) *Hunter-Gatherers in History, Archaeology, and Anthropology*, 57–66. Oxford, Berg.

Zvelebil, M. (2002) The invention of hunter-gatherers in seventeenth century Europe? A comment on Mark Pluciennik. *Archaeological Dialogues* 9(2), 123–129.

Chapter 4

The end of hunting and gathering

Bill Finlayson

Introduction

The social and economic transformations that took place in the late Pleistocene and early Holocene of Southwest Asia bring an end to a world solely occupied by people reliant on wild resources and introduce a gradual shift to food production. This is a unique moment in history, characterised by a huge autochthonous shift in lifeways for which we have no direct ethnographic analogy. This initial transformation to food producing societies lacks any of the key ingredients that have variously been identified as essential for ethnographic analogy (as summarised, for example by Binford 1972). It lacks direct historical continuity with any known hunter-gatherers by many thousands of years, lacks environmental congruity with recent or modern hunter-gatherers, and lacks good economic parallels with hunter-gatherers living in the modern world. However, despite this complete misfit, a general reliance on ethnography and analogy continues to provide a substantial foundation to the interpretative framework employed in Southwest Asia. The general problems with this use of such an ethnographic framework have been critiqued before (e.g. Zvelebil & Fewster 2001; Hodder 1982; Wobst 1978), including its specific relationship to the Neolithic transformation in Southwest Asia (Finlayson & Warren 2010). Here I want to draw out some specifics where it seems that the anthropology of hunter-gatherers, and even more so, the subset that is commonly deployed by archaeologists, limits and restricts our archaeological understandings – which in turn reduces the potential contribution of archaeology to hunter-gatherer studies.

The brilliance of matching Morgan's (1877) social scheme with the European three-age system, and the power of Childe's vision of a Neolithic revolution (Childe 1935), simultaneously affecting all aspects of society and economy as a single package in a rapid shift, have left us handicapped as they established a deeply stadial approach to the Neolithic transition. The scale and rapidity of change is emphasised by the idea that a Neolithic revolution occurs suddenly in many places over a short period of time around the world (Cohen 2009). This established model has remained exceedingly powerful, and has led to an acceptance that food production is revolutionary, global, and creates the modern world. Renfrew summarises this model by stating that 'humans, through the development of agriculture, were able to turn away from a life of hunting and gathering and to live in villages and then in towns' (Renfrew 2007, vii–viii). It is simple and catchy, and has led to a proliferation of revolutionary moments, such as the sedentary revolution (Renfrew 2007), the symbolic revolution (Cauvin 2000) and even a cognitive revolution (Watkins 2005). Such an approach encourages an opposition between hunting and gathering and farming ways of life which crucially leaves no space for anything in between. The approach may, at least to an extent, work in a European context, where it can be argued that the Neolithic does arrive ready-made as a package, whether it was transmitted by migration or assimilation, but given the absence of any space between hunting and gathering, it excludes all of the interesting initial transition in Southwest Asia. The conflation of the Southwest Asian and the European conceptions of the Neolithic is problematic, although both derive from Childe's definition. The Southwest Asian Neolithic is an entirely different context, where indigenous hunter-gatherers transform themselves over the course of an incredibly long period, by the end of which they have developed many of the traits later used to define Neolithic as it appears in Europe. For the Southwest Asian Neolithic, it is only by using hindsight that we can even recognise the nature of the transition that was taking place, and Neolithic societies were only transitional in a long-term perspective.

Our unfamiliarity with such an autochthonous transformation leaves us bereft of analogical parallels to call on. It is too modern for much reliance on primate analogy, although there are calls made on Dunbar's work on social groups to understand the requirements of maintaining society in increasingly large settled communities (e.g. Watkins 2005), and there are no parallels within anthropological ethnography. It is notable that in volumes on hunter-gatherers, whether archaeological or anthropological, while there may be substantial sections devoted to the relations between hunter-gatherers and farmers, whether in the modern world or the European Mesolithic/Neolithic transition, there is very little on transitional societies – see for example in the recent Oxford Handbook (Cummings *et al.* 2014). Even in the introductory section to this Handbook, attention is drawn to the contact between hunters and gatherers and farmers, and the role played by hunter-gatherers in the transmission of farming (Jordan & Cummings 2014, 38). We stumble at the first actual transition, where our archaeological imaginations largely lead us to see the early Neolithic in terms of farming societies.

There are only three chapters on the initial transition in this Oxford Handbook, a volume that is composed of 61 chapters, with considerably more discussion of hunter-gatherers within a farming world (e.g. Cummings 2014). Rather strikingly, in contrast to most of the other chapters, the chapters on initial transition are not focused on society, but comprise a chapter on the domestication of plants (Harris 2014), one on the domestication of animals (Outram 2014) and a few pages within a chapter on the general transition process (Moore 2014). Moore believes in a 'mature mixed farming economy by 8,000 BP' (2014, 461), but many of the staples of Mediterranean farming, perhaps most strikingly the olive, are not fully incorporated until considerably later (Finlayson

2013). Outram and Harris both observe the long time this transition takes, with Harris proposing a 3000 year time span. The slow pace of transition is well-worth restating, the length of time involved is often invisible to people working outside the Southwest Asian context. The timescale suggested by Harris for the transitional period is actually quite short, I have argued elsewhere for a period of at least 8000 years of transition, which is a longer timescale than the distance that separates us from the end of the Neolithic in Southwest Asia, about 6500 years ago (Finlayson 2013). However, even this is still a short chronology; others have argued that the process goes back to 23,000 years BP at Ohalo II on the shore of the Sea of Galilee, where there is evidence for both small seed harvesting and architecture (Nadel 2004). There are problems with such long chronologies, some of which relate to the difficulties associated with 'origins research' as discussed by Gamble (2007), others of which relate to our own difficulties of classification.

Outram reminds us of the difficulties in deciding what domestication really is, casting us back to Ingold (1980) and the importance of the social relations of production. Both agriculture and domestication are imprecise concepts that cause confusion due to a lack of definition coupled with an assumption that we all know what they mean (Harris 2007, 18). The closer we are able to look at the biological processes involved, the harder it becomes to observe a revolutionary, category changing, moment. Zeder (2009, 38), following Ingold, has argued that no particular domestication moment can be identified, and that our interest should be in the long process of interaction between humans and potential domesticates, rather than trying to identify a particular moment of domestication or artificial threshold between hunting and gathering and farming. Few would now argue that morphological shifts are a key indicator of the leading edge of domestication (Zeder 2009; Makarewicz 2013). Similarly, the construction of shelters such as the brush huts, floors, post-holes and hearths at sites such as Ohalo II, Ein Gev I and Kharaneh IV (Maher *et al.* 2012) in the early Epipalaeolithic, while important and a reminder that construction has a long history, are not really architecture in a meaningful way. They long pre-date the emergence of the built environment and the novel forms of settlement that are a hallmark of the Neolithic, although these also appear long before the mature mixed farming economy coalesces (Watkins 2005). This incredibly long, slow, and undirected process is ill suited to a simple classification that jumps from hunting and gathering to farming societies. Even if we insert intermediary categories, such as the complex hunter-gatherer, such devices simply add additional steps in the process.

Analogy, archaeology and anachronism

There have been numerous discussions of the application of ethnographic analogy in archaeology over the years (Zvelebil & Fewster 2001; Finlayson & Warren 2010; Hodder 1982), and there is no need to rehearse these in detail. The classic description of a hunter-gatherer society, with its characteristics of egalitarian social structure, the importance of sharing, the role of mobility and less than 5% reliance on domesticated foods, is a thoroughly modern definition (Panter-Brick *et al.* 2001). It describes an adaptation, often to marginal environments, that is always part of a modern world, where the hunter-gatherers have either previously farmed, or at least are in contact with farming societies and perhaps work for them. They form a desperately poor analogy for societies 10,000, still less 23,000 years ago, living in a rich environment with no contact with farmers. However, despite this body of argument and the enormous development in archaeological knowledge, analytical techniques and models, we still discuss the Neolithic transformation within an extremely basic framework of simple to complex hunter-gatherer, followed by farmer, which permits us to fall back on oversimplified ethnographic analogy.

In part this use of analogy continues to rely on a processualist approach that emphasises law-like assumptions regarding hunter-gatherer behaviour, even where the research context is far removed from processualism (cf. Zelebil & Fewster 2001), and in part requires we maintain sharply defined boundary shifts between hunter-gatherers, farmers and their intermediaries, so that they remain visible in a qualified terminology of 'complex' or 'incipient'. Although not always made explicit, such analogous reasoning is largely based upon the universal generalisations that were the hallmark of much processual archaeology (see Kuijt 2008 for a clearly argued case where synthesised anthropological generalisations are deployed to study ritual behaviour in the early Neolithic). Developing the 'law-like' approach, Benz and Bauer have recently (2013) explicitly argued in the context of the Southwest Asian Neolithic transition that 'anthropological universals' exist, and these encourage certain decisions and actions, and make others less probable. They argue that recurring patterns identified in ethnographic accounts allow the formulation of probabilities concerning behaviour, such as generalised reciprocity, and emotional reactions, such as fear of strangers. However, this misses the key issue regarding the Neolithic transition. The first transition to food producing societies is outside our anthropological knowledge. In the absence of any ethnographic knowledge of this period, the use of such universals requires highly circular reasoning. Many of these universal generalisations are too broad and bland, discussing concepts such as egalitarianism or sharing as simply being aspects of hunter-gatherer behaviour (e.g. Benz 2010). This generalisation of behaviour also runs through reconstructions of European Mesolithic societies (e.g. Robb 2013; Thomas 2013). Such behaviours have a complicated relationship with hunter-gatherer societies, as they have become part of the definition of what a modern hunter-gatherer is (Bird-David 1988). Even the proponents of globalisation in archaeological interpretation, such as Renfrew, recognise that the generalised view that allows global comparisons require a level of abstraction that becomes meaningless, where 'cross-continental comparisons may at first seem to risk superficiality' (Renfrew 2003, 32).

Classification and categorisation

Hunter-gatherer as a classification has been, and remains, a surprisingly elusive concept with definitions evolving over time (Lee & Devore 1968; Ingold 1988;

Bird-David 1988). The classification currently employed only really emerges in the middle of the 20th century (Barnard 2004). The 'revisionist' descriptions of modern hunter-gatherers, describing how their current way of life is the product of resistance to neighbouring farmers (e.g. Schrire 1984), or is part of a history that includes farming (e.g. Wilmsen & Denbow 1990), undermines the very concept of a common hunter-gatherer way of life. Widlok has recently proposed that in the contemporary world we should be studying hunter-gatherer 'situations' rather than hunter-gatherer societies (Widlok 2016). This is in part a response to the association of hunter-gatherers with marginality and deprivation, which currently characterises many hunter-gatherer societies. Arguably, food-producing societies will have marginalised hunter-gatherers since their first development, except in very specific contexts of natural resource abundance (typically marine) or within ecological niches where farming is impossible (for example, arctic or desert contexts). Prior to the development of farming there was no such degree of marginalisation (although economic inequality is always likely to have existed between hunter-gatherers), and this incompatibility with the modern hunter-gatherer situation should provide an alarm-call for any simple analogy made between societies living in the world before farming and the present or recent past. The modern ethnographically derived understanding that there is a distinct gap between hunting and farming societies and economies (e.g. Panter-Brick *et al.* 2001) does not allow us to address the significant transitional period where societies, and economies, were very different and in some senses in-between what we would now classify as either hunter-gatherer or farmer. In recent years the quest for completely 'pure' hunter-gatherers has declined (Barnard 2014, 43), but archaeological definitions still require that subsistence input from domesticated resources must be marginal to avoid reclassification as something other than 'hunter-gatherer'. Arguably, within anthropology there has been a change of emphasis in hunter-gatherer research with the focus on economy being replaced by, for example, definitions dependent on social organisation (Pluciennik 2014). This change has rarely penetrated archaeological analogy. Ironically, within Southwest Asian Neolithic archaeology, we appear to be less tolerant of the introduction of elements of food production within hunting and gathering economies than we are within modern ethnography or anthropology. This may be understandable, perhaps inevitable, within a context where we actively seek the roots of farming societies, flagging up every minor shift as a first, incipient step on the road to modernity – and consequently as a step away from hunting and gathering.

The concept of the complex hunter-gatherer, mostly based on recent Northwest Coast societies is often deployed in archaeology, especially to describe the late Pleistocene Early Natufian society in Southwest Asia (Price & Brown 1985). Complex hunter-gatherer societies have been argued to be highly stable and, especially in Northwest Europe, as being resistant to farming. Complex hunter-gatherers are usually assumed to have been hierarchical in structure, more sedentary, and often dependent on seasonally abundant stored food. The archaeological evidence from Natufian settlements has been argued to indicate the presence of such a combination of traits, allowing the complex hunter-gatherer type to be used to fill the theoretical analogical gap between a presumed simple, mobile and egalitarian Epipalaeolithic hunter-gatherer society and the early Neolithic farmer. However, this has required a role reversal for complex hunter-gatherers, who are described in the Southwest Asian context as being an unstable stage (despite a 3000 year duration) that almost automatically led the way to farming. This contrasts with their definition elsewhere and the assumption that complex hunter-gatherers formed a transitional link, or that their progression to farming was inevitable, appears to be retrofitted by hindsight to the otherwise very successful Natufian societies (cf. Rowley-Conwy 2004; Finlayson 2009; Finlayson & Warren 2010).

The insertion of this hierarchical hunter-gatherer type leads to a number of other logical problems with early Neolithic narratives, in particular arguments that social behaviour in the early Neolithic was often intended to maintain an egalitarian hunter-gatherer way of life, despite the burdens of the new economy and community size. Moore, for example, regards the Pre-Pottery Neolithic A (PPNA) as a 'new agricultural economy', yet has no problems in seeing the Pre-Pottery Neolithic B (PPNB) as egalitarian even in its largest settlements (Moore 2014). Social structures designed to maintain an egalitarian society are assumed to represent continuity from a simple hunter-gatherer past (Kuijt 2008). Unfortunately, this seems to step back to an imagined hunter-gatherer past, not reckoning on the thousands years of the Epipalaeolithic, especially the 'complex hunter-gatherer' Natufian society. In effect, complex Natufian hunter-gatherers seem to be deployed to bridge a gap, but to then be dismissed from the narrative once that role is complete.

Rather than introducing 'complex-hunter-gatherers' as a category, we may be better off recognising that there are different forms of complexity, and that complexity is relative, allowing us to discuss a wider range of societies within a broad hunter-gatherer definition (cf. Fewster & Zvelebil 2001). However, apart from maintaining a 'hunter-gatherer' label, it is not clear what the benefit of continuing to describe these societies as hunter-gatherers is, as the flexibility of the definition at this point means that some, or all, of what we typically believe to be properties of hunter-gatherers no longer apply. This creates a challenge for contemporary research, as in the absence of 'pure' hunter-gatherers, all ethnographic work now goes 'beyond the received hunter-gatherer framework' (Widlock 2016, 140), and the transitional societies around the Neolithic transformation also lie outwith this framework.

The use of hunter-gatherer and the savage in the creation of the 'other' is well known and has been extensively debated elsewhere (see Finlayson & Warren 2010). What has received less attention is the other side of the division, the people like us, the farmers. Our imagined modern connection to farming is projected back into the past, where Neolithic societies are interpreted as farming societies familiar from our recent past, and then brought back into the present. For example, the account of the excavations at Abu Hureyra was published with a cover anachronistically showing camels at the water hole and a herder on a donkey (Moore *et al.* 2000), with neither animal having been domesticated in the Neolithic. The message is clear, the Neolithic revolution creates a modern agricultural economy and village society. A similar process has occurred in francophone literature, for example in Cauvin's explicit linkage of Southwest Asian Neolithic populations to Catholic peasants in France (Cauvin 2000). A timeless romantic image of the farmer links us directly to the idea of the Neolithic, as opposed to the 'other' of the Palaeolithic. Categorisation into food production and food procurement, although seeking to remove some of the dichotomies present in most models, continues to preserve boundaries. Smith (2001) and Harris (2007) have discussed the intermediate zone between hunting and gathering and farming, but almost exclusively in economic terms. One terminological solution has been the introduction of the concept of 'low-level food producing' societies (Smith 2001), which gives us a short-hand descriptor for the economies of extensive periods of history and a useful escape from dichotomy. However, this definition is not extended to social structures, indeed perhaps cannot be extended, as so far the social structures for the transitional period have all been provided by analogy from modern ethnography. Most archaeological low-level food producers probably fell within Panter-Brick's gap between hunter-gatherers and farmers in the modern world. Is such a universal terminology as low-level food producer even useful, or does it simply mask the important and interesting detail of specific contexts?

Much as we can push back the start of the process that in Barnard's terminology reduced the economic 'purity' of the hunter-gatherers concerned, we also have to pull forward its completion and the point when we believe we can truly identify the first 'farmers'. Identifying a fully farming society turns out to be quite difficult. Pearsall has argued that the issue is not when domestication first appears, but when dependence on the domesticate occurs (Pearsall 2009). In terms of identifying farming, as distinct from hunting and gathering, this seems a more constructive approach than just identifying first domesticates, but it still depends on a simplistic opposition of two modes of subsistence that are hard to identify archaeologically. We can now identify some of the leading edges of animal domestication, for example in kill patterns as an indication of the management of wild herds (e.g. Makarewicz 2013). Similarly, through the presence of weed flora we can suggest a long period of the cultivation of wild plants (Colledge *et al.* 2005). But the debate over the point at which we describe what has happened as domestication – the active management, or the emergence (or dominance) of domesticated traits – is ongoing. This gentle slope, where low-level food production is a continuum, beginning with such processes as fire management of the environment, as practiced by several recent hunter-gatherer societies, is not amenable to simple stadial definition. Even once there are clear examples of domesticated plants and animals, they do not immediately dominate the diet, which continues to include wild, rather than only produced, food. In Southwest Asia, it is not until at least the later, or ceramic Neolithic (starting around 8000 cal BP) that we can see a farming economy in place (Finlayson 2013). But even this society may not yet really be farming in the way we understand it. Farming is a deep-rooted concept that is central to many conceptions of society today, employed in the romanticized recent past, and even in the bucolic myths used to sell factory farmed foods in supermarkets (Finlayson & Warren 2010). The various tropes used in the archaeological literature, for example the idea that by the Middle PPNB elements familiar to us in contemporary Middle Eastern settlements had become established, or affinities between the PPN and medieval European peasant societies, or the concept of a standard Eurasian farming package, or even the conceit that near eastern village architecture has not changed since the Neolithic (Bar-Yosef & Meadow 1995; Cauvin 2000; Barker 2006; McCarter 2007), all play to the same idea that farmers are somehow completely ahistorical. The identification of early farmers with modern farmers is a fundamental part of the idea that in some way farming societies are people like us, in stark contrast to the otherness of hunter-gatherers.

The Pre-Pottery Neolithic

The Pre-Pottery Neolithic A (PPNA, 12,000–10,800 cal BP) is often seen as the key moment of transition, the first Neolithic society. It is sometimes divided into an early part, still part of the Epipalaeolithic, still really hunting and gathering, and a second part, living in villages, farming (if only through the cultivation of wild plants), and somehow really Neolithic (Cauvin 2000; Goring-Morris & Belfer-Cohen 2010). Does this mean that the PPNA conforms perfectly to a stadial model, the point where we can actually divide history between hunter-gatherers and farmers? Or are we simply imposing a rather crude definition onto the evidence, not least because we deploy modern analogies onto a context where they do not apply. If this is the last moment of a world solely inhabited by hunting and gathering societies, what do the transitional societies tell us, and can they be relevant to Widlok's challenge?

The division of the PPNA into a not so real and then somehow real Neolithic appears largely as an attempt to refine the moment of transition, but we should query whether such a moment ever actually happened. Over the period of transition, change occurred at different speeds and trajectories throughout the region, creating a number of substantial difficulties in using ethnographic data to provide points of analogy during the process of the Neolithic transformation in Southwest Asia. Different areas changed through their own versions of the transition, economically, technologically and socially. The historical processes that occur in northern Syria on the Middle Euphrates are not the same as those that happen in the Jordan valley, which is different again from what takes place in southern Jordan (Finlayson & Makarewicz in press). The more we discover about the period the richer the local historical contexts become. Although there are clear unifying features, the degree of diversity between PPNA sites and regions is remarkable, and there is little sign of a major fissure that runs through the PPNA to divide hunter-gatherers from farmers.

PPNA economies are within the range of variation that might be accepted as hunter-gatherer in the present, as it seems unlikely that their dependence on food production, certainly on domesticates, played a significant economic role. It appears likely that wild plants were cultivated during the PPNA, and it is possible that hunting of wild animals was conducted in a selective manner. Neither process necessarily indicates a step on the road to domestication. Indeed, the hunting strategies that we can observe are not the same as those at the leading edges of domestication (Finlayson *et al.* 2014). Fundamentally, people still relied on hunted meat, and generally on wild plants and this early Neolithic economy seems to be a hunting and gathering economy, which continues into the PPNB.

Food storage has been understood as an important economic development within the transition, with the idea of delayed return hunter-gatherer economies taking hold as part of the idea of the Natufian as a stepping stone to farming. Testart (1982) in a very influential paper, presented a strong case for the importance of food storage and delayed return amongst complex hunter-gatherers, and the social consequences of storage, with the subsequent rise in concepts such as privacy and private property, and the end of classic hunter-gatherer behaviours such as sharing, all being important parts of the model. The relevance of using Testart's approach to study the transition in Southwest Asia is undermined by more recent general agreement that the concept of storage in the Natufian has been overstated (cf. Bar-Yosef 1998). There is better evidence for PPNA storage, however, in contrast to the role attributed to storage by Testart where it is a vital part of a trajectory towards private property and an end to sharing, the various stores and granaries that have been identified, appear to be very good examples of communal architecture being deliberately employed to maintain shared access to food (cf. Kuijt & Finlayson 2009). It is clear that the anthropological model developed by Testart is not showing the full range of behavioural variation amongst past hunter-gatherers.

Architectural permanence is a phenomenon that develops over a long period, from shelters built at Ohalo II *c.* 23,000 years ago, to the two storey, densely packed architecture of large Neolithic settlements in the Late PPNB (9200–8700 cal BP). The early Epipalaeolithic structures were flimsy shelters, but by the Early Natufian (14,500–12,800 cal BP), substantial stone, mud and plaster constructions had appeared (cf. Byrd 2005). The first 'Neolithic revolution', Renfrew's sedentary revolution, is therefore often assumed to be in place before or by the start of the Neolithic, although Olszewski (1991), Bar-Yosef (1998) and Finlayson (2011) have all argued that the evidence for Natufian sedentism has been overstated. Furthermore, the evidence for substantial settlement architecture declines during the Late Natufian, suggesting greater mobility had returned (Belfer-Cohen & Bar-Yosef 2000). The substantial architecture at PPNA Jericho, especially the wall and tower, originally interpreted as defensive, supported the idea that sedentism had returned and was well established by the PPNA (Kenyon & Holland 1981). The defensive role is now generally dismissed, with the monumentality of the architecture seen as more significant (Ronen & Adler

2001). At Gobekli Tepe, despite the scale of monumental architecture, its symbolic form and decoration has led to the site being interpreted as a regional seasonal gathering location (Schmidt 2005).

Sedentism and mobility lie on a spectrum (cf. Goring-Morris & Belfer-Cohen 2008), and the increasingly substantial architecture that is a trait through the PPNA is no longer seen as an abrupt shift to sedentary lifeways, but as part of an ongoing process of increasingly sedentary behaviour, yet still with a significant degree of mobility within the population. The binary opposition between mobile hunter-gathers and sedentary farmers, once arguably bridged by the complex hunter-gatherers of the Natufian, has been undermined. It does however appear clear that major architectural developments, in very different forms, are occurring across the region, at Jericho on the west bank, at Gobekli Tepe on the Middle Euphrates, and elsewhere, as in southern Jordan at WF16 where a small settlement is dominated by a large communal structure (Finlayson *et al.* 2011). People are investing heavily in their built environment within societies that are barely, if at all, food producing.

Is there any evidence that PPNA society was in some way transformed, and can no longer be captured as 'hunter-gatherer'? If not by the economy, then the biggest alternative potential shift would lie in the nature of society or community. Is there something different about Neolithic communities? The Neolithic in Southwest Asia has generally been described as a village culture, when people developed the social mechanisms (and, some would argue, the cognitive abilities) to sustain large group communities (Watkins 2005).

A key feature of these villages is the house, or indeed the home, interpreted as evidence of a radically new way of living in the PPNA (Watkins 1990; Wilson 1988) from the PPNA onwards. There is an assumption that the majority of buildings are houses and this lies behind an uncritical extension of the evidence to argue that the household is a key social unit, that people had domesticated themselves, and moved on from the basic shelters that hunter-gatherers live in. The discussion of Neolithic houses is ubiquitous, from the PPNA at Qermez Dere (Watkins *et al.* 1989), the MPPNB in the southern Levant (Banning & Byrd 1987), and the Late PPNB complex house in southern Jordan (Gebel 2006), and the house continues to be a default perspective on early architecture. In particular, the pattern of stability at Çatalhöyük, where the same houses were repeatedly rebuilt, redecorated and used in an apparently constant manner over a long time, has been argued to reflect constant human behaviours, which permit the use of ethnographic data. The archaeological emphasis on 'houses' leads to the interpretation of society as 'house-based' (Bloch 2010). The high profile of Çatalhöyük means that ideas developed there are given a wider significance, however, the architectural patterns of continuity at Çatalhöyük appear geographically fairly restricted, and of course the central Anatolian Neolithic is relatively late in the wider Neolithic sequence. The modern 'house-based' society, the Zafimaniry, used as an analogue to the Çatalhöyük is also unusual in their time and location in the world. They place much emphasis on house construction while their neighbours build 'flimsy, temporary, and plain' houses (Bloch 2010), indicating that despite their high profile, neither Çatalhöyük nor the Zafimaniry represent good 'universal' examples. As more detailed research has accumulated around central Anatolian examples, it has become apparent that at least at Asikli Hoyuk, and probably in the earlier levels at Çatalhöyük, houses were not an organizing principle (During & Marciniak 2006).

In the earliest Neolithic, the architectural evidence from southern Jordan in the PPNA from the sites of Dhra' and WF16, suggests an emphasis on shared communal storage buildings, open food-processing shelters, large communal structures and an absence of obvious residential buildings (Finlayson *et al.* 2011). There is no clear evidence for a standard 'house' at all. Rather, the settlement appears to be constructed around a series of special purpose buildings, including storage buildings and workshops, and, at WF16, one spectacular large communal building. It appears that settlements were built around communal principles (Finlayson *et al.* 2011). At Dhra' evidence from phytoliths and voids in soil thin sections suggests that the substantial quantities of barley available may have been produced with human assistance – the cultivation of wild plants that is the hallmark of a low level food producing economy. The presence of highly visible large store buildings and publicly visible food processing structures suggests that the architecture may have been being used to help enforce food sharing (cf. Flannery 1972). But this cannot be the simple maintenance of 'traditional hunter-gatherer practices'. Such a communal organization principle suggests that a shift to a household society has not taken place, and that the PPNA may be either maintaining aspects of (complex) Natufian society, or indeed developing something entirely *sui generis.* In contrast to Çatalhöyük (and also Bloch's account of the Zafiminary) where there are no other apparent meeting places other than the 'houses', the southern Levant, from the large communal structure at Wadi Faynan 16, the tower at Jericho and then large and distinctive buildings in the PPNB, appears to be full of meeting places. It seems clear that early settlements were tightly knit communities with very strong local identities.

Another potential critical step change in the Neolithic that might separate it from its hunter-gatherer past is the idea of a revolution of symbols, or a cognitive revolution, or maybe the beginnings of religion. This has been one of the major foci of Southwest Asian Neolithic research over the last decades (Cauvin 2000). Much of the evidence used to support this argument has been based on evidence from the Middle Euphrates, where there appears to have been a substantial increase in the production of apparently symbolically charged objects and structures, now most obvious at Gobekli Tepe. This is not entirely echoed in the PPNA of the southern Levant, which may look a little impoverished in its repertoire of symbolic, or art, objects compared to the preceding Natufian. However, the southern Levant is where, from the Natufian onwards, the treatment of the dead includes the removal of skulls, and ultimately to the plastered skulls of the PPNB, along with plaster statues and figures, and monumental construction such as the tower at Jericho. Again, it is not so much revolutionary, as part of a longstanding gradually changing tradition, with no obvious boundary moment.

Conclusion

The existing framework for the Neolithic transition in the southern Levant is that the Natufian emerges as a complex hunter-gatherer society, which is replaced by a very simple farming society in the PPNA. The stadial systems of early 20th century archaeology were highly receptive to anthropological categorization – but this forced archaeological thought patterns into a very particular way of seeing and understanding society and change. The terminology still forces our narratives, and remains hard to escape, despite complications such as variation between what Neolithic means, its use as a term for a culture history period, and as an evolutionary process. These alternatives don't sit very well together, and have an even poorer match with our ethnographic terminology.

Wobst's call against the tyranny of the ethnographic record (1978) is a plea that has not been heeded in many corners of Southwest Asian Neolithic research. Southwest Asian Neolithic archaeological research maintains a strict definition of hunting and gathering, where the identification of anything that might represent a shift away from food procurement to production is recognised as indicating a transition – initially to complex hunting and gathering and then to low level food production. There is more tolerance for modern hunter-gatherer societies obtaining some of their subsistence from food production or domesticates, than for ancient societies. This is because we see no middle ground, no intermediate zone, in the modern world, but a clear gap between farmer and forager. The world 12,000 years ago contained a far greater diversity of societies than the surviving, generally marginal and highly adapted, hunter-gatherers who live today, and hunter-gatherers who engineered the first transition to food producing societies. Rather than borrowing and simplifying modern ethnography to study the past, archaeology should attempt to make a contribution to wider hunter-gatherer studies from study of the past.

Kusimba (2005, 354), amongst others, has wondered about the utility of the category of hunter-gatherer, and whether it set up a circularity of interpretation, where the nature of society is assumed from the start. That problem affects Neolithic research. The transitional Neolithic is an area that might be really fruitful for hunter-gatherer studies, containing many examples of societies who do not fit the impoverished ethnographic base. The recognition that hunter-gatherers are not unnaturally resistant to change (Lane 2014, 136) is surely another important area where archaeology can play an important role in demonstrating how dynamic hunter-gatherer society can be. What appears to have been the real shared characteristic between present and past is a huge capacity for flexibility, experimentation and consequent variation in lifeways.

References

Banning, E. B. & Byrd, B. F. (1987) Houses and the changing residential unit: domestic architecture at PPNB 'Ain Ghazal, Jordan. *Proceedings of the Prehistoric Society* 53, 309–325.

Barker, G. (2006) *The Agricultural Revolution in Prehistory*. Oxford, Oxford University Press.

Barnard, A. (2004) Hunting-and-gathering society: an eighteenth-century Scottish invention. In A. Barnard (ed.), *Hunter-gatherers in History, Archaeology and Anthropology*, 31–43, Oxford, Berg.

Barnard, A. (2014) Defining hunter-gatherers: Enlightenment, Romantic, and Social Evolutionary perspectives. In V. Cummings, P. Jordan & M. Zvelebil (eds), *The Oxford Handbook of the Archaeology and Anthropology of Hunter-Gatherers*. 43–54, Oxford, Oxford Uuniversity Press.

Bar-Yosef, O. (1998) The Natufian Culture in the Levant, threshold to the origins of agriculture. *Evolutionary Anthropology* 6(5), 159–177.

Bar-Yosef, O. & Meadow, R. (1995) The origins of agriculture in the Near East. In T. D. Price & A. B. Gebauer (eds), *Last Hunters-First Farmers: New Perspectives on the Prehistoric Transition to Agriculture*, 39–94. Santa Fe, School of American Research.

Belfer-Cohen, A. & Bar-Yosef, O. (2000) Early sedentism in the Near East: A bumpy ride to village life (13,000–8,000 BP). In I. Kuijt (ed.), *Life in Neolithic Farming Communities: Social Organization, Identity, and Differentiation*, 19–37, New York, Academic/Plenum Press.

Benz, M. & Bauer, J. (2013) Symbols of power – symbols of crisis? A psycho-social approach to Early Neolithic symbol systems *Neolithics* 2(13), 11–24.

Binford, L. (1972) *An Archaeological Perspective*. New York, Seminar Press.

Bird-David, N. H. (1988) Hunters and gatherers and outsiders. In T. Ingold, D. Riches & J. Woodburn (eds), *Hunters and Gatherers I: History, Evolution and Social Change*, 17–72. Oxford, Berg.

Bloch, M. (2010) Is there religion at Çatalhöyük ... or are there just houses? In I. Hodder (ed.), *Religion in the Emergence of Civilization. Çatalhöyük as a Case Study*, 146–162. Cambridge, Cambridge University Press.

Byrd, B. (2005) *Early Neolithic Life at Beidha, Jordan: Neolithic Spatial Organisation and Vernacular Architecture*. British Academy Monographs in Archaeology. Oxford, Oxford University Press & Council for British Research in the Levant.

Cauvin, J. (2000) *The Birth of the Gods and the Origins of Agriculture*. Translated by T. Watkins. Cambridge, Cambridge University Press.

Childe, V. G. (1935) *New Light on the Most Ancient East: The Oriental Prelude to European Prehistory*. London, Kegan Paul.

Cohen, M. N. (2009) Introduction: rethinking the origins of agriculture. *Current Anthropology* 50(5), 591–595.

Colledge, S., Conolly, J., & Shennan, S. (2005) The origins of European farming from SW Asian origins to NW European limits. *European Journal of Archaeology* 8(2), 137–156.

Cummings, V. (2014) Hunting and gathering in a farmers' world. In V. Cummings, P. Jordan & M. Zvelebil (eds) *The Oxford Handbook of the Archaeology and Anthropology of Hunter-Gatherers*, 767–786, Oxford, Oxford University Press.

Cummings, V., Jordan, P. & Zvelebil, M. (eds) (2014) *The Oxford Handbook of the Archaeology and Anthropology of Hunter-Gatherers*, Oxford, Oxford University Press.

During, B. S. & Marciniak, A. (2006) Households and communities in the central Anatolian Neolithic. *Archaeological Dialogues* 12(2), 165–187.

Finlayson, B. (2009) The 'complex-hunter-gatherer' and the transition to farming. In N. Finlay, S. McCartan, N. Milner & C. Wickham-Jones (eds), *From Bann Flakes to Bushmills, Papers in Honour of Professor Peter Woodman*, 175–199. Prehistoric Society Research Papers 1. Oxford, Prehistoric Society & Oxbow Books.

Finlayson, B. (2011) Archaeology, evidence and anthropology: circular arguments in the transition from foraging to farming. In M. Benz (ed.), *The Principle of Sharing. Segregation and Construction of Social Identities at the Transition from Foraging to Farming*, 19–34. Studies in Early Near Eastern Production, Subsistence, and Environment 14. Berlin, ex Oriente.

Finlayson, B. (2013) Imposing the Neolithic on the past. *Levant* 45(2), 133–148.

Finlayson, B. & Makarewicz, C. (in press) The Neolithic of Southern Jordan. In O. Bar-Yosef & Y. Enzel (eds), *The Quaternary of the Levant*, 743–752. Cambridge, Cambridge University Press.

Finlayson, B. & Warren, G. (2010) *Changing Natures: Hunter-gatherers, First Farmers, and the Modern World.* Duckworth Debates in Archaeology. London, Duckworth.

Finlayson, B., Makarewicz, C., Smith, S. & Mithen, S. (2014) The transition from PPNA to PPNB in southern Jordan, *Studies in the History and Archaeology of Jordan* 11, 105–119.

Finlayson, B., Mithen, S., Najjar, M., Smith, S., Maricevic, D., Pankhurst, N. & Yeomans, L. (2011) Architecture, sedentism and social complexity. Communal building in Pre-Pottery Neolithic A settlements: new evidence from WF16. *Proceedings of the National Academy of Science* 108(20), 8183–8188.

Flannery, K. V. (1972) The origins of the village as a settlement type in Mesoamerica and the Near East: a comparative study. In P. J. Ucko, R. Tringham & G. W. Dimbleby (eds), *Man, Settlement and Urbanism,* 23–53. London, Duckworth.

Gamble, C. (2007) *Origins and Revolutions: Human Identity in Earliest Prehistory.* Cambridge, Cambridge University Press.

Gebel, H. G., Kinzel, M., Nissen, H. J. & Zaid, Z. (2006) Summary and conclusions. In H. G. Gebel, H. J. Nissen & Z. Zaid (eds), *Basta II: The Architecture and Stratigraphy,* 203–224. Berlin, ex Oriente.

Goring-Morris, A. N. & Belfer-Cohen, A. (2008) A roof over one's head: developments in near eastern residential architecture across the Epipalaeolithic-Neolithic transition. In P. Bocquet- Appel & O. Bar-Yosef (eds), *The Neolithic Demographic Transition and its Consequences,* 229–286. Berlin, Springer.

Goring-Morris, A. N. & Belfer-Cohen, A. (2010) 'Great Expectations', or the inevitable collapse of the early Neolithic in the Near East. In M. Bandy & J. Fox (eds), *Becoming Villagers: Comparing Early Village Societies,* 62–77. Tuscon, University of Arizona Press.

Harris, D. R. (2007) Agriculture, cultivation and domestication: exploring the conceptual framework of early food production. In T. Denham, J. Iriarte & L. Vrydaghs (eds), *Rethinking Agriculture,* 16–35. One World Archaeology Series. Walnut Creek, Left Coast Press.

Harris, D. R. (2014) Plant domestications. In V. Cummings, P. Jordan & M. Zvelebil (eds), *The Oxford Handbook of the Archaeology and Anthropology of Hunter-Gatherers,* 729–748, Oxford, Oxford University Press.

Hodder, I. (1982) *The Present Past: An Introduction to Anthropology for Archaeologists.* London, Batsford.

Ingold, T. (1980) *Hunters, Pastoralists and Ranchers: Reindeer Economies and their Transformations.* Cambridge, Cambridge University Press.

Ingold, T. (1988) Notes on the foraging mode of production. In T. Ingold, D. Riches & J. Woodburn (eds), *Hunters and Gatherers I: History, Evolution and Social Change,* 267–285. Oxford, Berg.

Jordan, P. & Cummings, V. (2014) Analytical frames of reference in hunter-gatherer research. In V. Cummings, P. Jordan & M. Zvelebil (eds), *The Oxford Handbook of the Archaeology and Anthropology of Hunter-Gatherers,* 33–42, Oxford, Oxford University Press.

Kenyon, K. & Holland, T. (1981) *Excavations at Jericho: The Architecture and Stratigraphy of the Tell* III, London, British School of Archaeology, Jerusalem.

Kuijt, I. (2008) The regeneration of life. Neolithic structures of symbolic remembering and forgetting, *Current Anthropology* 49(2), 171–197.

Kuijt, I. & Finlayson, B. (2009) Inventing storage: evidence for the earliest pre-domestication granaries 11,000 years ago in the Jordan Valley. *Proceedings of the National Academy of Sciences* 106(27), 10966–10970.

Kusimba, S. B. (2005) What is a hunter-gatherer? Variation in the archaeological record of eastern and southern Africa. *Journal of Archaeological Research* 13(4), 337–366.

Lane, P. (2014) Hunter-gatherer-fishers, ethnoarchaeology and analogical reasoning. In V. Cummings, P. Jordan & M. Zvelebil (eds), *The Oxford Handbook of the Archaeology and Anthropology of Hunter-Gatherers,* 104–150, Oxford, Oxford University Press.

Lee, R. B. & Devore, I. (1968) *Man the Hunter.* Chicago, Aldine.

Maher, L., Richter, T. & Stock, J. (2012) The Pre-Natufian Epipaleolithic: long-term behavioral trends in the Levant. *Evolutionary Anthropology* 21, 69–81.

Makarewicz, C. (2013) Bridgehead to the *Badia*: new biometrical and isotopic perspectives on Early Neolithic caprine exploitation systems at 'Ain Ghazal. *Levant* 45(2), 117–131.

McCarter, S. F. (2007) *Neolithic*. London, Routledge.

Moore, A. (2014) Post-glacial transformations among hunter-gatherer societies in the Mediterranean and western Asia. In V. Cummings, P. Jordan & M. Zvelebil (eds), *The Oxford Handbook of the Archaeology and Anthropology of Hunter-Gatherers*, 456–478, Oxford, Oxford University Press.

Moore, A. M., Hillman, G. C. and Legge, A. J. (2000) *Village on the Euphrates*. Oxford, Oxford University Press.

Morgan, L. D. (1877) *Ancient Society*. London, Macmillan.

Nadel, D. (2004) Wild barley harvesting, fishing, and year-round occupation at Ohalo II (19.5 KY, Jordan Valley, Israel), in Le Secrétariat du Congrès (eds) *Acts of the XIVth UISSP Congress, University of Liege (September 2001): Section 6: The Upper Palaeolithic* (General Sessions and Posters) 135–143. British Archaeological Report S1240. Oxford, Archaeopress.

Olszewski, D. I. (1991) Social complexity in the Natufian? Assessing the relationship of ideas and data. In G. A. Clark (ed.), *Perspectives on the Past. Theoretical Biases in Mediterranean Hunter-gatherer Research*, 322–40. Philadelphia, University of Pennsylvania Press.

Outram, A. K. (2014) Animal domestication. In V. Cummings, P. Jordan & M. Zvelebil (eds), *The Oxford Handbook of the Archaeology and Anthropology of Hunter-Gatherers*, 749–763, Oxford, Oxford University Press.

Panter-Brick, C., Layton, R. H. & Rowley-Conwy, P. (2001) Lines of enquiry. In C. Panter-Brick, R. H. Layton & P. Rowley-Conwy (eds), *Hunter-gatherers: An Interdisciplinary Perspective*. Cambridge, Cambridge University Press.

Pearsall, D. M. (2009) Investigating the transition to agriculture. *Current Anthropology* 50, 609–613.

Pluciennik, M. (2014) Historical frames of reference for 'hunter-gatherers'. In V. Cummings, P. Jordan & M. Zvelebil (eds), *The Oxford Handbook of the Archaeology and Anthropology of Hunter-Gatherers*, 55–68. Oxford, Oxford University Press.

Price, T. D. & Brown, J. A. (eds) (1985) *Prehistoric Hunter-gatherers: The Emergence of Cultural Complexity*. Orlando, Academic Press.

Renfrew, C. (2007) *Prehistory: the Making of the Human Mind*. London, Weideneld & Nicolson.

Renfrew, C. (2003) *Figuring it out*. London, Thames and Hudson.

Robb, J. (2013) Material culture, landscapes of action, and emergent causation: a new model for the origins of the European Neolithic. *Current Anthropology* 54(6), 657–683.

Ronen, A. & Adler, D. (2001) The walls of Jericho were magical. *Ethnology and Anthropology of Eurasia* 2(6), 97–103.

Rowley-Conwy, P. (2004) How the west was lost. A reconsideration of agricultural origins in Britain, Ireland and Scandinavia. *Current Anthropology* 45, S83–S113.

Schmidt, K. (2005) 'Ritual Centres' and the Neolithisation of Upper Mesopotamia, *Neolithics* 2(5), 13–21

Schrire, C. (ed.) (1984) *Past and Present in Hunter-Gatherer Studies*. Orlando, Academic Press.

Smith, B. D. (2001) Low-level food production. *Journal of Archaeological Research* 9, 1–43.

Testart, A. (1982) The significance of food storage among hunter-gatherers: residence patterns, population densities, and social inequalities. *Current Anthropology* 23(5), 523–537.

Thomas, J. (2013) Comment on: 'Material culture, landscapes of action, and emergent causation: a new model for the origins of the European Neolithic'. *Current Anthropology* 54(6), 657–683.

Watkins, T., Baird, D. & Betts, A. (1989) Qermez Dere and the early aceramic Neolithic of N Iraq. *Paléorient* 15(1), 19–24.

Watkins, T. (1990) The origins of house and home? *World Archaeology* 21(3), 336–346.

Watkins, T. (2005) The Neolithic revolution and the emergence of humanity: a cognitive approach to the first comprehensive world-view. In J. Clarke (ed.), *Archaeological Perspectives on the Transmission and Transformation of Culture in the Eastern Mediterranean*, 84–88. Levant Supplementary Series 2. Oxford, Oxbow Books and Council for British Research in the Levant.

Widlok, T. (2016) Hunter-gatherer situations. *Hunter-Gatherer Research* 2.2, 127–143.

Wilson, P. (1988) *The Domestication of the Human Species.* New Haven, Yale University Press.

Wilmsen, E. & Denbow, J. (1990) Paradigmatic history of San-speaking peoples and current attempts at revision. *Current Anthropology* 31, 489–524.

Wobst, M. (1978) The archaeo-ethnology of hunter-gatherers or the tyranny of the ethnographic record in archaeology. *American Antiquity* 43(2), 303–309.

Zeder, M. (2009) The Neolithic macroevolution: macroevolutionary theory and the study of culture change. *Journal of Archaeological Research* 17, 1–63.

Zvelebil, M. & Fewster, K. J. (2001) Pictures at an exhibition: Ethnoarchaeology and hunter-gatherers. In K. J. Fewster & M. Zvelebil (eds), *Ethnoarchaeology and Hunter-Gatherers: Pictures at an Exhibition.* British Archaeological Report S955, 143–157. Oxford, Archaeopress.

Chapter 5

Okhotsk and Sushen: history and diversity in Iron Age Maritime hunter-gatherers of northern Japan

Mark J. Hudson

Although the place and time discussed in this chapter will be unfamiliar to many readers, the basic problem considered here is widely shared across research on hunter-gatherer diversity: how do we analyse that diversity without being forced into preconceived categories of difference? In this essay, I will use the example of the Okhotsk culture of Iron Age northern Japan. In writing that previous sentence I have already brought the problem of this chapter to the fore. What, for instance, do we really mean by the archaeological concept of the 'Okhotsk culture', a concept that was only developed in the 20th century even though the society it purports to classify existed from about the 4th to the 12th centuries AD? Furthermore, in that sentence and in the title of this chapter I have deliberately employed the term 'Iron Age', even though that periodisation is not normally used in Japan. On one level this is a question of convenience: how to highlight the period discussed in a way that will be quickly understood by as many readers as possible. In this case, several alternatives would be available including 'late prehistoric', 'protohistoric' or 'early historic'. Period names commonly used in Japanese archaeology, such as Kofun, Nara and Epi-Jōmon, might also have been used (and these latter terms will indeed appear in the main body of the paper). Depending on the reader, the use of the term 'Iron Age' here will generate images – perhaps of Celts in southern France importing wine from the Mediterranean – that may or may not be helpful in understanding the diversity of the Okhotsk culture. In the European context, of course, the very notion of 'Iron Age hunter-gatherers' sounds strange. As discussed below, however, I have decided to use this term to emphasise the importance of iron to the history of the Okhotsk and neighboring societies. Finally, geographically, I have spoken of 'northern Japan' even though most of the discussion will focus on Hokkaido, an island that did not officially become part of Japan until 1869. Here again, the gloss 'northern Japan' seems appropriate because the Okhotsk people were also exploring south into the Tohoku region of northern Honshu and the early states of the Kofun and Nara periods in western Japan played such an important role in Iron Age Hokkaido.

Hunter-gatherer diversity can be explored in many ways but one such axis is certainly the historical problem of how *difference* was perceived in past societies. The economic alterity of hunter-gatherers in the modern world was not necessarily shared by past civilisations which often possessed quite different views of the relationship between forager and farmer (Kreiner 1993; Ölschleger 2013; Pluciennik 2014). People that can possibly be linked with the Okhotsk culture appear in both Japanese and Chinese histories as 'devils' rather than humans. In AD 640, for example, Chinese records note that envoys from a northern land called Liugui 流鬼 reached the Tang capital of Chang'an. The name Liugui is written with characters meaning 'flowing devils'. There has been a long debate over the location of Liugui. It is by no means irrelevant to the topic of this chapter to note that an influential paper by Dutch Sinologist Gustaaf Schlegel (1893) placed Liugui in Kamchatka. At a time when there was little archaeological knowledge of the Sea of Okhotsk region, the ethnographic writings of Georg Steller on Kamchatka provided Schlegel with what seemed like the most appropriate context to frame the Liugui. Although the problem of the Liugui will not be discussed in detail here, Kikuchi (2009) has recently used archaeological evidence in addition to textual critique to argue that the Liugui can be associated with the Okhotsk culture.

The Okhotsk in archaeology

The Okhotsk culture spread south from Sakhalin around the 4th century AD. In Hokkaido, the predominant areas of Okhotsk settlement were the islands of Rebun and Rishiri, the Sea of Okhotsk coast of eastern Hokkaido and the Kuril Islands (Fig. 5.1). In the archaeological literature, the Okhotsk are widely characterised as maritime hunter-gatherers and stable isotope studies (Tsutaya *et al.* 2014) support Maeda's (2002) conclusion that the Okhotsk was the most maritime adapted culture in Japanese history.

In reading about the Okhotsk, it is easy to form the conclusion that it was a culture 'apart' from anything else. Skeletal remains show that the Okhotsk people were physically different from the Epi-Jōmon populations who lived in the rest of Hokkaido at the same time and there is little doubt that the Okhotsk were indeed immigrants from the north (Ishida 1988; 1994). Most maps of Okhotsk settlement show a clear geographical separation between the Okhotsk culture and the Epi-Jōmon. Given the distinctive maritime focus of Okhotsk subsistence, it is widely assumed that they occupied a unique niche of coastal tundra landscapes that were of little interest to Epi-Jōmon groups. In fact, the tundra zone of eastern Hokkaido had seen only a minimal human occupation in the Jōmon period itself (Fukuda 2013). Archaeologically, the Okhotsk culture is also characterised by a range of more or less distinctive forms of

Figure 5.1. Location map showing key regions discussed in text.

pottery, bone tools, house plans, burial customs and ritual activities. The relative lack of evidence for trade between the Okhotsk and neighbouring cultures also reinforces the impression of Okhotsk apartness (Hudson 2004).

The history of research on the Okhotsk culture with its legacies of colonialism and the Cold War have been a further factor in promoting distinctive interpretations of the archaeology. With Cold War tensions in the Sea of Okhotsk region by no means totally resolved today (cf. Hara 2007), joint research between Russian and Japanese scholars remains the exception rather than the rule. In the early postwar period, an influential paper by Befu and Chard (1964) set the tone for many later understandings of the Okhotsk in its emphasis on maritime hunting connections with the Bering Sea. Russian scholars, by contrast, tend to place the Okhotsk culture in a more complex regional context centered on the Sea of Okhotsk (e.g. Deryugin 2008).

The Okhotsk in Japanese historical accounts

Despite the many distinctive aspects of Okhotsk culture, recent research is beginning to reevaluate the role played by the Okhotsk in the post-Jōmon history of Hokkaido. This research suggests a much more complex picture than has been accepted so far, moving the Okhotsk from a marginal to a more central position in Hokkaido history. In attempting to place the Okhotsk culture in a more historical framework, one place to begin is with written records found in early Japanese chronicles. The *Nihon Shoki* (AD 720) includes the following entry for the year 544:

> At Cape Minabe, on the northern side of the Island of Sado, there arrived men of Su-shen in a boat, and staid (sic) there. During the spring and summer they caught fish, which they used for food. The men of that island said they were not human beings. They also called them devils, and did not dare to go near them. (Aston 1972, II, 58)

This entry describes a seasonal visit to Sado in the Sea of Japan by a people so strange that they were not even considered as human beings. The account goes on to record that when the islanders 'having gathered acorns, were preparing to cook them for eating' the acorn shells suddenly turned into two men 'who fought together, to the great wonder of the villagers' (Aston 1972, II, 58–59). Although it is not clear if the acorn spirits were also Sushen people, it is clear that this entry does not regard 'hunter-gathering' as a special category: the fishing Sushen were considered as devils but the local islanders were also eating acorns, even if nuts are unlikely to have been their main staple by the 6th century.

Who were these 'Sushen'? The name is written with Chinese characters referring to a people from Manchuria who appear in Chinese records as early as the 6th century BC. The name Sushen is believed to denote a Tungusic people who were ancestral to the Mohe and Jurchen (Aston 1972, II, 58). In ancient Chinese texts such as the *Guoyu* ('Discourses of the States'), gifts of 'archaic' stone arrowheads from the Sushen to the emperor are interpreted as auspicious signs of the ruler's virtue (Kikuchi 2009, 100–101). The anachronistic use of 'Sushen' in Japanese records a thousand years after the name was first used in China was no doubt an attempt to give legitimacy to Japan's early state. In the Japanese context, the term Sushen is probably best interpreted as a traditional label for a 'northern people' rather than a specific ethnic group from Manchuria. According to later entries in the *Nihon Shoki*, the Sushen also lived in Hokkaido. During the reign of the empress Saimei (r. 655–661), Abe no Omi, Warden of the Province of Koshi (the modern Hokuriku region), was sent on several military expeditions to the north by the Yamato state based in western Japan. During these expeditions, the main enemy of Abe no Omi was the Sushen, who were attacking the Emishi people. In the third month of 660:

> Abe no Omi was sent on an expedition with a fleet of 200 ships against the land of Su-shen. Abe no Omi made some Yemishi of Michinoku embark on board his own ship. They arrived close to a great river. Upon this over a thousand Yemishi of Watari-shima assembled ... saying:- 'The Su-shen fleet has arrived in great force and threatens to slay us.' (Aston 1972, II, 263–264)

Here Yemishi – usually written in modern Japanese as Emishi – is a name meaning 'barbarian' which was applied by the Japanese state to people living in northern Honshu and Hokkaido who were outside state control. The Emishi certainly included people who later became the Ainu, but ethnic Japanese groups were probably also included in this category which was essentially political and did not differentiate between hunter-gathering and farming economies. In the previous quotation, Abe no Omi forced Emishi from Michinoku (northern Honshu) to join his expedition to Watari-shima, which was the name given by the Japanese to Hokkaido during this period. According to the *Nihon Shoki*, the Emishi of Hokkaido were under attack from the Sushen and sought help from the Japanese to defeat them. Although this account may over-emphasise the role of the Yamato state in 'protecting' the Emishi, it seems likely that conflict did exist between the Emishi and the Sushen at this time.

The *Nihon Shoki* account of the Abe no Omi expeditions has been widely debated by Japanese historians and various interpretations exist as to the places and peoples mentioned. If the Emishi of Hokkaido can be associated with the archaeological culture known as Epi-Jōmon, then who were the Sushen? Archaeologically, the only real candidate is the Okhotsk culture. A detailed argument supporting the identification of the Okhotsk with the Sushen has recently been published by Segawa (2011, 47–81). Although there is not space here to rehearse all of Segawa's conclusions, I want to explore how this identification between the Sushen and the Okhotsk might affect our understanding of hunter-gatherer diversity in northern Japan.

The Sushen and ethnic/cultural frameworks

Although the *Nihon Shoki* account of the Sushen represents little more than a few ethnohistoric 'snippets' about the people of that name, the account is important in forcing us to imagine new frameworks for understanding Iron Age Hokkaido. As used in the *Nihon Shoki*, the term 'Sushen' may not necessarily refer to a fixed ethnic group; it may alternatively have been a broader term for northern peoples who were biologically and culturally different from the Ainoid Epi-Jōmon. This possibility already introduces an element of ambiguity that is, if not absent, at least more deeply buried in the archaeological concept of the 'Okhotsk culture'. Secondly, the *Nihon Shoki* accounts of the Sushen describe a people living in or visiting areas well outside the 'textbook' area of Okhotsk settlement in eastern Hokkaido. Sado

Island is located at about the same latitude as Fukushima City and was part of the area of Kofun culture. Although there has been debate over the precise location of the 'great river' and other place names mentioned in Abe no Omi's campaigns in Watari-shima, most scholars are in agreement that the account describes southwest Hokkaido (Kodama 1968).

It is true that most Okhotsk culture archaeological sites are located along the coastal zone of eastern Hokkaido (including Rebun and Rishiri Islands) and out into the Kuril Islands. However, there are also a number of Okhotsk sites or finds of pottery in western Hokkaido down the coast of the Sea of Japan. One of the most important of these is the Aonae Dune Site on Okushiri Island, discussed in English by Matsumura *et al.* (2006). Segawa (2011) argues that Herobe island, the Sushen base mentioned in the *Nihon Shoki*, was Okushiri. Other important Okhotsk sites down the Sea of Japan include Kojima Tatehama at the southern end of Hokkaido and Seno in northern Aomori across the Tsugaru Strait. Skeletal remains of Okhotsk type have been found in association with Epi-Jōmon cultural remains at the Chatsu 4 site on the western coast of Hokkaido (Matsumura *et al.* 2006, 18).

Acknowledging an Okhotsk presence in southwest Hokkaido makes it much easier to explain DNA evidence that brown bear (*Ursus arctos*) remains from Okhotsk deposits at the Kafukai site on Rebun Island were transported from southern Hokkaido (Masuda *et al.* 2001). The authors of this DNA analysis argue that southern Hokkaido was outside the area of Okhotsk settlement and was occupied only by the Epi-Jōmon, but it is far more parsimonious to assume that brown bears were captured in areas where Okhotsk people were actually living or visiting and then carried to Rebun, presumably as cubs.

The Okhotsk and the Epi-Jōmon: Iron Age migrations in northern Japan

If we accept that early Okhotsk settlements, at least before the Abe no Omi campaigns of the 7th century, were found in western as well as eastern Hokkaido, then we need to consider the relationship between the Okhotsk and the Epi-Jōmon cultures in more detail. From this perspective, the Okhotsk changes from being a 'marginal' culture that occupied parts of Hokkaido that nobody else was interested in, into something far more diverse and complex. In fact, the more we consider this question, the more it becomes clear that we cannot consider the history of the Epi-Jōmon or indeed the northern Kofun culture, without also considering the Okhotsk.

Diversity and the Epi-Jōmon Culture

The name 'Epi-Jōmon', first coined in the 1930s based on the continued use of cord marking as a ceramic decoration, is misleading because it completely hides the cultural diversity that characterises this period. Not only were the Early and Late phases of the Epi-Jōmon very different, this archaeological culture also had numerous substantial regional differences between Hokkaido and the Tohoku. Yagi (2010, 35) has proposed the term 'Proto-Emishi culture' for the Tohoku region in this phase, but no widely accepted alternative exists for Epi-Jōmon Hokkaido.

The Epi-Jōmon period is usually divided into two stages, Early and Late. The Early Epi-Jōmon in Hokkaido was characterised by localised ceramic cultures and subsistence economies based largely on ecological zones, although there was also an island-wide increase in fishing activities (Takase 2014). From around the 3rd century AD, however, a new pattern of hunter-gatherer diversity developed which was no longer based primarily on ecology. Late Epi-Jōmon groups started to move south into the northern Tohoku where they interacted with Yayoi and then Kofun period societies over a broad area of settlement that included several ecological zones. The desire to access iron tools was almost certainly the main motivation for this Epi-Jōmon migration (Segawa 2005; 2011, 53–54). Unlike in Hokkaido, where stone tools remained common until the 8th–9th centuries, stone tools were already much rarer and stone arrowheads very unusual in Epi-Jōmon sites in the northern Tohoku (Yagi 2010, 28–29). With no house remains discovered from the Late Epi-Jōmon in the Tohoku, Ishii (1998) has argued that this culture developed a nomadic subsistence economy based on trade with the Kofun state in salmon and deer and bear skins. A related phenomenon occurred in the Ryukyu Islands to the south of Japan at this time: although Yayoi culture and agriculture were not present in the Ryukyus, local hunter-gatherers began long-distance trade in tropical shells with chieftains in Kyushu (Kinoshita 2003; Hudson & Barnes 1991; Takamiya *et al.* 2016). Such trade-based hunter-gatherers had not existed in the Jōmon period itself and mark a new development in hunter-gatherer diversity in Japan.

Contacts with the Kofun State

As the Epi-Jōmon expanded south into the northern Tohoku region, it encountered the Late Yayoi and then the Kofun cultures of Japan. The Kofun (AD 250–710) is known as the time when an early state developed based in the Kinai (Kyoto-Nara-Osaka) region of western Japan (Barnes 2006; Mizoguchi 2013). The name 'Kofun' derives from the mounded tombs that characterised the period and such tombs are found in eastern Japan as far as the Sendai area. The presence of these tombs does not necessarily mean that a unified state controlled all of eastern Honshu at this time (Barnes 2012). The Kofun culture of the Tohoku was, however, very different from the Epi-Jōmon in many respects: its economic base was agriculture, which supported a system of social stratification, and Kofun people lived in pit houses which were no longer used by Epi-Jōmon groups in the Tohoku (Yagi 2010, 34). Horses were also used by Kofun people in the Tohoku (Matsumoto 2006, 17–28).

Despite the clear archaeological differences between the Kofun and Epi-Jōmon cultures in the Tohoku region at this time, the Yamato state in western Japan increasingly began to classify the people of the north as marginal 'barbarians' termed 'Emishi'. The considerable archaeological diversity of the Emishi people, studied in recent years by Matsumoto (2006; 2011), Yagi (2010) and others, became subsumed within the 'political' identity of a people who opposed state power. Under pressure from the expansion of the Yamato state, the people of the Kofun and Epi-Jōmon traditions experienced a complex process of both mixing and separation. From the 5th through to the 7th centuries, Epi-Jōmon pottery became increasingly rare in the Tohoku and the people of this culture appear to have begun to move back to Hokkaido (Segawa 2011, 54). Ono (1998) argues that the expansion of the Kofun state was the main cause of this reverse migration. However, this change in settlement seems to have been associated with an increasingly systematic pattern of trade that saw greater quantities of iron reaching Hokkaido (Sasada 2013, 100–101; Segawa 2011, 55–57). Although the actual site(s) involved have not yet been identified, Segawa (2011, 57) speculates that trading centres responsible for the distribution of iron to Hokkaido were found on the Pacific coast of Aomori at the very north of the Tohoku. In terms of the classification of ancient trade developed by Renfrew (1975), Segawa's argument would seem to be that the 5th–7th centuries saw a shift from a 'reciprocity' pattern of trade to one involving 'central place redistribution'. Further archaeological studies are required to test this hypothesis.

Following the movement of Epi-Jōmon hunter-gatherers back to Hokkaido, from the late 7th to the 9th centuries groups of Japanese farmers from the northern Tohoku migrated into the Ishikari plain in southwest Hokkaido. In addition to agriculture, these groups brought iron tools, spindle whorls and pit houses with *kamado* ovens (Segawa 2005, 21–24; Matsumoto 2006). Millets and other cultivated crops are known from several sites in Hokkaido at this time, mainly in the Ishikari region (Crawford 2011). These migrants had a major impact on the ancestral Ainu culture known as the Satsumon, a culture which differed from the Epi-Jōmon in displaying strong links with the Japanese culture of the Late Kofun, Nara and early Heian eras.

The Okhotsk: from ecology to history

The dynamic background sketched above changes our understanding of the expansion of the Okhotsk culture. Rather than simply explaining the Okhotsk through ecology, as a group of maritime hunter-gatherers whose technology enabled them to occupy a previously uninhabited coastal zone (cf. Befu & Chard 1964), the historical context takes on a new importance. The movement of Epi-Jōmon groups south from Hokkaido in search of iron was mirrored by a similar migration of Okhotsk people from Sakhalin into Hokkaido. Unlike the Epi-Jōmon, whose sites are found far inland in the northern Tohoku, the Okhotsk people occupied the islands and coasts of western Hokkaido and down into the Tohoku region. The maritime subsistence focus of the Okhotsk may have enabled the exploitation of a different ecological niche from Epi-Jōmon and Kofun populations, a pattern suggested by the *Nihon Shoki* description of the Sushen on Sado Island quoted above. As the Epi-Jōmon moved back to Hokkaido and perhaps came to rely on coastal trade 'central places' in Aomori, they probably came into more conflict with the Okhotsk from the 6th century. The 7th century campaign of Abe no Omi and the Emishi against the Sushen fits well with this scenario of a changing power balance in Hokkaido over access to trade (Segawa 2011). The diminished power of the Sushen in western Hokkaido led to the renewed vigour of the Okhotsk expansion along the eastern coast of Hokkaido and down into the Kuril Islands.

Conclusions

In most accounts of Japanese archaeology, the Okhotsk culture stands out for its *difference* from other cultures of prehistoric Japan but also for its internal *homogeneity* as a maritime hunter-gatherer adaptation. This chapter has attempted a preliminary critique of both of these points, arguing that the Okhotsk is much more diverse than these traditional frameworks suggest. The *Nihon Shoki* accounts of the Sushen people were used as one point of departure for this critique. The writers of the *Nihon Shoki* had little idea who the people they termed 'Sushen' really were, yet a connection with the people of what archaeologists know as the 'Okhotsk culture' seems highly likely. This link with the Sushen enables us to re-imagine the diversity of the Okhotsk culture. The point here is not that the Sushen were or were not the same as the Okhotsk; rather, both Sushen and Okhotsk were part of the same historical process of hunter-gatherer expansion south into northern Japan, an expansion that appears to have been primarily fueled by a desire for iron.

Acknowledgements

Research for this paper was supported by the Advanced Core Research Center for the History of Human Ecology in the North, the Social Sciences and Humanities Research Council Canada for the Baikal-Hokkaido Archaeology Project and JSPS grant-in-aid No. 24242030.

References

Aston, W. G. (1972) *Nihongi: Chronicles of Japan from the Earliest Times to AD 697*. Rutland, Tuttle.

Barnes, G. L. (2006) *State Formation in Japan: Emergence of a 4th-Century Ruling Elite*. London, Routledge.

Barnes, G. L. (2012) The emergence of political rulership and the State in Early Japan. In K. F. Friday (ed.), *Japan Emerging: Premodern History to 1850*, 77–88. Boulder, Westview.

Befu, H. & Chard, C. S. (1964) A prehistoric maritime culture of the Okhotsk Sea. *American Antiquity* 30, 1–24.

Crawford, G. W. (2011) Advances in understanding early agriculture in Japan. *Current Anthropology* 52(S4), S331–S345.

Deryugin, V. A. (2008) On the definition of the term 'Okhotsk Culture'. *Archaeology, Ethnology and Anthropology of Eurasia* 33, 58–66.

Fukuda, M. (2013) Hokkaidō to Saharin, Chishima: Nichiro nikoku no kōkogaku kara mita Jōmon buka no hokuhen [Hokkaido, Sakhakin and the Kurils: The northern frontier of Jōmon culture as seen from the archaeology of Japan and Russia]. *Kikan Kōkogaku* 125, 62–65.

Hara, K. (2007) *Cold War Frontiers in the Asia-Pacific: Divided Territories in the San Francisco System.* Abingdon, Routledge.

Hudson, M. J. (2004) The perverse realities of change: World system incorporation and the Okhotsk Culture of Hokkaido. *Journal of Anthropological Archaeology* 23, 290–308.

Hudson, M. J. & Barnes, G. L. (1991) Yoshinogari: A Yayoi settlement in northern Kyushu. *Monumenta Nipponica* 46, 211–235.

Ishida, H. (1988) Morphological studies of Okhotsk crania from Omisaki, Hokkaido. *Journal of the Anthropological Society of Nippon* 96, 17–46.

Ishida, H. (1994) Skeletal morphology of the Okhotsk People on Sakhalin Island. *Anthropological Science* 102, 257–269.

Ishii, J. (1998) Kōhokushiki-ki ni okeru seigyō no tenkan (Subsistence changes in the Kōhoku phase). *Kōkogaku Jānaru* 439, 15–20.

Kikuchi, T. (2009) *Ohōtsuku no kodaishi [The Ancient History of the Okhotsk]*. Tokyo, Heibonsha.

Kinoshita, N. (2003) Shell trade and exchange in the prehistory of the Ryukyu Archipleago. *Bulletin of the Indo-Pacific Prehistory Association* 23, 67–72.

Kodama, S. (1968) Abe no Omi Hirafu no Watarishima Ensei ni Kansuru Shomondai I: Watarishima Emishi to Michinoku Emishi [Several Problems relating to the Expedition attempted by Hirafu Abe-no-Omi to the Watarishima I: Watarishima Emishi and Michinoku Emishi]. *Hoppō Bunka Kenkyū* 3, 95–140 (in Japanese with English summary).

Kreiner, J. (1993) European Images of the Ainu and Ainu Studies in Europe. In J. Kreiner (ed.), *European Studies on Ainu Language and Culture*, 13–60. Munich, Iudicium.

Kuzmin, Y. V., Yanshina, O. V., Fitzpatrick, S. M. & Shubina, O. A. (2012) The Neolithic of the Kurile Islands (Russian Far East): Current state and future prospects. *Journal of Island & Coastal Archaeology* 7, 234–254.

Maeda, U. (2002) *Ohōtsuku no kōkogaku [The Archaeology of the Okhotsk]*. Tokyo, Dōseisha.

Masuda, R., Amano, T. & Ono, H. (2001) Ancient DNA analysis of brown bear (*Ursus arctos*) remains from the archeological site of Rebun Island, Hokkaido, Japan. *Zoological Science* 18, 741–751.

Matsumoto, T. (2006) *Emishi no kōkogaku (The Archaeology of the Emishi)*. Tokyo, Dōseisha.

Matsumoto, T. (2011) *Emishi to wa dare ka (Who Were the Emishi)*. Tokyo, Dōseisha.

Matsumura, H., Hudson, M. J., Koshida, K. & Minakawa, Y. (2006) Embodying Okhotsk ethnicity: human skeletal remains from the Aonae Dune site, Okushiri Island, Hokkaido. *Asian Perspectives* 45, 1–23.

Mizoguchi, K. (2013) *The Archaeology of Japan: From the Earliest Rice Farming Villages to the Rise of the State.* Cambridge, Cambridge University Press.

Ölschleger, H. D. (2014) Ainu ethnography: historical representations in the West. In M. J. Hudson, A. E. Lewallen & M. K. Watson (eds), *Beyond Ainu Studies: Changing Academic and Public Perspectives*, 25–44. Honolulu, University of Hawai'i Press.

Ono, H. (1998) Hokkaidō ni okeru Zoku Jōmon bunka kara Satsumon bunka e (*The transition from the Epi-Jōmon to the Satsumon in Hokkaido*). *Kōkogaku Jānaru* 436, 4–10.

Pluciennik, M. (2014) Historical frames of reference for 'hunter-gatherers'. In V. Cummings, P. Jordan & M. Zvelebil (eds), *The Oxford Handbook of the Archaeology and Anthropology of Hunter-Gatherers*, 55–68. Oxford, Oxford University Press.

Renfrew, C. (1975) Trade as action at a distance. In J. Sabloff & C. C. Lamberg-Karlowsky (eds), *Ancient Civilization and Trade*, 1–59. Albuquerque, University of New Mexico Press.

Sasada, T. (2013) *Hokkaidō ni okeru tetsu bunka no kōkogakuteki kenkyū [Archaeological Research on the Iron Culture of Hokkaido]*. Sapporo, Hokkaidō Shuppan Kikaku Sentā. (In Japanese with English summary).

Schlegel, G. (1893) Problèmes géographiques: Lieou-Kouï Kouo. *T'oung Pao* 4, 335–343.

Segawa, T. (2011) *Ainu no sekai [The World of the Ainu]*. Tokyo, Kōdansha.

Takamiya, H., Hudson, M. J., Yonenobu, H., Kurozumi, T. & Toizumi, T. (2016) An extraordinary case in human history: prehistoric hunter-gatherer adaptation to the islands of the Central Ryukyus (Amami and Okinawa Archipelagos), Japan. *Holocene* 26, 408–422.

Takase, K. (2014) Zoku-Jōmon bunka no shigen, tochi riyō [Use of resources and land in the Epi-Jōmon culture]. *Kokuritsu Rekishi Minzoku Hakubutsukan Kenkyū Hōkoku* 185, 15–61.

Tsutaya, T., Naito, Y., Ishida, H. & Yoneda, M. (2014) Carbon and nitrogen isotope analyses of human and dog diet in the Okhotsk Culture: perspectives from the Moyoro site, Japan. *Anthropological Science* 122, 89–99.

Yagi, M. (2010) *Kodai Emishi Shakai no Seiritsu (The Formation of Ancient Emishi Society)*. Tokyo, Dōseisha.

Chapter 6

Comparative analysis of the development of hunter-fisher-gatherer societies of Tierra Del Fuego and the Northwest Coast of America

Jordi Estévez and Alfredo Prieto

Introduction

This paper proposes some general methodological reflections for the study of hunter-fisher-gatherer societies (HFG) and presents, as an example and case study, a comparative analysis of the development of two societies considered in the literature as representing two extremes in the social organisation of HFG.

Despite long lasting discussion (Sassaman 2004), the tension between historical (cultural history) and evolutionary perspectives (neo-evolutionism, cultural ecology, cultural materialism) on cultural variation and change of HFG over time continues to be the main epistemological and ontological conflict amongst researchers. At one extreme, biological determinism reduces history to adaptation to environmental conditions or to bags of genes competing for reproduction. On the other, particularist extremism, the idealistic vision and denial of the existence of regularities or claims of the impossibility of an objective approach, leaves archaeology reduced to a mere descriptive and dilettante discipline, unable to have social significance. Here we present a comparative and explanatory essay from a different perspective (Argeles *et al.* 1995; Vila 2006): historical materialism as developed in Spain and Latin America (Mcguire 2008). We consider dialectical materialism the most convenient method for explaining complex (social) phenomena. The existence of different scales and dialectical jumps (breaks) in the levels of explanation and time scales (Bailey 1981; Holdaway & Wandsnider 2008) are recognised, while ontological limits are assumed (Gándara 2011).

We have tried to simplify the search for explanations integrating our understanding of sudden changes by distinguishing three levels of causal relationships: a dominant causal factor, a determinant and a triggering effect (Estévez 2005). The first can be a long-term relationship, the last a little disturbance. Sudden changes (i.e. environmental disturbances) create special conditions in the state of the determinant factors and may have a deeper effect on development and change in societies. The nature of these causes can change and even alternate, but what matters is the relationship between those causal levels. For instance, a long period of the oldest human past was the consequence of the biological relationships between humans and their predators, and the determinant factor of change was the relationship between the development of brain and technology. Mastery of fire ended the dominance of these conditions and later the relationship between the development of technology and population growth became the dominant factor: human reproduction and technological (extractive) capability could overrun resource production and endanger the reproduction of prey. Thus the increase in resource exploitation or population increase threatens the sustainability of society: more exploitation of resources (labour investment and technological development) means less population increase and social sustainability. This is what we (Estevez *et al.* 1998) called the 'principal contradiction' in extant human HFG societies and concluded that in later HFG societies, the relations of reproduction dominate the relations of production.

If we do not assume a strictly particularistic position the question may be raised as to why we should make comparisons between societies. From our historical materialist perspective, the analysis of the contrast between similarities and differences, considering the issue of scale, is a scientific strategy to identify and distinguish the essential causalities from their particular phenomenal expressions. This study must be addressed primarily through the analysis of the dynamics of social processes and relationships rather than comparing the discrete examples and traits in space or time. In this paper we will discuss a coarse-grained comparative analysis of two extremes of the American Pacific coast (Fig. 6.1). We will focus on the best-known areas, the central Northwest Coast (NWC) and the Magellan's region and Tierra del Fuego archipelago (TdF) (Estévez & Vila 2010). Our goal is to gain some insights into general trends in social development (considering social relationships as the critical issue) of HFG by comparing the dynamics of societies considered as examples of the two extremes of socially simple and complex HFG (cf. Estévez & Vila 2012), although they share a very similar environment and main subsistence resources (fish, shellfish, marine mammals and birds).

We have used uncalibrated dates in this paper as a reminder that our chronology is very approximate. Most radiocarbon determinations are made on either charcoal from unidentified samples, leaving great uncertainty regarding old wood effects, or on molluscs where the reservoir effect is not properly controlled. Calibration of these determinations would introduce a spurious sense of accuracy.

Theoretical issues

Before we proceed to the comparative analysis we would like to raise some issues. First, we need to analyse the choice of the object of analysis. The correspondence of

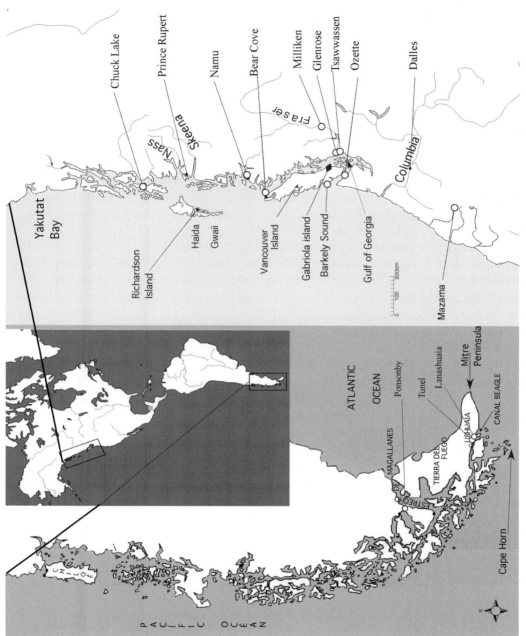

Figure 6.1. Map showing TdF and NWC at the same scale showing sites discussed in text.

the NWC geographical region with a coherent social-cultural unity has been much discussed (cf. Moss 2011), however almost all authors who have worked from both functionalist/adaptationist or historicist perspectives have found it difficult to escape that delimitation. This is reflected in the titles of the most comprehensive works. The southern region is sometimes based on geographic criteria, Southern Patagonia, Magallanes-Tierra del Fuego, establishing divisions based on ecological criteria and on the mode of transport of human groups (pedestrian/terrestrial steppe hunters, and western, eastern or southern canoeists) or by extrapolating the ethnical classifications from the main ethnographic sources (M. Gusinde, see also Blumauer, this volume). In both cases, demarcating limits between 'interior or terrestrial' societies and 'coastal societies' beyond the historical and ethnographic information is problematic.

Although some accounts were produced during the first contacts and reports of navigators, early settlers and missionaries, basic ethnographic information in both cases was generated in the late nineteenth and early twentieth centuries (two or three centuries later than first contact). It was elaborated from a particularist and anti-evolutionist theoretical perspective by two ethnographers, M. Gusinde and F. Boas, rooted in the German cultural environment of the late 19th century. This reveals significant bias in these accounts and the need to establish a critical perspective. On one hand we have to consider androcentric bias and on the other we can ask to what extent the divisions established between groups corresponded to reality or rather to a need to simplify, define and embrace an object of study – originally dynamic but basically almost vanished by the time of study (Vila & Estevez 2010).

Since the common objective of these two ethnographers was opposition to simple environmental determinism, it is legitimate to ask if the proper equal classification of these as hunter-gatherer societies is adequate (Estévez & Vila 2010). Moss (2011) has described NWC groups as 'fisher-food producers', recognising the management of salmon reproduction, the clam gardens (a feature just rediscovered in 2002), the cultivation of food crops documented archaeologically (Turner & Deur 2005) and tobacco, which were described by Boas himself (Boas 1902).

Another substantive issue is how far back in time we can trace these features and relations described in the ethnographic information (see also Grier this volume). Ethnographic information has weighed decisively in the inferences made from the archaeological evidence. The problem here is that, although we have independent evidence for climate and natural resources, human strategies must be inferred.

Complexity or simplicity

The concept of social complexity, often attributed to NWC societies, has been much discussed (Sassaman 2004; Moss 2011). Some scholars insist on its continuous relative and comparative character (Fitzhugh 2003). A list of features has been associated with 'complex' HFG but the substantive distinction relates complexity with the existence of 'institutionalised labor (*sic*) relations whereby some people must perform work for others under the direction of nonkin and inherited privileged status' (Arnold 1993, 78). Thus inequality is defined as opposed to the equality of 'simple' HFG.

Although with differing emphases and directions of causality, the complexity of the NWC has been associated with fishing (mainly of salmon), conservation and possible ways of managing the stock of stored food (for an overview see Estévez & Vila 2010). The predominance of environmental archaeology approaches has generated a number of proposals for scientific explanation linking the object of labour, the resources, with strategies for subsistence that determine the rise of forms of social organisation. Based on use of strategic locations on the main river courses, or the presence of consumed salmon remains (i.e. Milliken on the Fraser, or Dalles on the Columbia and the site of Namu on the central coast), some authors argue for specialised exploitation and conservation in the NWC since the oldest archaeological sites in the region (Cannon & Yang 2006), well before 5000 BP. They advocate a stability of the exploitation of salmon and an 'extensification' for other fish species (Butler & Campbell 2004). A stable adaptive exploitation of coastal resources (which culminates in the ethnographically described society) has also been considered to have been installed in TdF since 6500 BP (Orquera & Piana 1999). In contrast, it has been postulated that the high salmon dependence of the NWC (Butler 2000), and the simplicity of social organisation in TdF documented by ethnography, could have been the indirect result of native mortality caused by Europeans (Ocampo & Rivas 2000, Yesner 2004).

The problems of induction and generalisation

In Tdf and the NWC, archaeological research began by trying to establish culture-historical sequences (see Estevez & Vila 2010; Vazquez & Prieto 2014). The development of processual archaeology, especially from the late 1970s, tried to establish adaptive and environmentally deterministic explanations (e.g. Burley 1980; Croes & Hackenberger 1988; Piana 1984). There have been eclectic trials mixing elements of both theoretical currents (e.g. Orquera & Piana 1999; O'Connor & Maschner 1999). Since the beginning of the 21st century, the collection of new data and the post-processualist critique has produced a new relativism and scepticism regarding the above explanations, and has generated new alternative explanations (e.g. Moss 2011, 96).

The aforementioned environmental-cultural predominance of the materialist approach has produced an archaeological record that has targeted the subsistence basis of past societies, collecting wildlife and environmental data. Despite the problems of inferring subsistence from faunal and botanical samples (see Estevez 1991) and discussion since the 1970s about the problem of operating with differing types of counting units in archaeozoology, authors continue to draw conclusions from comparisons of different faunal assemblages by NISP (number of identified specimens, i.e. bones and bone fragments) while it is obvious that, for instance, a higher NISP of a small fish (like herring) does not imply a dietary predominance of that species over larger fishes (e.g. rockfish or salmon).

Another problem is the character and representativeness of the sample. This refers to both the temporal and the spatial spectrum. Our excavations at two European contact-time sites in TdF that can be attributed to the same ethnic group (the Yamana) and are *c.* 60 km distant, have exposed the need for an appropriate and tested sampling system for each site (Estevez *et al.* 2013). Our analysis has shown that apparently similar shell-middens were built by a number of successive occupations at Tunel VII (Estevez & Vila 1995; 2006), and by one more prolonged occupation at Lanashuaia (Verdún *et al.* 2015). The analysis of faunal remains has shown that conclusions drawn from each sample rely heavily on a fine stratigraphy, because of the sequence of different activities carried out. Moreover, the same people at the two sites exploited different types and proportions of animals, adjusting to their availability given specific environments (Mameli & Estévez 2004).

Some archaeozoological studies of the NWC have emphasised the importance of herring for the development of NWC societies, playing down the role of salmon (McKechnit *et al.* 2014). This is especially based on evidence from the sites on the east coast of Vancouver Island, contrasting with sites near the mouth of the main salmon rivers like the Fraser and Skeena. The first discussion of the relative over-estimation of the relevance of salmon by archaeologists (Monks 1987), however justified, was formulated from a site that documented mass exploitation of herring. There are ethnographic accounts for different activities at specific places and times. The effects of canoe travel has also been underestimated (see Blake 2010), for example a salmon catching site and one of herring exploitation may be only one-days canoeing distance, as with Gabriola Island (herring) and Tsawwassen (salmon).

The location of processing activities and refuse disposal should also be taken into account. Indoor or out-door activities for example could be organised according to the season and the conditions required for working (e.g. Estevez *et al.* 2013; Lepofsky *et al.* 2000). The distribution of refuse is also conditioned by the social status of consumers and by social norms. A recurrent social organisation of space and unequal distribution of consumption both within the living units and between the various households can result in unequal composition of different samples from the same site, as at Ozette (Samuels 2006). We could, for example, hypothesise (cf. Moss 1993) that salmon was a prestige food in comparison with more everyday foods such as shellfish, herring and vegetables. The interpretation of the social and political dynamics and conflicts may vary substantially.

We have defined Yamana subsistence as a specialisation in a non-specialised subsistence strategy elsewhere (Gassiot & Estévez 2006). This distinguishes two types of what other scholars might define globally as collectors. For us it is important to distinguish between non-specialised opportunistic hunter and gathering and a technologically specialised but opportunistic hunting, fishing and gathering system. The former does not exclude the possibility of having very species specific, seasonal or sporadic depredation episodes, taking advantage of concentration of many prey individuals (e.g. reindeer, goat or aurochs herds in some Middle Palaeolithic sites). The second, like the Mesolithic or the TdF canoeist, uses highly specialised technological gear to cope intensively with a wide range of resources.

All these arguments demonstrate the danger of assuming identical samples can be interpreted to mean the same, or of making general conclusions just from archaeozoological analysis. Before making direct comparisons of fauna from each site, the character of the site should be established, including its function in the wider system of subsistence strategies, and the character of the sample in the wider distribution, consumption and disposal system. This requires a temporal, contextual and spatial analysis of all material remains, from products to the instruments, as well as infrastructural constructions. We would be sceptical of drawing equivalences between the societies of two sites showing the same sample of resources residues and perhaps the same technology but very separate in time.

Some theories of social causality explaining the development of societies have been developed. But there are few studies on social evolution which have a solid empirical basis for unambiguous inductions (see Sutherland 2004). Very little social explanation can be effectively compared with the archaeological record generated until now (cf. Ames & Martindale 2014). Some habitation structures have been excavated and a change from little huts to big houses seems clear in the NWC. In some sites the internal spatial distribution of activities has been analysed (e.g. Coupland & Banning 1996, Sobel *et al.* 2006) and some ideas about changes in social organisation have arisen (i.e. based on the disposition of the fireplaces). But our understanding of the structure and the dynamics of society before contact time are still reliant on the ethnographic data. Large areas of shell-midden structures were interpreted differently according to the ethnography in the two areas. In TdF in principle they are regarded as the accumulation of successive occupations of one or a few social units, while in the NWC they have instead been interpreted as structured villages. However, it has not been possible to demonstrate conclusively the coexistence of these units and the existence of large villages from the archaeological evidence alone, if we leave aside, in the NWC, the possible defensive structures of late chronology and the 'proto-historic' village of Ozette (Samuels 1991).

Another crucial point derives from the very classical definition of economy that involves the production *and distribution* of the produced goods. That means not just the resources available, but also the amount of labour invested to get them, the technology and the organisation of the labour force and the organisation of the consumers (which also implies the production and maintenance of people). These two organisations are not easy to visualise archaeologically. An egalitarian organisation with just sexual and age distribution of labour has often been suggested for simpler HFG societies (e.g. Arnold 1993, 84). However the equality, or egalitarianism, of 'simple' HFG has been questioned since the 1970s from a gender perspective (Begler 1978, Estevez *et al.* 1998). Work is not necessarily equally distributed in 'simple' HFG societies. Gender differentiation (unlike age distinction) is a universal feature, fixed from birth for each person. If the distribution is uneven between the sexes it means

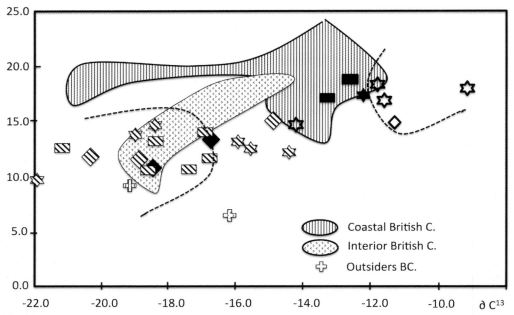

Figure 6.2. Plot of isotope values for ∂N15 (vertical axis) and ∂C13 (horizontal axis) in human remains. The areas comprise individuals from British Columbia. The crosses indicate the outsiders situated out of their range (redrawn from Schwarzc et al. 2014, fig. 5.) For the Island Grande of Tierra del Fuego, stars represent females, diamonds males, rectangles indeterminate. Samples from terrestrial hunters are hatched, those from the SE of the Island are white, and canoeists of the Beagle Channel, black. Dotted lines separate terrestrial diet at left and maritime at right (after Schinder et al. 2003, fig. 3). Although there are still a few segregated analyses, isotopic content points to different tendencies between males and females in diet.

that there is a permanent exploitation of one part of the society by another. If we admit 'that the manipulation of labour required by enormous investments in low-rank resources exploitation and processing was central to emergence of complexity in NWC' (Arnold 1993, 97), then we can guess that the part of the workforce that could have been over-exploited, would carry a greater increase in the investment of labour. Differences in diet consumption between men and women (see Fig. 6.2) seen in stress markers or in the ideological treatment of both genders (i.e. in graves) could be good evidence for sexual inequality (i.e. Cybulsky *et al.* 1992).

The earlier paralel development in TdF and NWC

Keeping these issues in mind, we now present a comparison of the general trends in the sequence of both areas. We will consider technology and the subsistence record but also introduce the sexual division of labour and consider reproduction.

There is a striking similarity of the landscape in the two regions. The only substantial difference is the existence in the NWC of large rivers like the Columbia,

Fraser, Skeena or Nash and thus the number of seasonal anadromous fish-runs. In both regions we can observe a not consistent, but persistent population growth (assuming that the increase of sites could be interpreted in this sense), and the intensification of resource exploitation, leading to the use of massive fishing devices or (opportunistic) whale hunting in both regions and to shellfish and plant gardening in the NWC. We can also observe the persistence through time of some of the same extractive technologies (canoes, harpoons) despite some social 'crashes' or hiatuses in the chronology. Another common issue for both regions is the existence and maintenance of different languages and some permeability of people across 'language frontiers'. Both areas show similar starting points in terms of chronology and the types of resources they initially exploited, but reproductive strategies did not have the same final effect in TdF and the NWC, and at some point these processes diverged.

At both ends of the Pacific there is evidence of human presence, albeit tenuous, before 12,000 BP. The pre-Holocene people exploited animals that became extinct. In both regions there are important chronological gaps between the Late Glacial and Holocene archaeological evidence. The time scale and the slight evidence do not allow correlation of the natural changes and some catastrophic events (volcano eruptions and glacial lake outbursts) as triggering or causal effects on societies.

The fauna exploited at the Holocene sites of both regions is very similar to the modern fauna. Some of the oldest sites on the coasts of both regions share particular characteristics. In Tierra del Fuego at Tunel-I and in the NWC at Glenrose on the Fraser delta, Gbto23 in Prince Rupert, and Bear Cove, on the north of Vancouver Island, there is evidence of an initial occupation which did not involve intensive exploitation of shellfish, and does not seem to have had a specialisation on any particular type of resource. In the south, subsistence was of terrestrial animals such as guanaco and *Rhea*, despite the fact that the sites dated between 8000 and 6500 BP (e.g. Tunel I and Ponsonby) are close to the modern coast (Prieto 1991). All of the sites seem to represent incursions by people who hunted terrestrial fauna, without any specialisation on littoral environments (Orquera & Piana 2006). In the centre of the NWC there is more evidence of fishing and exploitation of marine animals during the early Holocene (e.g. Haida Gwaii, Chuck Lake, Namu before 5000 BP, Bear Cove and Glenrose before 4500 BP). This has sometimes been characterised as a specialised littoral exploitation, but it could be perhaps better interpreted as the occasional exploitation of such resources within an opportunist strategy of catching a local resource that was seasonally abundant (e.g. Matson 2010; Coupland *et al.* 2010).

In the south after a break in occupation that followed an important eruption of the Hudson Volcano around 6980 BP, there was a change towards intensive exploitation of littoral resources from the island of Chiloe to Tierra del Fuego, 1500 km to the south (Prieto *et al.* 2014). From that time (around 6500 BP) onwards, coastal sites were based on the exploitation of littoral resources, specifically the collection of mussels, hunting pinnipeds and fishing, hunting birds and occasionally land mammals (especially guanaco or huemul), and the collection of crustaceans, fruits and fungi (Estévez & Vila 1998). In a similar fashion, there were volcanic episodes in the NWC such as the eruption of Mazama (around 7500 BP), but there has been little exploration of their effect on the surrounding societies. The collection of molluscs began, or increased spectacularly, around 5500–4500 BP (Moss *et al.* 2007). This was a general trend in sites from the Gulf of Georgia to the north of British Columbia. In the NWC this trend coincided with a rapid increase in the numbers of sites (see Grier 2003). This has been interpreted as being the result of intensification in the exploitation of the environment (Ames & Maschner 1999), or as an option to support an increasing population (Croes & Hackenberger 1988).

The beginning of broad spectrum exploitation aimed specifically at littoral resources is related to the appearance of harpoons and a technology developed for fishing and hunting in the water, with a pattern of annual exploitation and a high degree of logistical mobility, shown by the presence of little rounded huts without permanent structures (Matson & Coupland 1995; Orquera & Piana 1999). In both regions bone and stone artefacts appear with engraved decoration, or even small, sculpted figures in the case of the Saint Mungo period (5500–3500 BP after Matson & Coupland 1995) at the mouth of the Fraser River. According to the Argentinian authors and in the view of some Canadian authors, from this time onwards in the Beagle Channel and in the NWC basic subsistence strategies consolidated into adjustments to local littoral resources with some local variations. Nevertheless, despite the general stability in the non-biological conditions and an identifiable continuity of occupation in some sites, and in the qualitative nature of the exploited resources, there was actually no simple, fixed and stable adaptation to the environment from the mid-Holocene in either region. There are obvious changes and hiatuses in the archaeological record that demonstrate that there were crises and readjustments, some of which affected a whole region. Sometimes, but not always, these breaks were related to possible trigger effects of sudden changes in nature, or were due to geological activity or tsunami (i.e. Ocampo & Rivas 2000; Moss 2011).

Subsistence in broad regions of both American coasts relied on mussels as the key resource, although it was sustained mainly by marine mammals and generally by fishing. The variety of resources and the abundance of mussels contributed to increased security and predictability of subsistence. These, together with a higher mobility and capability of transport provided by canoeing, allowed a relaxation of reproductive controls, thus achieving relatively high rates of population growth and an increasing pressure on resources. There were attempts to maintain stability within a precarious equilibrium (Butler & Campbell 2004), but it was not always possible to achieve this successfully. The problem lay in the reliability of the basic resources, especially in the easy availability, but rapid depletion of mussels, which, although they appear in large quantities and are easy to collect, also have a relatively slow recuperation, especially if they are intensively exploited. The dependence on mussels also means that red tides might interrupt the food supply (Spencer 1951).

In the southern sequence, one marked break in the sequence occurred shortly before 5000 BP (Rivas & Ocampo 2006). The most visible break (Gassiot & Estévez 2006), which is also the most controversial to interpret, occurred between 4500 and 4100 BP (Orquera & Piana 1999; Stern & Prieto 1991) and produced a short period of use of a new type of instrument and an emphasis on the exploitation of terrestrial fauna. In the NWC there were also stratigraphic breaks in most of the sites (Vila & Estevez 2010). The reduction or disappearance of mussels in many locations after 3500 BP, probably caused by over-exploitation or because of environmental change (Butler & Campbell 2004), would have led to a major crisis. The chronology of the major breaks in the two zones is out of step by about the same extent as the difference in time for the generalisation of first intensive mollusc exploitation (that began about 6500 BP in TdF and about 5500 BP in the NWC). From this time onwards, behaviour in our two regions (north and south) diverged increasingly quickly.

The divergence

In TdF, after 3300 BP the basic features of tools and archaeologically documented strategies remained unchanged until the arrival of Europeans. From the first coastal exploitation right through the following period, the tool set remained essentially the same; the only changes were its simplification, the disappearance of decoration on bone artefacts, and the incorporation (perhaps around 2600 BP but certainly before 1400 BP) of bows and arrows. People used a great variety of particular strategies to adjust to slight geographic and temporal environmental variations. A successful social control of human reproduction, together with flexibility and a high supply of marine resources which flowed in from breeding grounds located outside the normal reach of groups, maintained the balance between resources and population until the arrival of Europeans (Vila & Ruiz 2001). There is little seasonal variation in the flux of resources. The major variations were not regular but chance events of whale or massive fish strandings. The mussels continued to be the staple resource, and probably the minimal threshold that could not be crossed. Increasing the level of food production would have required a huge improvement of technology and of men's effort to access the distant pinnipedia breading grounds, fish banks and whales. Evidence for the intensification in resource extraction is ambiguous. The documented fish traps have not been dated. The (opportunistic) hunting of whales is difficult to document (although it is related by one ethnographic source and the enormous harpoon heads in the ethnographic collections could be indirect proof), but it may have developed after European influence. On the other hand, a significant increase of population in TdF (cf. Rivas & Ocampo 2006) is not visible. The efforts made to demonstrate archeologically the aggregation of people, as described by the earliest sailors, have so far been unsuccessful (Zangrando 2009; Briz *et al.* 2009) or not conclusive (Yesner 2004).

In contrast, in the NWC the dynamic of change was a spiral (Estévez & Vila 2010). Around 3500 BP there was an important change of emphasis in gathering strategies from collecting mussels, to collecting molluscs from sandy deposits, which required major investment in gathering effort. This change is documented in many places from the north of British Columbia (Mitchell & Donald 1988) through the Gulf of Georgia and much further south, towards the coast of Santa Barbara in California (Erlandson & Moss 1999). This has been attributed to factors such as the transformation of coasts and their stabilisation and the advance of deltas, or to cultural factors of over-exploitation. Around the Gulf of Georgia this change was accompanied by an emphasis on fishing for large fish. Evidence of massive salmon or other fish exploitation does not automatically imply the existence of storage, but conservation techniques must have been developed at some time, somewhere (Burley 1980) and have to be demonstrated archaeologically (Matson 2010).

Almost all authors agree that from around 2500 BP, only 1000 or 1500 years after the change in the most abundant mollusc species, the main elements of the distinctive NWC model are already present: intensive exploitation and storage of salmon and other fish species such as herring and candlefish, large/long houses, and social complexity, which most authors equate to the production of objects of great added subjective value including, for example, stone sculpture. However, not everything was unchanging. There was another intriguing break between 1700 BP and 1500 BP when, more or less at the same time, there is evidence of a generalised war-oriented settlement pattern, defensive structures and obvious signs of conflict such as weapons of war (Angelbeck & Grier 2012), and stone sculpture disappeared. Later on there was a substantive change in burial practice: in the coastal zone from about 700 BP the dead were no longer buried in shell middens (Cybulski *et al.* 1992).

In sum, the crisis that occurred around 4500 BP in TdF was not solved in the same way as the crisis about 1000 years later in NWC. There were several options for intensifying the exploitation of different resources from among the large number of possible resources already known. Developing fishing to a greater extent was a good solution in both areas. The people had the experience and the techniques needed on one hand and, on the other hand, fish stocks had the advantage of being difficult to overexploit with existing technology. The traditional systems were not effective enough to completely deplete the stocks, and therefore people could overcome the problems of decreasing yields without reaching an immediate limit.

Nevertheless, in the NWC extending the massive fish extraction system was, in principle, the least-cost solution because it did not need a great investment in new technology. Using the traditional systems of capture (fish traps and weirs were probably already present long before 3000 BP) allowed HFG to overcome the problems of diminishing returns without encountering any immediate limits. Evidence for depletion of resources is ambiguous (cf. Butler 2000). It could affect high rank marine mammals and perhaps even salmon, but this is not clearly visible in the fish samples (McKechnitt *et al.* 2014). Massive fishing did not require a spectacular increase in extractive labour. Once the preservation techniques for fish (drying, smoking, oil extraction) were implemented, the only problem was that all of the captured fish (which could theoretically supply the bulk of annual food needs) had to be processed quickly and this required a significant increase in the amount and concentration of labour force in processing, preparing and maintaining the infrastructure (hearths, drying facilities, etc). As different authors have already pointed out, and as the history of the 'iron chink' machine clearly demonstrates (Vila & Estevez 2010), the ability to process the fish captured was the real 'bottleneck' in an economy reliant on anadromous fish. The apparently inexhaustible supply of fish, despite the traditional mass capture techniques and the relative slight effort invested in their capture, produced a new contradiction.

The limit within the system shifted from the environment to the processing capacity. This would create a demographic trap, which could spiral out of control. More women were needed, as workers (if we accept the gendered distribution of labour described in ethnographic sources) but also as producers of more people, in order to increase the labour force as this would generate more reproduction, but in turn that would generate more demand, and then further intensify the exploitation of other resources. In these circumstances there would be a spiralling increase in demand. It is probable that this system was freed of the central contradiction between production and reproduction. The more labour invested in processing the fish capture, the more product was obtained because a large amount of biomass could potentially be extracted without threatening the continuity of the reproduction of the main resource. The system favoured groups of people with access to the best fishing spots, but above all those groups that could better mobilise the necessary labour force to take advantage of their moments of over-abundance. Thus the society would be transformed into an expanding system (as an agricultural system does) and would end up competing and taking over the neighbouring societies. Setting free the power of reproduction became the dominant factor that underlies all other causes that determined or triggered all the developments in the NWC. Despite the abundance of resources exploitable with the available technology, these societies were subject to socio-economic stress. The great potential of production (and storage) was conditional on the availability of a big enough (female) labour force. This put pressure on reproduction and as a side effect on social organisation that invested huge efforts into managing, controlling and capturing labour forces, ultimately including slaves, and resources (Vila & Estévez 2010).

In areas like the Columbia River, the Fraser River and perhaps the Nass and Skeena rivers, an expansive system would affect other neighbouring areas through escalating violence and the widespread coercion not only against women but also against other segments of the population. This violence and coercion would also provoke counter-reactions (Grier & Angelbeck 2012). With the entry of the Europeans in the play, NWC societies redirected the over-production to exchange, and to the increase of wealth and power for the old managers. The system of subjective value radically changed, elaborating old tendencies including violence and a struggle to obtain (or retain) a labour force (slaves). The alternative development by the southern HFG that solved the contradiction by restricting reproduction and resulting in a relative lower population, led to a fast extinction process triggered by European sickness and overexploitation and depletion of strategic resources, in particular sea-lions (Orquera *et al.* 1991).

Conclusion

We have tried to illustrate the complex interplay of different causal levels and the need to further develop methodology. The contradiction within HFG societies, between a dominant relationship between the tendency to demographic growth and the reproductive rhythm of natural resources, can be solved by setting different social strategies. The parallel development of the early sequences and the subsequent relatively fast divergence at the extremes of the American Pacific coast is an example. One strategy was to reduce human reproduction to a sustainable level as in Tierra del Fuego, the other was intensification of the exploitation of resources that led to a spiral development like the late NWC development. It depended partially on the available resources, but also on prior experience, social strategies of production and reproduction, which are articulated around the relationships between men and women, and development, coupled with the triggering effect of environmental disturbances.

Adopting a comparative archaeological analysis of the general trends in the development of societies, taking into account the different levels of causal explanations and emphasising the relevance on reproduction, produces new insights that can transcend more simple environmental explanations.

References

Ames, K. M. & Martindale, A. (2014) Rope bridges and cables: a synthesis of Prince Rupert Harbour Archaeology. *Canadian Journal of Archaeology/Journal Canadien d'Archéologie* 38, 140–178.

Ames, K. M. & Maschner, H. D. G. (1999) *Peoples of the Northwest Coast : their Archaeology and Prehistory.* New York, Thames and Hudson.

Angelbeck, B. & Grier, C. (2012) Anarchism and the archaeology of anarchic societies: resistance to centralization in the Coast Salish region of the Pacific Northwest Coast. *Current Anthropology* 53(5), 547–587.

Argeles, T., Bonet, A., Clemente, I., Estévez, J., Gibaja, J., Lumbreras, L. G. & Piqué, R. (1995) Splendor realitatis. Teoría para una praxis. *Actas dos Trabalhos de Antropologia e Etnologhia* 35(1), 501–507.

Arnold, J. E. (1993) Labor and the rise of complex hunter-gatherers. *Journal of Anthropological Archaeology* 12, 75–119.

Bailey, G. N. (1981) Concepts, time scales and explanations in economic prehistory. In A. Sheridan & G. N. Bailey (eds), *Economic Archaeology*, 97–117 Oxford: British Archaeological Report S96. Oxford, British Archaeological Reports.

Begler, E. B. (1978) Sex, status and authority in egalitarian society. *American Anthropologist* ns 80, 571–588.

Blake, M. (2010) Navegación y definición de territorios en la NWC un ejemplo Coast Salish. In A.Vila & J. Estévez (eds), *La excepción y la norma: las sociedades indígenas de la Costa Noroeste de Norteamérica desde la Arqueología,* 111–123. Treballs d'Etnoarqueología, 8. Madrid. CSIC.

Boas, F. (1902) *Tsimshian texts.* Washington. Governmentt Printing Office microform.

Briz, I., Álvarez, M., Zurro, D. & Caro, J. (2009) Meet for lunch in Tierra del Fuego: a new ethnoarchaeological project. *Antiquity*, 83(322): http://antiquity.ac.uk/projgall/briz322/. (accessed 11/11/2010)

Burley, D. (1980) *Marpole: Anthropological Reconstructions of a Prehistoric Northwest Culture Type.* Burnaby. Department of Archaeology, Simon Fraser University.

Butler, V. L. (2000) Resource depression on the Northwest Coast of NorthAmerica. *Antiquity* 74, 649–661.

Butler, V. L. & Campbell, S. K. (2004) Resource intensification and resource depression in the Pacific Northwest of North America: a zooarchaeological review. *Journal of World Prehistory* 18(4), 327–405.

Cannon, A. & Yang, D. (2006) Early storage and sedentism on the Pacific Northwest Coast: ancient DNA analysis of salmon remains from Namu, British Columbia. *American Antiquity* 71, 123–140.

Coupland, G. & Banning, E. B. (eds) (1996) *People Who Lived in Big Houses: Archaeological Perspectives on Large Domestic Structures.* Monographs in World Prehistory 27. Madison, Prehistory Press.

Coupland, G., Stewart, K. & Patton, K. (2010) Do you never get tired of salmon? Evidence for extreme salmon specialization at Prince Rupert Harbour, British Columbia. *Journal of Anthropological Archaeology* 29(2), 189–207.

Croes, D. R. & Hackenberger, S. (1988) Hoko River archaeological complex: modelling prehistoric Northwest Coast economic evolution. In L. I. Barry (ed.), *Prehistoric Economies of the Pacific Northwest Coast,* 19–85. Research in Economic Anthropology. Supplement 3. Greenwich, JAI Press.

Cybulski, J. S., Balkwill, D., Young, G. S., Sutherland, P. D., Canadian Museum of Civilization and Archaeological Survey of Canada (1992) *A Greenville Burial Ground: Human Remains and Mortuary Elements in British Columbia Coast Prehistory.* Hull. Canadian Museum of Civilization. Mercury Series 146.

Erlandson, J. M. & Moss, M. L. (1999) The systematic use of radiocarbon dating in archaeological surveys in coastal and other erosional environments. *American Antiquity* 64(3), 431–443.

Estévez, J. (1991) Cuestiones de fauna en Arqueología. In A. Vila (ed.), *Arqueologia,* 57–81. Madrid, Consejo Superior de Investgaciones Científicas.

Estévez, J. (2005) *Catástrofes en Prehistoria.* Barcelona. Editorial Bellaterra.

Estévez, J. & Vila, A. (eds) (1995) *Encuentros en los concheros fueguinos. Treballs d'Etnoarqueologia,* 1. Bellaterra. UAB Departament d'Antropologia social i de Prehistòria, CSIC.

Estévez, J. & Vila, A. (1998) Tierra del Fuego, lugar de encuentros. *Revista de Arqueología Americana* 15, 187–219.

Estévez, J. & Vila, A. (2006) Variability in the lithic and faunal record through 10 reoccupations of a XIX century Yamana hut. *Journal of Anthropological Archaeology* 25(4), 408–423.

Estévez, J. & Vila, A. (2010) Introducción: el porqué de este libro y de nuestra ida a la Costa Noroeste. In A.Vila & J. Estévez (eds.), *La excepción y la norma: las sociedades indígena de la Costa Noroeste de Norteamérica desde la Arqueología,* 9–61. Treballs d'Etnoarqueologia 8. Madrid, CSIC.

Estévez, J. & Vila, A. (2012) On the extremes of hunter-fisher-gatherers of America's Pacific Rim. *Quaternary International* 285, 1–10.

Estévez, J., Vila, A. & Piqué, R. (2013) Methodological reflections on shell midden archaeology: issues from Tierra del Fuego ethnoarchaeology. In G.N. Bailey, K. Hardy & A. Camara (eds) *Shell Energy. Mollusc Shells as Coastal Resources,* 107–122. Oxford, Oxbow Books.

Estevez, J., Vila, A., Terradas, X., Piqué, R., Taulé, M., Gibaja, J. & Ruiz, G. (1998) Cazar o no cazar, ¿es ésta la cuestión? *Boletin de Antropología Americana,* 33, 5–24.

Fitzhugh, B. (2003) *The Evolution of Complex Hunter-Gatherers: Archaeological Evidence From the North Pacific.* Plenum. New York.

Gándara, M. (2011) Los límites de la explicación : la 'ontologización' y sus consecuencias éticas y políticas en arqueología. In E. Williams, M. G. Sánchez, P. Weigand & M. Gándara (eds), *Mesoamérica. Debates y perspectivas*, 45–56. Zamora, Colegio de Michoacán.

Gassiot, E. & Estévez, J. (2006) Last foragers in coastal environments: a comparative study: cantabrian Mesolithic, the Yámana of Tierra del Fuego and archaic foragers in Central America Coasts. In C. Grier, J. Kim & J. Uchiyama (eds), *Beyond Affluent Foragers. Rethinking Hunter-Gatherer Complexity. Proceedings of the 9th conference of the International Council of Archaeozoology, Durham, August 2002*, 90–105. Oxford. Oxbow Books.

Grier, C. (2003) Dimensions of regional interaction in the prehistoric Gulf of Georgia. In R. G. Matson, G. Coupland & Q. Mackie (eds), *Emerging from the Mist: Studies in Northwest Coast Culture History*, 170–187. Vancouver, UBC Press.

Grier, C. (2010) Probables pasados y posibles futuros: sobre la reconstruccion de cazadores-recolectores complejos de la NWC. In A. Vila & J. Estévez (eds), *La excepción y la norma: las sociedades indígenas de la Costa Noroeste de Norteamérica desde la arqueología*, 147–166. Madrid, CSIC.

Holdaway, S. & Wandsnider, L. (eds) (2008) *Time in Archaeology. Time Perspectivism Revisited.* Salt Lake City, University of Utah Press.

Lepofsky, D., Blake, M., Brown, D., Morrison, S., Oakes, N. & Lyons, N. (2000) The archaeology of the Scowlitz site, SW British Columbia. *Journal of Field Archaeology* 27, 391–416.

Mameli, L. & Estévez, J. (2004) *Etnoarqueozoología de aves: el ejemplo del extremo sur americano.* Treballs d'Etnoarqueologia 5. Madrid, CSIC.

Mannino, M. A. & Thomas, K. D. (2002) Depletion of a resource? The impact of prehistoric human foraging on intertidal mollusc communities and its significance for human settlement, mobility and dispersal. *World Archaeology* 33(3), 452–474.

Martinic, M. (1996) La Cueva del Milodon (Ultima Esperanza, Patagonia chilena). Un siglo de descubrimientos y estudios referidos a la vida primitiva en el sur de America. *Journal de la Société des Américanistes* 82, 311–323.

Matson, R. G. (2010) Los orígenes de la cultura de la Costa Noroeste. In A. Vila & J. Estévez (eds), *La excepción y la norma: las sociedades indígenas de la Costa Noroeste de Norteamérica desde la Arqueología*, 63–85. Treballs d'Etnoarqueologia 8. Madrid, CSIC.

Matson, R. G. & Coupland, G. (1995) *The Prehistory of the Northwest Coast.* San Diego: Academic Press.

McGuire, R. (2008) Marxism. In R. A. Bentley, H. D. G. Maschner & C. Chippindale (eds), *Handbook of Archaeological Theories*, 73–93. New York, AltaMira Press.

McKechnie, I., Lepofsky, D., Moss, M. L., Butler, V. L., Orchard, T. J., Coupland, G., Foster, F., *et al.* (2014) Archaeological data provide alternative hypotheses on Pacific herring (*Clupea pallasii*) distribution, abundance, and variability. *Proceedings of the National Academy of Sciences*, 111(9), Published online February 18, 2014 | E807–E816 PNAS.

Mitchell, D. H. & Donald, L. (1988) Archaeology and the study of Northwest Coast economies. In B. L. Isaac (ed.), *Prehistoric Economies of the Pacific Northwest Coast, Research In Economic Anthropology*, 293–351. Greenwich, JAI Press.

Monks, G. G. (1987) Prey as bait: the Deep Bay example. *Canadian Journal of Archaeology* 11, 119–142.

Moss, M. L. (1993) Shellfish, gender, and status on the Northwest Coast: Reconciling archeological, ethnographic, and ethnohistorical records of the Tlingit. *American Anthropologist* 95 (3 Sept.), 631–652.

Moss, M. L. (2011) *Northwest Coast. Archaeology as Deep History.* Washington, SAA Press.

Moss, M. L., Peteet, D. M. & Whitlock, C. (2007) Mid-Holocene culture and climate on the Northwest Coast of North America. In D. G. Anderson, K. A. Maasch & D. H. Sandweiss (eds), *Climate Change and Cultural Dynamics: A Global Perspective on Mid-Holocene Transitions*, 491–529. New York, Elsevier.

Ocampo, C. & Rivas, P. (2000) Nuevos fechados 14C de la costa norte de la isla Navarino, costa sur del canal Beagle, provincia Antártica chilena, región de Magallanes. *Anales del Instituto de la Patagonia* 28, 197–214.

Orquera, L. A. & Piana, E. L. (1999) *Arqueología de la región del canal Beagle (Tierra del Fuego, República Argentina.* Buenos Aires, Publicaciones de la SAA.

Orquera, L. A. & Piana, E.L. (2006) El poblamiento inicial del área litoral sudamericana sudoccidental. *Magallania* 34(2), 21–36.

Orquera, L. A., Piana, E. L., Vila, A. & Estévez, J. (1991) El fin de un sistema: Un sitio de canoeros del siglo XIX. *Actas del XII Congreso Nacional de Arqueología Chilena (Temuco, 14 al 19 de octubre), boletin 4, tomo 1. Simposios*, 89–94. Temuco, Museo Regional de la Araucania.

Piana, E. L. (1984) *Arrinconamiento ó adaptación en Tierra del Fuego.* Buenos Aires. Antropología Argentina.

Prieto, A. (1991) Cazadores tempranos y tardíos en Cueva del Lago Sofía 1. *Anales del Instituto de La Patagonia* 20, 75–99.

Prieto, A., Stern, Ch. R. & Estévez J. (2013) ThepPeopling of the Fuego-Patagonian fjords by littoral hunter–gatherers after the mid-Holocene H1 eruption of Hudson Volcano. *Quaternary International* 317, 3–13.

Rivas, P. & Ocampo, C. (2006) La Adaptación Humana al Bosque en la Isla de Chiloé. Estrategias Adaptativas en el Litoral Septentrional de Los Canales Patagónicos. Unpublished Paper presented at the XVI Congreso de Arqueología Chilena. Simposio Arqueología En Zonas Boscosas: Propuestas Metodológicas y Teóricas.

Samuels, S. R. (ed.) (1991) *Ozette Archaeological Project Research Reports,* 177–284. Reports of Investigations 63. Pullman, Washington State University, Department of Anthropology.

Sassaman, K. E. (2004) Complex hunter–gatherers in evolution and history: a North American perspective. *Journal of Archaeological Research* 12(3), 227–280.

Schinder, G., Guichón, R., Comparatore, V. & Burry, S. (2003) Inferencias paleodietarias mediante isotopos estables en restos oseos humanos provenientes de Tierra del Fuego, Argentina. *Revista Argentina de Antropologia Biológica* 5(2), 15–31.

Schwarcz, H. P., Chisholm, B. S. & Burchell, M. (2014) Isotopic studies of the diet of the people of the coast of British Columbia. *American Journal of Physical Anthropology* 155(30), 460–468.

Sobel, E. A., Gahr, D. A. T. & Ames, K. M. (2006) *Household Archaeology on the Northwest Coast.* Ann Arbor, International Monographs in Prehistory.

Spencer, B. (1951) *Spencer's Last Journey, Being the Journal of an Expedition to Tierra del Fuego by the Late Baldwin Spencer, with a Memoir,* (R. R. Marret and T.K. Penniman compilers). Oxford. Balfour, Clarendon Press.

Stern, Ch. & Prieto, A. (1991) Origin of the green obsidian of Magallanes. Anales del Instituto de la Patagonia (Serie Ciencias Humanas). *Anales Del Instituto de La Patagonia* 20, 89–97

Sutherland, P. D. (2004) Variability, Historical Contingency, and Cultural Change in Northern Archaeological Sequences. Unpublished PhD Thesis, University of Alberta.

Turner, N. J. & Deur, D. (eds) (2005) *Keeping it Living Traditions of Plant Use and Cultivation on the Northwest Coast of North America.* Vancouver, UBC Press.

Vázquez, M. & Prieto, A. (2014) Búsqueda sin término: breve historia dela Arqueología en Tierra del Fuego. In *Cazadores de Mar y Tierra. Estudios recientes en arqueología fueguina,* 15–49. Ushuaia, Argentina, Editora Cultural Tierra del Fuego.

Verdún, E., Estevez, J. & Vila, A. (2015) Ethnoarcheology of Tierra del Fuego hunter-fisher-gatherer societies. The site of Lanashuaia. In S. Sálzelovál, M. Novák & A. Mizerová (eds), *Forgotten Times and Spaces: New Perspectives in Paleoanthropological, Paleoethnological and Archaeological Studies,* 532–541 Brno. Institute of Archeology of the Czech Academy of Sciences; Masaryk University.

Vila, A. (2006) Propuesta de evaluación de la metodología arqueológica. In Departament d'Arqueologia i Antropologia IMF-CSIC (eds), *Etnoarqueología de la Prehistoria: más allá de la analogía,* 61–76. Madrid, CSIC.

Vila, A. & Estévez, J (2010) El factor marginado en cazadores-recolectores: de la Tierra del Fuego a la Costa Noroeeste. In A.Vila & J. Estévez (eds), *La excepción y la norma: las sociedades indígena de la Costa Noroeste de Norteamérica desde la Arqueología,* 183–216. Treballs d'Etnoarqueologia 8. Madrid, CSIC.

Vila, A. & Ruiz, G. (2001) Información etnológica y análisis de la reproducción social: el caso yámana. *Revista Española de Antropología Americana* 31, 275–291.

Yesner, D. R. (2004). Prehistoric maritime adaptations of the Subarctic and Subantarctic Zones: the Aleutian/Fuegian connection reconsidered. *Arctic Anthropology* 41(2), 76–97.

Zangrando, A. F. (2009) Is fishing intensification a direct route to hunter-gatherer complexity? A case study from the Beagle Channel region (Tierra del Fuego, southern South America). *World Archaeology.* DOI: 10.1080/00438240903363848

Part 2: Diversity, comparisons and analogies

Chapter 7

Let's start with our academic past: the abandoned 'Vienna School' and our hunter-gatherer pasts

Reinhard Blumauer

This paper recapitulates an era of Austrian ethnology that has become famous as the *Wiener Schule der Völkerkunde* ['Vienna School of Ethnology']. The proponents of this school conducted extensive field research among hunter-gatherer societies and used them as analogies for the very beginning of our human past. This approach, however, was in many ways quite exceptional: it may be the only paradigm that was both abandoned and declared obsolete by its own followers. So why should we start thinking about it again half a century later? What can we learn from an abandoned paradigm? Just to make it clear – this paper is not about reviving this paradigm. Yet it seems worth taking a closer look at its pitfalls. After all, it is so much easier to detect dead ends in the approaches of others than in our own way of thinking. And when it comes to dead ends, the Vienna School has a lot to offer. Nevertheless, it is also an intriguing starting point that should not be overlooked just because the paradigm was declared obsolete. The following paper focuses only on some of the issues raised by the Vienna School, such as the comparative approach, categorisations, ideology, dogmatism and interdisciplinary cooperation.

A very short introduction to the 'Vienna School'

The defining moment for the so-called Vienna School of Ethnology was probably the year 1906, when Father Wilhelm Schmidt founded the journal *Anthropos* (for a biography of Schmidt see Brandewie 1990). It was his intention to bring together the ethnographic knowledge of missionaries from all around the world. The journal was based in the monastery of St Gabriel in Mödling, a small town near Vienna, Austria. Father Schmidt was able to encourage some missionary school students to help him with the journal. Soon they became his students and followers of his form of diffusionism which combined several premises under the theoretical *Kulturkreislehre* ['culture circle scheme']. When the *Institut für Völkerkunde*, today's *Department of Social and Cultural Anthropology*, was founded at the University of Vienna in 1928, its first head was Father Wilhelm Koppers, Schmidt's closest student and assistant in Mödling. *Kulturkreislehre* then became the central theoretical and methodological framework of academic ethnology in Vienna for the following 30 years. Moreover, the Catholic network enabled the *Kulturkreislehre* to also influence ethnological traditions outside German-speaking countries.

Premises of the 'Vienna School'

The concept of *Kulturkreise* was initially formulated by German ethnologist Leo Frobenius who immediately abandoned it. It was subsequently recognised on a much broader scale when the concept was introduced in the field of museum ethnology. In Germany, the most prominent adherents of the *Kulturkreislehre* were Fritz Graebner, Bernhard Ankermann and Wilhelm Foy, all of whom were museum ethnologists (cf. Ankermann 1905; Graebner 1905). In this context, the *Kulturkreis* concept was introduced as an opportunity to organise all the material in ethnographic museums. As material culture from all around the world was placed next to each other in the storage areas of such museums, the various items gave the impression that there might be parallels between certain items of different origin. The question was obvious: were these separate inventions or did they have a common origin? Evolutionists tended towards the first answer and argued that cultures take similar directions of development due to similar influences. Diffusionism, on the other hand, regarded human beings as insufficiently ingenious (*Ideenarmut*) to independently develop similar inventions. Therefore, such similar forms had to have common roots. This impression was supported even more when the near infinite number of museum objects still showed many parallels between different cultures. In their opinion, not only individual objects, but also entire sets of items seemed to belong together and appear in different places. These sets 'define certain areas and cultural stages' the so-called *Kulturkreise*.

Schmidt went even further, though. As a trained linguist, he combined this distribution of material culture with language areas and enjoyed an excellent reputation, not only in the field of linguistics in general, but also due to finding so-called *Sprachenkreise* ['language circles']. These *Sprachenkreise* defined the distribution of languages and the relations between them. By doing this he was able to find proof of migrations or contacts in the past, especially for Southeast Asia (cf. Schmidt 1926).

Under Schmidt's influence, Austrian prehistorian Oswald Menghin combined this scheme with prehistory in his book *Weltgeschichte der Steinzeit* ['World History of the Stone Age'] (1929). Similarly to Schmidt's ethnological *Kulturkreise* Menghin declared various prehistoric *Kulturkreise* based on tool use, as for example a bone-culture or the stone axe-culture. Characterised by constant generalisation, this is how the *Kulturkreislehre* was able, at least in Schmidt's mind, to reconstruct the entire history of the world.

This ambitious undertaking of combining archaeological and ethnological data in one frame of reference is essential. As Clyde Kluckhohn, who studied for some time in Vienna under Schmidt's auspices, said in defence of the *Kulturkreislehre*:

> 'Perhaps the central reason for careful examination of the *Kulturkreislehre* is that it attempts to provide a schematization for the archaeological and ethnological facts of the whole world – at a time when the recognition that even very early peoples were no respecters of continents is being forced upon us. The followers of the *Kulturkreislehre* have at least resolutely devoted themselves to the true task of scholars: they have endeavoured to ferret out and establish unperceived relationships between facts, and we will be unwise to condemn them too austerely if the relations they think to have discovered are not always approved in detail by their fellow scholars.' (Kluckhohn 1936, 196)

As Kluckhohn points out, the Vienna School developed a scheme for a universal world history that combined, at least theoretically, cultural anthropology and archaeology with a special focus, as we will see in the following, on hunter-gatherer societies.

Schmidt saw ethnology as a historical discipline and, therefore, part of the *Geisteswissenschaft* (humanities) instead of *Naturwissenschaft* (science). In consequence, he called his school and method *kulturhistorisch* ['culture-historical'] and claimed it to be founded on historical evidence: for the outlines of this method, see the English translation of Schmidt's book (Schmidt 1939). Still, his output was mainly interpretive and astonishingly evolutionistic. As Marvin Harris put it:

> 'The most striking feature of this scheme is its evolutionism. The succession of "grades" is nothing less than the familiar sequence of "stages" leading from hunting and gathering types of sociocultural systems through horticultural or pastoral types and on to complex stratified civilizations. The evolutionary significance of the *Kreise* is further strengthened by the fact that Schmidt attempted to associate the sequence of grades with the main European archaeological divisions of prehistory [...].' (Harris 2001, 385)

In assessing the evolutionary character of his thought, one has to keep in mind Schmidt's religiously motivated worldview, in which evolutionism, materialism and socialism – the archenemies of the Catholic Church – were one and the same. Yet, while he criticised evolutionists for ideological reasons, Schmidt's own work was not far away from evolutionism, especially in the speculative nature of his theories. One explanation for this contradiction comes from Schmidt himself. He denied the concept of unilinear evolutionism but did not do the same for evolution (cf. Schmidt 1937, vii). Although societies evolve, this process is a consequence of diffusion.

The concept of *Kulturkreise* was based on the idea of diffusion as the central force in human development. Schmidt defined four main *Kulturkreise*, which formed a chronological order of development. In attacking the evolutionary stage model for its unilinear approach, Schmidt postulated a connection and interplay between the various circles, which would then form a new circle. By applying a 'culture historical' method that focused on the form and quantity of cultural items, Schmidt believed in the possibility of reconstructing the various circles backwards, thus finally arriving at the so-called *Urkultur* ['primal culture']. Based on the assumption of a common ancestry for certain cultural items, it was not difficult for the historical method to apply a comparative approach to museum collections. No matter how far away they might be in terms of space and time, the cultures would appear as their origins were traced back.

> 'It was not the vaunted criteria of form and quantity, but the comparative method, upon which the German "historical" school rested. For their task was precisely the same as that of the evolutionists: they sought to derive from an inspection of contemporary peoples a knowledge of origins and of the successive modification which cultures had experienced. The *Kreise* were not only "Circles" but they were "Strata" – a part of a universal chronological scheme, which rested entirely on the assumption that contemporary cultures could be arranged according to degree of primitiveness. Schmidt made no attempt to conceal his dependence on the comparative method.' (Harris 2001, 388)

The 'Vienna School', hunter-gatherer societies and human history

Schmidt's theories began addressing hunter-gatherer societies, especially pygmies, at a very early stage. In his book *Die Stellung der Pygmäenvölker in der Entwicklungsgeschichte des Menschen* ['The Position of Pygmies in the Development of Mankind'] (1910), he claimed the pygmies of Central Africa, as well as the so-called negritos of Southeast Asia, to represent the *Urkultur*. Aside from the Fuegians, they seemed to Schmidt to be the most ancient peoples still alive that could be studied to get a glimpse into our human past (cf. Schmidt 1910, 285f.). Indeed, it appeared that ethnology showed an even greater potential to reconstruct human cultural history than prehistory because scholars of prehistory could only find evidence of the Stone Age. Ethnology had found proof of cultures without stone tools (*Eolithic*), a 'Wood Age' that, consequently, had to be older (cf. Schmidt 1910, 110).

Although the claimed antiquity of the pygmies was derived from their simplicity in technology, Schmidt was opposed to the evolutionist view of a general primitive state and subsequent development. Simplicity in material culture did not have to correlate with simplicity of other cultural items. In opposition to development and evolution, Schmidt also considered degenerations, especially in ethical and moral issues.

Schmidt was eager to state that the pygmies were neither regressive (*Kümmervölker*) nor half-human (cf. Schmidt 1910, 268). In his opinion, pygmies and early humans were equally human (*Vollmenschen*), and in those days, not everybody could share his view. In case of early humans, it is still an issue at stake, as Finlayson and Warren point out:

> '[...] one of the key functions of the concept of the hunter-gatherer, historically, has been to set up an "other" against which we can define our modern selves. It is therefore no surprise that a logical outcome of its use in discussing the Neolithic revolution is to assume that hunter-gatherers were not all like us. [...] we argue that people have been fully human for much longer than the ideas of these authors imply.' (Finlayson & Warren 2010, 15)

A special feature of the *Urkulturen* seemed to be strong cultural consistency (*Kulturkonstanz*). Given the perfect adaption to their environments, it was supposed that these hunter-gatherer-societies had no need for a cultural change. This would explain why they had not changed substantially, although the Vienna School claimed that there were no people without history.

Obvious differences between the pygmies and Fuegians were reflected in Schmidt's *Urkulturen*. Nevertheless, there were at least a few features all *Urkulturen* had in common, especially in the field of material culture and mode of subsistence. Schmidt defined these *Urkulturen* in terms of material culture, sociology and religion. Material culture was basically defined by the absence of certain items, such as stone/metal tools, animal husbandry or agriculture. *Urkultur* was also marked by an assumed 'primitive' state of other cultural traits, for example art or tools.

Aside from the materialistic, economic basis of Schmidt's *Urkulturen*, his main interest focused on the idealistic, ethical dimensions. The following three basic assumptions of Schmidt became infamously known as the 'three Ms': primal monotheism, primal monogamy and monogenesis. Schmidt came into contact with Andrew Lang's hypothesis that monotheism was situated at the beginning of religious evolution (cf. Lang 1898). In the eyes of a Roman Catholic priest, this notion seemed to be proof of the biblical Genesis. He devoted almost his whole life to prove this hypothesis in his 12-volume publication *Der Ursprung der Gottesidee* ['The Origin of the Idea of God']. This hypothesis, for Schmidt already a fact, was under attack from the very beginning and ultimately withdrawn by Schmidt's followers immediately after his death in 1954.

Another central element of his three Ms was primal monogamy. Once again, Schmidt saw this notion as proof of the biblical story of Adam and Eve. In the beginning, there was not the evolutionist's promiscuity, but the ideal Catholic family. Even after Schebesta had informed Schmidt of the tendency among hunter-gatherers towards serial monogamy, Schmidt still never retreated from this definition (cf. Thiel 1995).

The concept of *Kulturkreise* was also based on the third assumption of a monogenesis. From the perspective of diffusionists, the inventiveness of humans was limited. If they found similar traits in different cultures, it seemed clear to them that these societies had to have common roots, as separate invention was considered less likely. And after all, monogenesis was also in perfect harmony with Adam and Eve.

Schmidt never ventured out into the field himself. Instead of field research, he built up an institute with an impressive library and founded a journal to collect information from both missionaries and researchers from around the world. Based on this data, he published dozens of books and hundreds of articles. Apart from his exhaustive writing efforts, Schmidt also arranged for research funding, especially from the Roman Catholic Church and even from the Pope himself, for his scholars, so he could send them out to find proof for his hypothesis.

The two most prominent of his field researchers were Paul Schebesta and Martin Gusinde (for a short biographical sketch, see Dupré 1968; Anon 1969). Schebesta became one of the first and most famous pygmy and negrito specialists after conducting fieldwork among the Bambuti in the Ituri forest (1929/30, 1934/35) and the Semang/Senoi in Malaysia (1924/25, 1938/39). Martin Gusinde conducted fieldwork in Tierra del Fuego between 1918 and 1924, but later also in the Ituri, the Philippines, the Kalahari and the US. Although Schmidt was their teacher and mentor, both scholars produced work that differed from Schmidt's to some extent. Because of their ethnographic experience, they could not follow Schmidt's rigid generalisations. Schmidt, however, was not the kind of person to change his mind just because of some contradicting evidence. In the end, however, Schmidt seemed to retreat from some of his assumptions, as Schebesta suggested after Schmidt's death, 'Ich glaube, daß Schmidt, gerade durch meine Forschungen unter den Bambuti eines anderen belehrt, Abstriche an seine Lieblingsidee gemacht hat' ['Especially after my research among the Bambuti had proved him wrong, I believe that Schmidt accepted that he had to alter his favourite idea.'] (Schebesta 1954, 691; transl. R. B.)

In their scientific monographs, Schebesta and Gusinde mostly avoided *Kulturkreis* speculations and relied on empiric evidence. In consequence, their ethnographic books have remained important sources to this day. In this context, however, we have to keep in mind that even if the diffusionist paradigm has become obsolete, some of the particular interpretations belonging to this mind-set could still stand the test of time, as for example Schebesta's theory on blowpipe diffusion among the Senoi and Semang (cf. Schebesta 1952; 1957). He compared these weapons and quivers among different groups and observed that the incidence and absence of decorations and related myths varied between the groups. Based on this observation, Schebesta thought he could reconstruct the place of origin and subsequent transmission of the blowpipe. So we can say that this particular theory of diffusion of a specific object is perfectly acceptable without accepting the whole paradigm which underpinned Schebesta's research. In a nutshell, we always need to differentiate between the principles of a certain paradigm and the theories derived from it. Judging a paradigm by its faulty results may otherwise tempt us to overlook or even dismiss sound theoretical premises, theories and vice versa.

Hans Reichenbach's division between context of discovery and context of justification is a useful tool to analyse this issue and may result in a more objective view (cf. Reichenbach 1938, 6ff.). In his opinion, ideological bias can play a crucial role in the context of discovery. When it comes to justification, however, theories have to pass the test on empirical grounds. In line with this perspective, we may take some of Schmidt's theories and methods more seriously without accepting his faulty generalisations.

What can we learn?
Scientific anthropology vs. relativism/regression/revisionism
When talking about the reconstruction of our early human past based on comparison with today's hunter-gatherer societies, we are confronted with several objections: The most general one is a postulated relativism or particularism that challenges a

comparative approach. It is possible for paradigms applying a generalising approach to compare prehistoric and modern hunter-gatherer societies. At least in this point, the *Kulturkreislehre*, evolutionists and sociobiologists agree.

One of the main arguments against Schmidt's theories of *Urkulturen* is that today's hunter-gatherers and our prehistoric ancestors are not comparable. Today's hunter-gatherers were considered to be regressions, the product of being pushed towards marginal places, as the German term *Kümmervölker* ['degenerated peoples'] evokes as well. In the late 1980s, a similar objection reappeared in the form of the revisionist debate (cf. Stiles 1992). This type of relativism opposes comparisons between prehistory and today.

The notion that today's hunter-gatherers are 'real survivals' of prehistoric groups is, of course, not tenable anymore. However, *comparison* does not mean *equating*. Comparing hunter-gatherers to our prehistoric ancestors does not automatically entail that we transfer them back in time. From a scientific point of view based on generalisation, such a step is not even necessary to compare them to the earliest humans. What matters instead is the materialistic frame of reference for comparisons of material and economic culture that remains cautious concerning further reconstructions of sociological or religious culture.

It is somehow ironic that although Father Schmidt was fiercely anti-materialistic and anti-scientific, the basic features of his *Urkulturen*, except the 'three Ms', were defined in plain analytic, scientific and materialistic terms. In his earlier work, Schmidt was quite aware of these difficulties:

> 'Die Ethnologie beginnt diese Methode mit Recht vorerst auf dem Gebiete der materiellen Kultur zur Durchführung zu bringen, deren greifbare Natur mehr vor Subjektivität bewahrt und nicht solche Versuchungen zu tendenziösen Deutungen vielseitiger Möglichkeiten bietet.'

> ['Ethnology is absolutely right to start applying this method to material culture first, as its tangible nature keeps us away from subjectivity and does not lure us into making biased interpretations where there are many different possibilities.'] (Schmidt 1910, 285; transl. R. B.)

When it comes to the importance of economy, Schmidt and especially his colleague Koppers came even closer to their arch-enemy of Marxism:

> 'Es lässt sich nicht leugnen, dass die gesamte gesellschaftliche Entwicklung in hohem Grade mitbedingt ist durch die wirtschaftliche Lage. Aber nicht in dem ausschließlichen oder wenigstens ausschlaggebenden Maße, wie der Marxismus es will.'

> ['It cannot be denied that the overall development of society is also determined by economic conditions, but not in the exclusive or at least in such a decisive way as Marxism suggests.'] (Schmidt 1923, 56 f.; transl. R. B.)

Schmidt's economic comparison between today's hunter-gatherers and prehistoric ones was immediately criticised, as for example by Raymond Firth:

> 'To label the most primitive peoples now existing in diverse parts of the world as the representatives of the oldest sphere of culture, and on this basis lay down the characteristics

of what must have been the primal form of economy, the *Urwirtschaft*, is not a statement of historical fact but a pure assumption.' (Firth 1927, 331)

In his comment on Schmidt, Firth bundled up the relativist's point of view and, between the lines, mixes up comparing and equating. It is necessary to observe that this statement does not qualify as a comparative approach at all. It is an assumption, as all other reconstructions and analogies are. Nevertheless, some assumptions are logically sound and are more successfully supported by empirical evidence than others.

As already mentioned, Schmidt and Koppers as well as their Marxist counterparts were aware of the need to start with comparisons from the economic sphere. Keeping that in mind, and I would even argue only from this point on, comparing hunter-gatherer societies, past and present, is logically sound. The basic assumptions of the Vienna School as based on economic concepts could stand the test of time. In contrast, those hypotheses that came out of an idealistic position, as for example the 'three Ms', have already been abandoned.

Diversity and the troubles of categorisation

In accordance with the biblical account and the concept of monogenesis, Schmidt was looking for the 'original' *Urkultur*. Nevertheless, 'today's oldest reachable cultures' were not that homogeneous. So, one important achievement of the Vienna School was the recognition of diversity among hunter-gatherer societies. It was a rare instance, where Schmidt started from empirical data and then had to construct a model that allowed for these differences to exist. Schmidt and his followers knew that it was not possible to find a single general original culture that shaped human development. Moreover, there was no reason to assert a long-term homogenous beginning of mankind that would have shaped our whole mind-set – a point of view that still seems to be quite common among evolutionary psychologists or sociobiologists, for example in their use of the concept of the environment of evolutionary adaptedness (cf. Bowlby 1969).

Diversity in environment and climate are strong forces in the shaping of society. As humans spread all around the globe, adapting to the changing environment defined the evolution of societies. In this case, Schmidt would have supported the claim of Finlayson and Warren that '... we prefer to emphasise *variability*, rather than any supposed march of *progress*' (Finlayson & Warren 2010, 17). Once again, Schmidt's explanation for this diversity was a materialistic one, namely the adaption to specific environments that, nevertheless, foster similar economic and social patterns. The definition of what constitutes hunter-gatherer societies cannot include specific patterns relating to the environment, as for example, special hunting methods or plant usage.

The definition of hunter-gatherer societies is not an easy task. Schmidt's categorisation was still far too fixed and clear. Although he defined four types of

Urkulturen, the defining features were too specific for certain societies to generate a more general mode of subsistence. Schmidt focused on certain weapons, tools, housing and resources that depended on specific environments. One of the cultural features of all Urkulturen for Schmidt was the usage of bow and arrows (cf. Schmidt 1925). Nevertheless, whether a group lives behind wind breaks or in tents reflects environment and climate rather than any kind of specific cultural state.

Ideological bias

Schmidt also used his ethnological work for political agitation against the socialist city government of Vienna. In dozens of newspaper articles, he declared monogamy and monotheism to be the cornerstones of the natural and divine order. Just as his ethnographic knowledge shaped his political believes, his worldview also shaped his ethnographic work. Still, any critique against Schmidt that, as a priest, he was obviously too ideologically biased was defended or at least qualified by Clyde Kluckhohn in a quite interesting way:

> 'We must, I think, rigorously avoid the temptation to dismiss the *Kulturkreislehre* as founded upon a "bias". I sometimes wonder if it is not in part true that because its 'biases' are somewhat more apparent than those of some other ethnological schools that the doctrines are therefore perhaps the less dangerous.' (Kluckhohn 1936, 173f.)

Schmidt's school was not the only paradigm with a declared political agenda; what about Marxist or feminist anthropology? What is so 'dangerous' about being biased? Is it the general idea of being biased or do we despise only the 'wrong' version of it? In terms of the *Kulturkreislehre,* we must not forget that there was also a 'secular' version in Germany. Dismissing the whole *Kulturkreislehre* because of a supposed general religious motivation would thus be incorrect. Moreover, judging a paradigm only on behalf of the worldview of some of its proponents also neglects Reichenbach's distinction about contexts of discovery and justification (outlined above).

In this regard, another prominent 'defender' of Schmidt, Robert Lowie, points out:

> 'Anticlerical critics have suggested that the field work undertaken under Father Schmidt's auspices has been unduly colored (sic) by Catholic or personal prejudices. This is an unfair criticism; let him that is without bias cast the first stone.' (Lowie 1937, 193)

Lowie stresses the omnipresence of ideological bias. Hunter-gatherer studies, as all fields of social science, have always been vulnerable to the influences of political agendas. To some extent, our bias, or let us put it in a more neutral way and say ideological preferences, also becomes visible in our vocabulary. Consciously or unconsciously, some terms come with certain ideological implications, as for example 'primitive communism' or 'affluent society'. With Kluckhohn's remark in mind, we have to ask whether we should make such terms clearer. Simply avoiding such terms would only be another means of ideological camouflage.

Dogmatic deduction vs induction

Another obvious pitfall of the Vienna School was its dogmatic, deductive approach. Although pioneering fieldwork was conducted on which several still recommendable and valuable monographs were based, the empirical data produced was forced into a scheme, even if it did not fit at all. Against Schmidt's own claim that his theorising was fully based on empirical evidence, the opposite is too obvious. In the end, the applied dogmatism of these models was the final straw leading to the demise of this paradigm.

Again Kluckhohn:

> 'Nor is the *kulturgeschichtliche Methode* by any means purely inductive as many of its protagonists have maintained. These investigators start with observation, it is true, but presently they seem, ... to leap at synthesis before they have pursued exhaustive analysis. One searches in vain for a full and lucid explanation of how the ethnologist may know precisely which traits form a particular *Kreis*. Certain steps in the process do not seem to be made completely explicit. One has the sense of being confronted rather suddenly with the full grown *Kulturkreis*. And from the created *Kulturkreise* many deductions are made.' (Kluckhohn 1936, 168)

Keeping in mind the many fieldworkers who were part of the Viennese School, this appraisal seems somewhat unfair. It was primarily Schmidt's stubbornness and his clinging on to his own dogmatic framework that kept the Vienna School away from progress. Nevertheless, the field studies would have never been sufficient to satisfy Schmidt's overambitious undertaking. In this regard, a lesson we can learn is the need for fieldwork and the constant integration of empirical material into our theoretical development. When Schmidt first developed his *Kulturkreise*, the data he could rely on was rather poor, however he did not integrate any of the new yet contradictory empirical evidence into his reconstructions. Continuous feedback loops between deduction and induction are much more important than Schmidt, mainly due to ideological blinkers, was aware of.

Some of the researchers of the Vienna School worked among hunter-gatherer societies that were in the process of shifting towards horticulture, and an important research focus should have been on changes in modes of subsistence. However, the researchers only focused on what they thought to be the 'original' way of living and overlooked these very changes. This reflects a weakness of the concept of the *Kulturkreise*: the notion that intermingling *Kulturkreise* would lead to a new one did not shine enough light on the process itself. Therefore, the creation of the postulated *Kulturkreise* seemed to have taken place in a 'black box'. It was the theoretical framework that made the researchers overlook these transformations. The *Kulturkreis* concept implied quite a dynamic view of culture but, in fact, its application was based on a static notion of culture that would not mix or change anymore.

Interdisciplinary cooperation

Although Schmidt tried to develop a universal world history from the beginning of mankind, he focused too much on ethnology. As mentioned above, he was convinced that cultural anthropology had an advantage due to its direct contact to the *Urkulturen*. In consequence, ethnology should be a kind of master discipline with the disciplines of prehistory, linguistics and anthropology positioned under its auspices. This kind of disciplinary hierarchy is neither tenable nor necessary. Ethnographic analogies without reference to archaeological evidence are useless in regard to our very research interest. The interdisciplinary cooperation between archaeology and cultural anthropology is absolutely necessary to find answers to our questions. Theoretically, the Vienna School was aware of that, but could not come to terms with its own demands.

Another discipline that played an important role in Schmidt's search for various *Kulturkreise* was linguistics. Although the opportunities offered by linguistics in the reconstruction of migrations and culture contact had been known and applied, there was nobody before or after Schmidt trying so hard to combine linguitsics with evidence from other disciplines. This close cooperation between the disciplines seems to have only worked because it was primarily done by one single person.

We should also keep in mind another issue in this regard: the importance of a guiding principle under which all the different disciplines conduct their research. The *Kulturkreis* system, as faulty as it may was, had this very function. It was a framework in which all the ethnological, linguistic, prehistoric and anthropological data could be compared and provided a common ground for debate. Our own Conference on Hunting and Gathering Societies, for example, is a fantastic interdisciplinary conference but discussions between various disciplines are rather rare and tend to talk at cross-purposes. Nevertheless, there is no lack of a master discipline – it is a shared paradigm that is missing. Being sceptical about grand narratives must not keep us away from thinking about the necessity of shared reference systems in common research fields.

Conclusion

A critical reading of Schmidt's work is an interesting and even fruitful task. It can also be amusing, as for example, when reading Schmidt's self-conscious appraisal of his own culture-historical method as the final answer to the problems in ethnology. Decades later, most of his work has been proven wrong. We have to ask what will happen to our theories in the next decades?

The problems outlined in this article as questions of science, diversity or ideology have been keeping our disciplines busy for the last hundred years. Looking back in history, it seems that we have not come any further, as the discussions tend to be repeated again and again. Analysing former debates can help us to overcome such issues. Therefore, it is important for us to choose an objective point of view. Neither scientific nor ideological bias should keep us from having a closer look at paradigms we do not share, otherwise, we might risk dismissing useful theories and principles.

Our academic history can be seen by analogy to a roadmap as a guiding tool towards answers to our research questions. It shows us all the ways our predecessors have already taken and, therefore, can provide us with the directions of where we might expect solutions and where to be cautious of dead ends or obstacles. As our disciplines progress, this map gets more and more detailed. It is up to us to write and use this roadmap. This is why we should care about an abandoned paradigm.

Acknowledgements

I would like to thank Khaled Hakami for his comments on an earlier draft as well as Helmut Lukas and Andre Gingrich for prolific discussions on this topic.

References

Ankermann, B. (1905) Kulturkreise und Kulturschichten in Afrika. *Zeitschrift für Ethnologie* 37, 54–86.
Anonymous (1969) Martin Gusinde, S.V.D.: 1886–1969. *Anthropological Quarterly* 42, 354–356.
Bowlby, J. (1969) *Attachment.* New York, Basic Books.
Brandewie, E. (1990) *When Giants Walked the Earth. The Life and Times of Wilhelm Schmidt SVD.* Fribourg, Universitätsverlag.
Dupré, W. (1968) Paul Joachim Schebesta, 1887–1967. *American Anthropologist* 70, 537–545.
Finlayson, B. & Warren, G. (2010) *Changing Natures: Hunter-gatherers, First Farmers and the Modern World.* London, Duckworths.
Firth, R. (1927) The study of primitive economics. *Economica* 21, 312–335.
Graebner, F. (1905) Kulturkreise und Kulturschichten in Ozeanien. *Zeitschrift für Ethnologie* 37, 28–53.
Harris, M. (2001) *The Rise of Anthropological Theory: a History of Theories of Culture*, updated edition. Walnut Creek, Altamira Press.
Kluckhohn, C. (1936) Some reflections on the method and theory of the *Kulturkreislehre. American Anthropologist* 38, 157–196.
Lang, A. (1898) *The Making of Religion.* London, Longmans, Green.
Lowie, R. (1937) *The History of Ethnological Theory.* New York, Rinehart & Company.
Menghin, O. (1929) *Weltgeschichte der Steinzeit.* Vienna, Schroll.
Reichenbach, H. (1938) *Experience and Prediction. An Analysis of the Foundations and the Structure of Knowledge.* Chicago, University of Chicago Press.
Schebesta, P. (1952) *Die Negrito Asiens.* Vol. 2. Part 1. St Gabriel, St Gabriel.
Schebesta, P. (1954) Das Problem des Urmonotheismus. Kritik einer Kritik. *Anthropos* 49, 689–697.
Schebesta, P. (1957) *Die Negrito Asiens.* Vol. 2. Part 2. St Gabriel, St Gabriel.
Schmidt, W. (1910) *Die Stellung der Pygmäenvölker in der Entwicklungsgeschichte des Menschen.* Stuttgart, Strecker & Schröder.
Schmidt, W. (1923) Die sozialen Formen der einzelnen Kulturkreise. *Semaine d'ethnologie religieuse. Compte rendu analytique de la IIIe Session,* 48–67.
Schmidt, W. (1925) Das ethnologische Alter von Pfeil und Bogen. *Zeitschrift für Ethnologie* 57, 63–76.
Schmidt, W. (1926) *Die Sprachfamilien und Sprachenkreise der Erde.* Heidelberg, Winter.
Schmidt, W. (1937) *Handbuch der Methode der kulturhistorischen Ethnologie.* Münster, Aschendorff.
Schmidt, W. (1939) *The culture historical method of ethnology. A scientific approach to the racial question.* New York, Fortuny's.
Stiles, D. (1992) The Hunter-Gatherer 'Revisionist' Debate. *Anthropology Today* 8, 13–17.
Thiel, J. 1995 Der Urmonotheismus des P. Wilhelm Schmidt und seine Geschichte. In Rupp-Eisenreich, B. & Stagl, J. (eds), *Kulturwissenschaften im Vielvölkerstaat. Zur Geschichte der Ethnologie und verwandter Gebiete in Österreich, ca. 1780 bis 1918,* 256–267. Wien, Böhlau.

Chapter 8

Experimental ethnoarchaeology: studying hunter-gatherers at the uttermost end of the Earth

Robert Carracedo-Recasens and Albert García-Piquer

Introduction

Traditional archaeological and deterministic approaches have questioned the possibility of understanding the relevance of social and ideological organisation for explaining the past (cf. Trigger 1992; and e.g. the case of the development of the discipline in Spain in Estévez & Vila 1999). This has contributed to relativist and subjective approaches (for a detailed discussion e.g. Reybrouck 2012) and to a stress on the use of ethnographic analogies (see e.g. Hardy 2010). Similarly, the relationships between past individuals who were carrying out social production and reproduction (group or inter-group) are also considered hard to access. In short, everything that remains outside the reductionist definition of *the material* is seen as having little evidential basis for archaeological inference. As a result, the study of prehistoric societies is considered to be a field of speculations and of social inferences without real corroboration, relying consciously or unconsciously on analogies: basically, ethological analogies for the first human societies, and ethnographic for more recent ones.

The use or abuse of ethnographic analogy was a recurrent subject of debate in the archaeological literature in the second half of the 20th century (Wobst 1978; Gould & Watson 1982; Gándara 1990). In addition, ethnographic analogy has generally been reduced to taking biased comments and observations and transferring them uncritically into the past, forcing and homogenising the diverse ethnographic data: for example from the traditional categories proposed for lithic tools to the forager-collector model proposed by Binford (1980) or the Man The Hunter/Women The Gatherer model (see discussion in Wylie 1985). Thus, the social organisation of prehistoric societies has been extrapolated from certain general laws which result from particular theoretical approaches regarding hunter-fisher-gatherer societies. These laws relied on 'a static fossilised vision of current societies and on a self-confirmation of the character of fossilised societies for the modern ethnographic societies' (Vila & Estévez 2010, 10). As well, these laws also attempted to explain an essential, universal and actual 'human nature'. The outcome has been a relative consensus about the 'egalitarianism' of prehistoric hunter-fisher-gatherer societies, in the same way and for the same reasons that present or recent hunter-fisher-gatherer societies are considered to be 'egalitarian'; even if 'egalitarian' is usually accompanied by the recognition of 'sex and age divisions'.

However, the direct or indirect use of ethnographic analogies has to consider two fundamental biases. First, the androcentricity of early ethnographies resulted in 'a (male) normative picture of the society' (Begler 1978, 577). Second, societies studied by ethnography are not primitive or prehistoric; they are contemporary and have long historical trajectories. Despite that, few ethnographic descriptions have tried to find the causes of the particular observed situations within the earlier history of these same societies. The result is that many of the situations of inequality or alleged labour complementarity have been justified by reference to immutable biological difference. The subjective position of the observers made this detected inequality appear as a logical, normal and natural situation; or even to downplay it in contrast to the clearly existing inequality in their own society (Endicott & Endicott 2012).

Nevertheless, we should not reject the use of analogies in general, not least because they are constitutive of all archaeological inference, as discussed by Gándara (1990). If we understand analogy as a general procedure of logical inference, the use of analogy is not just permitted or legitimated; it is the main component of inference in archaeology and, ultimately, science. Furthermore, ethnographic sources and, in a broad sense, ethnoarchaeology, are fundamental tools when generating archaeological hypotheses, and therefore to the evaluation and reconsideration of archaeological methodologies.

In this sense, the ethnoarchaeological experimentation in Tierra del Fuego discussed in this paper was developed as a contribution to the methodological development of archaeology and ethnography through a historical case-study: 'by making both sources interact dialectically, as manifestations of the essential relationships, they become enriched in a new synthesis' (Estévez *et al.* 1998, 21). The first section of the paper is a critical review of ethnoarchaeological research and the theoretical basis behind the aforementioned methodological proposal. The following sections summarise the suitability of Tierra del Fuego as a case study, the main features of the Yamana society, and the results of the developed projects undertaken during the last two decades by the AGREST (*Archaeology of the Management of Social and Land Resources*) research group. The last sections of the paper are dedicated to outline two analytic proposals based on quantitative approaches, as well as the lines of research that are being currently developed (e.g. Social Simulation).

What is experimental ethnoarchaeology and why we need it

Archaeology and ethnology were often considered completely separate subjects, on account of the differences in their objects of study and methodological approaches.

This differentiation prevented the holistic study of historical phenomenon, and, therefore caused a lack of understanding of the development of different forms of social being. We argue that all of the social sciences, in common with archaeology, share the same object of study: social being, which involves a multiplicity of phenomena and is therefore converted into different objects of study, which in turn can be artificially separated, politically and for convenience, into different social science disciplines. In our understanding, the conventional limits between disciplines have to be blurred, and following this, we should scientifically study the historic development of social being. Thus, we understand archaeology as the science that studies social processes and their development through the material record of social activities. Through archaeology we try to find laws that explain social phenomena: which is, what happened, when did it happen, how did it develop, and why did it happen. Archaeological explanation should also be based on the principle that human societies are structured in a complicated hierarchical network of relationships, due to the need to ensure the material basis that satisfies the need for survival and reproduction of the group. The social relations of production and reproduction are the ones which constitute the essence of the socio-economic formations.

The early stages of archaeological activity in many areas were restricted to the creation of collections of objects, which were held far away from the subjects of ethnographic analysis. The material collected was analysed, described and categorised, and the synchronic extension and diachronic expansion of artefact typologies was seen as a way to follow the ideas of their makers. However, contemporary society wanted a more dynamic picture of the world that was being exposed than that provided by archaeological analysis within this 'official paradigm', so it was enlivened with ethnographic analogies, frequently without any explicit acknowledgment.

It was not until the late 1970s that ethnoarchaeology was first named as a distinct field of practice, within New Archaeology and in the context of middle range theory in particular (middle-level generalisations to connect the static archaeological material with past social dynamics). Overall, this approach developed the study of contemporary small-scale societies in order to derive useful analogies for understanding the way of life in prehistoric times (e.g. Binford 1978). However, this did not imply the discovery of global explanations for the processes of change that these prehistoric societies had undergone.

Archaeologists have resigned themselves to not being able to interpret the type of society they were studying unless an ethnographic analogy could be made. But if interpretations about prehistoric societies – how they were organised to produce and reproduce themselves, how and why they were changing, what alternatives there were and why they made those decisions – could not be made, how Archaeology could understand the causes of social development unless a purely ecological determinant is assumed is not clear (Estévez & Vila 1998). If we assume a non-mechanically deterministic position, the pretence of achieving a comprehensive representation of prehistoric societies from only environmental and subsistence information cannot be sustained. Therefore, such analyses could not reach the goal of knowing the historical processes that explain the development of today's reality (Argelés *et al.* 1995).

If we base our practice on alternative assumptions, for example contending that economic and social aspects of life are inseparable, then archaeology must aim to recover all aspects of social life without distinction. This requires an advance in forms of archaeological interpretation, seeking conceptual and methodological instruments based on the possibility that these relationships can be understood and eliminating the archaeological use of simplistic ethnographic analogies.

Facing these challenges, the AGREST project was developed, aiming to implement an archaeological methodology for social explanations. To do that, it was argued that the archaeological study of an ethnographically documented hunter-gatherer society could be a way to develop these conceptual instruments (Piana *et al.* 1992). So, we return to ethnographic observations again, not with the objective of refining a particular analogy, but to define the essential features of hunter-gatherer societies and to see how they could be materialised in the ethnographic and archaeological records of the same society. This definition of ethnoarchaeology differs from the New Archaeological approaches outlined above, which served to extrapolate middle-range theories for Archaeology. On the contrary, our approach contrasts the two sources of information on the same object of study: a concrete hunter-gatherer society. Ethnoarchaeology would therefore, in our framework, be an interface between the methodological development of both archaeology and ethnology (Estévez & Vila 1995).

'Experimental ethnoarchaeology', as it was called, therefore implied a dialectic confrontation between the theory and practice of archaeology and ethnology. Based on the results, we propose an archaeological methodology that allows us to get closer to prehistoric social formations in all aspects, economic and social, because one cannot be understood without the other. Putting experimental ethnoarchaeology into practice meant that we tried to recover an objective picture taken from both ethnographic information (which can be described as indirect because they have been filtered by the subjectivity of some authors) and archaeological (that can be described as direct because they have been generated without this subjective filter).

Having provided the background to the aims and worries that led us to the development of our approaches, a quick and synthetic definition is useful: Experimental ethnoarchaeology is an alternative archaeological methodology involving comparative use of archaeological and ethnographic evidence for the same social phenomena that enables us to formulate an adequate basis for socio-economic studies of hunter-gatherer societies (Piana *et al.* 1992; Estévez & Vila 1995). Therefore, the archaeological experimentation in Tierra del Fuego was developed along the following axes: 1) studying specific issues concerning archaeological methodology (Verdún *et al.* 2010); 2) identifying archaeological markers and quantitative/objective ways of evaluating inequality in prehistory; 3) exploring the use of sexual division of labour as a social mechanism to manage the balance between potential demographic growth and limited resource availability (the so-called 'thesis of the principal contradiction or internal mobilising factor', see Estévez *et al.* 1998).

Why Tierra del Fuego?

Since 1986, a large research team mainly formed by researchers of the Spanish National Research Council (CSIC) and the Autonomous University of Barcelona, has developed several Spanish-Argentinean research projects in Isla Grande de Tierra del Fuego, Argentina (see Piana *et al.* 1992; Vila *et al.* 2007). These projects have been funded by state research institutions, CSIC and the Argentinean National Scientific and Technical Research Council (CONICET), the Spanish ministries of culture and education and the European Union. The fundamental objective of these projects was to carry out an evaluation of archaeological methods and techniques applied in the archaeology of hunter-fisher-gatherers, reassessing theory as well as methodology.

The proposal was to address the analysis of a recent hunter-fisher-gatherer society that disappeared at the beginning of the 20th century, from both ethnographic and archaeological sources. The objective of the opposition of respectively indirect and direct sources was to study the essential features of a mode of production-reproduction and how hunter-fisher-gatherer social relationships are materialised in the archaeological record. The final objective was to reach a methodological formulation suitable to the socioeconomic study of prehistoric hunter-fisher-gatherer societies (Vila 2011).

The choice of Tierra del Fuego was the result of several existing circumstances. First, there are multiple and varied sources of information about the local groups from travellers, missionaries and ethnographers for over four centuries (see Martial 2007; Legoupil 2008; Orquera & Piana 1999a). The diversity of informants of different periods makes it easier to recognise the subjective bias in these sources. Another important factor was the absence of elements of agrarian or industrial societies in the area almost until the 19th century, unlike other hunter-fisher-gatherer societies. Last, previous archaeological research carried out by the Argentinean part of the team allowed a time depth for analysis of more than 6000 years, going back to the first colonisation of the area, showing exploitation strategies homologous to those historically documented (Orquera & Piana 1999b; Orquera *et al.* 2011; Orquera & Piana 2009; Prieto *et al.* 2013). This was important because it opened the possibility to carry out analysis from the perspective of the historical process developed in the area.

Concerning Yamana

The hunter-fisher-gatherer groups known in the ethnographic literature as *Yamana* or *Yaghan* (Fig. 8.1) lived in constant movement, spread out in basic social units along the southern coastline of the archipelago of Tierra del Fuego. These social units, isolated

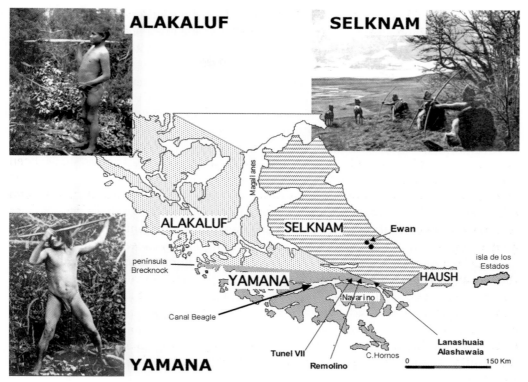

Figure 8.1. *The sites excavated by our research group in Tierra del Fuego.*

or connected to only a few other units, mainly pursued strategies of exploitation of coastal resources by means of canoe sailing (Hyades & Deniker 1891; Gusinde 1986; Orquera & Piana 1999b).

The existence of an unequal division of labour strictly based on sex is well documented ethnographically, and has even been evaluated quantitatively (Barceló *et al.* 2006; Vila *et al.* 2010). In summary, women gathered molluscs, sea urchins, crabs and spent a lot of time fishing from the canoes. They hunted cormorants, ducks and other birds; and with the aid of dogs they sometimes hunted even the biggest terrestrial prey, the guanaco. Women did the maintenance work for the canoe; they had to paddle, berth and untie it; they had to take care of the fire inside the canoe and recover from the water prey hunted by the men. Women were also responsible for making the fishing tools and getting the water; for all the food-processing, from butchering to cooking, and hut maintenance; and for various manufacturing tasks (including hide working, baskets, ropes, ornaments). Finally, women had to care for the health and well-being of neonates, children, men and the elderly.

Men fished with harpoons and hunted guanacos, sea mammals and birds. They butchered large game and chopped wood; they built canoes and made paddles, as well as weapons (harpoons, bows and arrows), stone and other tools. Men also cut the leather of pinnipeds into long strips and they made the *kina* ceremonial masks.

The rest of the work was done by both sexes equally. Finally, it should be noted that women were constantly at work, and their reputation depended on this persistence and diligence, while men alternated isolated tasks with long rests.

It should be noted that working processes were not explicitly established by social norms. They were part of daily life and were learned in childhood by means of a parental sexually-segregated education from 4–5 years old. These behaviour patterns were reinforced only once in life, during the *Ciexaus* ceremony, a puberty ritual where the teenage candidates (the so-called *ushwáala*) were instructed about their social roles as women or men (see Gusinde 1986, 836–844).

Yamana had no vertical social differentiation, besides some people who conducted the *Ciexaus* and *Kina* ceremonies (both exhaustively documented; see a summary in Vila & Ruiz 2001). Male dominance was sustained by the father's authority in every social unit. This social order, based on discrimination against women, was periodically restated during the *Kina*, a men's ceremony, and was explicitly reinforced by means of myths and legends (Pedraza Marín 2014).

Thus, the main social norms affecting social relations were essentially those related to social and biological reproduction, that is, norms controlling procreative behaviour (when, how and who they could marry or have sexual relations with). Among Yamana marriage was a means to control sexuality. Marriage was arranged by men: women could not decide to whom they got married and widows had to marry their brother-in-law. Heterosexuality, exogamy and incest taboo were social norms. Polygamy was common, even if a man rarely had more than four wives. Sexuality, especially women's sexuality, was focused on reproduction. Female premarital sexuality was controlled and women's infertility was penalised by abandonment or by taking another wife. Further mechanisms by which sexuality was controlled included education as well as intimidation (physical or ideological violence). Kidnapping of women existed, even of married women.

Accounts of the number of children per woman depends on the source consulted (Orquera & Piana 1999a, 469–470): Hyades and Deniker (1891, 189) proposed an average of four surviving children per woman, while these numbers are considered low by Gusinde (1986, 698), who discusses about six children. Both sources mention women with 7–14 children, although most died. Although infant mortality was high, the recorded potential Total Fertility Rate (Pennington 2001) would produce a high demographic increase, and thus additional management of reproduction would have been necessary to avoid significant population growth. We return to this point below. In any case, women suffered from great physical demands since there was little care or attention for women in labour or who had just given birth. Intentional abortion and infanticide of girls and of children with disabilities was usual and consented. Despite the greater amount of work invested by women they were explicitly marginalised from the decision-making group. Yamana society thus constitutes an asymmetrical reality based on social division of labour, value inequality and the control of reproduction exerted by men over women (Vila & Ruiz 2001).

Far from the image built by the 19th century ethnography, Yamana are not a paradigm of a 'simple society', a first step on the social evolutionary scale. Their social system was neither the consequence of degeneration nor of isolation. It was the historical product of successful sustainability. The canoe people of Tierra del Fuego had a specialised system of exploitation of a broad spectrum of the most abundant, ubiquitous and predictable resources (Gassiot & Estévez 2006; Alvarez *et al.* 2009). Sustainability in their organisational strategies is demonstrated by 6000 years of living on the archipelago island's coastal resources. In effect, after thousands of years of success and failure (observed in the archaeological record, Estévez & Vila 2013b) and of accumulating experience, the Yamana achieved a certain sustainability by optimising food production, avoiding the over-exploitation of the environment by regular strategies of management of critical resources (molluscs), as well as by regulating their own reproduction thanks to a social organisation based on constant mobility by canoe and by asymmetrical relationships between men and women. This asymmetrical relationship was implemented by a strict social/sexual division of labour, at least in ethnographic times. The products of the productive – and in a broader sense, reproductive – activity could be easily identified and, therefore, undervalued. In this way, women themselves could be also undervalued and consequently controlled in order to regulate sexual reproduction, making demographical stability or, at least, a short-term reduction of the population growth rate, possible. Ceremonies, sex-segregated education and myths or moral legends all made control effective (Estévez & Vila 2013a). Since social relationships surrounding social reproduction (the division and subjective value of work) are more conservative than other techniques and productive relationships (see Estévez & Vila 2007), the successful self-regulation of the population continued even after the landing of Europeans, bringing diseases, malnutrition and all kinds of violence. The result was the virtual extinction of the 3000 Yamana recorded in 1836 (Estévez & Vila 2013a).

Synthesis of the ethnoarchaeological experimentation

The project began in 1986 and it is still running today. Within this overarching framework, we have been implementing a series of specific research projects with a basic objective: to explore the process of change in hunter-gatherer societies (Vila *et al.* 1995).

First, an analysis of the ethnographic information on the Yamana society was required, investigating how social reproduction and the contradiction between potential demographic growth and limited resource availability works in societies that do not control the reproduction of resources. A critical analysis and systematisation of the iconographic and written sources, as well as re-visiting and re-describing from an archaeological viewpoint of all the relevant collections of materials deposited in ethnographic and archaeological museums, was conducted (see for details Estévez & Vila 2006).

A second phase of the research included the excavation of five daily settlements, two ceremonial burials and two cabins belonging to two of the Fueguian indigenous groups, the Yamana and a group from the northern coast, the Selk'nam (Vila *et al.* 2004; Fig. 8.1). Of particular ethnoarchaeological interest amongst these was the excavation of three recent (18th and 19th century) Yamana settlements on the north coast of the Beagle Channel: Túnel VII (Fig. 8.2), Lanashuaia and Alashawaia (Estévez

Figure 8.2. The site of Túnel VII on the Beagle Channel.

2009; Estévez & Vila 2000). Moreover, the excavation of the ritual hut from *Estancia Remolinos* (Vila *et al.* 2004) where the ceremony of the *Ciexaus* recorded by Gusinde was conducted, as well as of the funerary burial of a woman in Mischiuen III (Vila *et al.* 2006), allowed the exploration of aspects of social reproduction.

This phase of the research also involved a complete archaeological survey of the east–central coast of Tierra del Fuego, including GPS positioning of 131 sites; and gathering of information on the environmental context, stratigraphic sampling and subsequent radiocarbon dating. The palaeoclimatic curve and temperature over the past 6,000 years was investigated and an overall approach to the system of exploitation of resources over this period was reconstructed. Continuity was demonstrated in littoral ecosystems (Gassiot & Estévez 2006). Specific taphonomic processes and preservation conditions in Tierra del Fuego were considered and documented to extrapolate and predict the type of objects or portion of them that could be preserved in the archaeological record. Further consideration was given to which parts of the process might be inferred from sub-products, waste or other contextual information. Finally, most working procedures were experimentally replicated for a more quantitative and objective perspective.

Finally, a third phase involved comparing the ethnographic information with the experimental and archaeological data. The contextualisation of all the information obtained from studies of the archaeological material allowed us to construct a reasonable representation of the work processes involved in the production and consumption of goods (see below). Undeniably, in the archaeological component, the taphonomy and local creation of the material register is very important for understanding the actual use of space, the work processes and the time invested in them. The previous studies of the ethnographic collections were useful to evaluate how many objects of consumption would be well represented in the archaeological record, providing comparative information for our excavation and subsequent social inferences. Although some objects could not be completely or directly represented, they could be inferred through hypotheses based on the technical and ecological context. Of course, the existence of other objects would be very difficult to verify through archaeological evidence alone (e.g. perishable technological items, Fig. 8.3).

First attempts to develop an objective quantification of social organisation

Combining all the previous information, a quantitative approach to the level of inequality was proposed through the evaluation of the '*real value*', that is, the study of effort/time spent in the production of goods for every social segment of the population (Barceló *et al.* 2006). The aim of the proposed model was to reconstruct the main stages of production of all products (from acquisition of raw materials to the finished goods, ready for use or consumption) and the calculation of rates to quantify the relative work invested at each stage of the production of

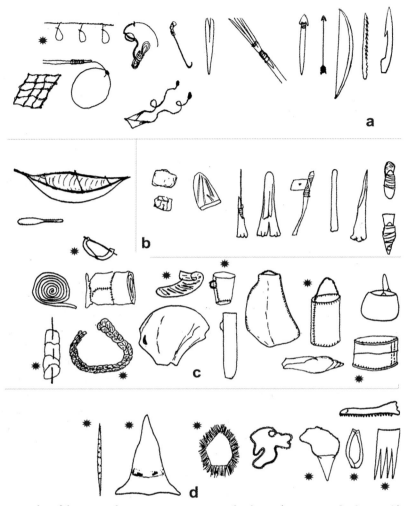

Figure 8.3. Examples of the most relevant Fueguian material culture a) extractive food items; b) instruments for the production of other goods, c) tools; and d) social-ideotechnic objects. Those marked with an asterisk are the ones that would be more difficult to infer from the archaeological record.

every object: 1) extraction of raw material; 2) preparing and transforming the raw material; several quantified parameters (Table 8.1), which later were aggregated to get a final score for each product (the *'real value'*).

The data analysis for the case of Raw Materials obtained by a Categorical Principal Components Analysis (CatPCA) and a non-hierarchic cluster analysis (k-means) allowed us to confirm the validity of the used parameters and make seven distinct groups on the basis of the work invested. From lower value (1) to higher (7): Group 1: low intensity gathering of materials with predictable availability e.g. eggs, vegetables,

Table 8.1. Parameters involved in procurement and production. Of the seven only the last three are relevant for manufacturing goods work processes

Parameters	Quantitative indexes
Time access	1 = up to 500 m 2 = 500 m to 5 km 3 = 5 km to 20 km 4 = more than 20 km
Temporal availability	1 = constant 2 = frequent 3 = seasonal/cycle 4 = sporadic/random
Spatial availability	1 = continuous 2 = discontinuous 3 = concentrated 4 = scarce
Physical effort involved in transportation	1 = up to 5 kg 2 = 5 to 20 kg 3 = 20 to 40 kg 4 = more than 40 kg
Technical complexity	1 = simple direct – without instrument (e.g. *collecting water or a cobblestone-hammer*). 2 = simple indirect passive – one instrument (*e.g. hunting birds with traps*). 3 = simple indirect active – one instrument (*e.g. knapping a scraper or weaving a basket*). 4 = simple indirect passive – multiple instruments (*e.g. fishing with fish-line*) 5 = simple indirect active – multiple instruments (*e.g. extracting bark*) 6 = complex with multiple instruments (*e.g. hunting a pinniped; elaborating a bow or a canoe*)
Labour force	1 = one person 2 = two persons 3 = a simple reproductive unit (*e.g. family*) 4 = multiple reproductive units
Acquisition time	1 = direct (*e.g. collecting fruits*) 2 = partial day 3 = complete day 4 = more than one day

algae; Group 2: more intensive work gathering materials whose availability is not always predictable: e.g. cutting down trees, hunting birds, fish caught at the beach; Group 3: collection of materials originally concentrated in space and time, collectively obtained with specific instruments: e.g. deep water shellfish, bark from certain trees; Group 4: collection of exotic European material, exchanged or collected e.g. glass, sheep; Group 5: hunting land animals e.g. guanaco, carnivorous; Group 6: e.g. systematic organised scavenging, stranded whale; Group 7: sea lion hunting. Figure 8.4 demonstrates that the real value of the obtained Raw Materials is the result of three

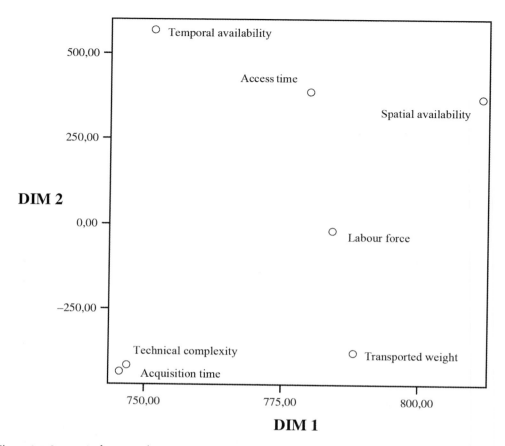

Figure 8.4. Categorical principal components analysis of the variables used to describe the work collection actions. The significant correlation between the variables Access time, Temporal availability and Spatial availability should be noted, on one hand, and the correlation between Acquisition time and technical complexity, on the other. The lack of relation between the latter and the transported weight suggests that the real value of the materials is related to weight, acquisition time and technical complexity.

independent components: the Nature of the Material (weight), the Availability of the Resources and the Technical Complexity of the Work Process. The fact that the Labour Force is placed at the centre of the graph reinforces the general impression that the amount and intensity of work depends on these three factors. Furthermore, the analysis of the different scores for working and obtaining raw material (Fig. 8.5) allowed us to obtain a statistically significant classification, grouping them in terms of the amount of work required for each one (Barceló *et al.* 2006).

In a second phase, the produced elements contained in the ethnoarchaeological database were assigned to the social agent responsible for the production (male labour, female labour, child labour male, child labour female and collective work), and who benefits from its use or consumption (man, woman, boy, girl, etc.). Using

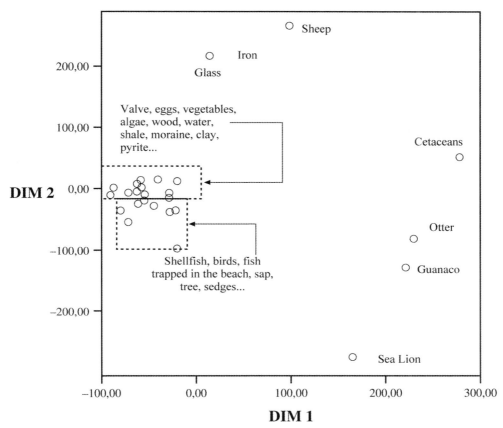

Figure 8.5. Categorical principal components analysis (CATPCA). Labour actions represented: gathering: eggs, vegetables, algae, wood, water, shale, sedges, stone, clay, pyrite, shellfish, deep water shellfish. Felling trees; obtaining bark from certain trees. Hunting: birds (with harpoon, with bow and arrows, trapping, or beating them), fish caught at the beach, fish caught with line. Hunting: guanaco, carnivorous, cetaceans, sea lion. Getting colonial resources: sheep, glass, iron.

these variables the social differentiation grade can be calculated in reference to all the items assigned in each stage of the production. The final calculation is simply a weighted sum of the relative estimations of the amount of work, corrected by the necessary amount of each material and/or product in each time of the cycle:

$$\frac{Amount\ of\ product\ generated \times Calculated\ value}{Amount\ of\ product\ consumed}$$

For this approach to the degree of social differentiation a first test was performed using the work process data concerning food obtained from sea lions: 1) collection (hunting, transportation); 2) extraction (evisceration, skinning, chopping) and 3) processing of raw materials (segmentation, chemical transformation).

Table 8.2. Data matrix of the total amount of value generated and appropriated in the process of obtaining food from sea lions

Action	Social category	Sum of generated value	Sum of appropriated value
Sea lion acquisition	Man	6	6
	Woman	7	5
	Boy	1	6
	Girl	1	6
Sea lion meat extraction	Man	2	5
	Woman	6	5
	Boy	1	6
	Girl	2	4
Sea lion meat transformation	Man	1	6
	Woman	7	5
	Boy	0	7
	Girl	2	5

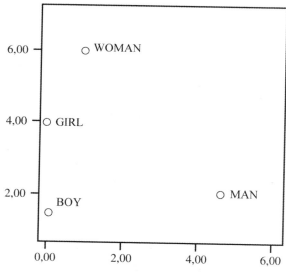

GENERATED VALUE

APPROPRIATED VALUE

Figure 8.6. Non-linear graphic model showing relationship between generation and appropriation of goods by sex between Yamana production units.

To this a second analytic dimension was added related to the appropriation of this real value, based on ethnographic information (Table 8.2). Grouping the activities related to each of the social categories (man, woman, boy, girl) allows us to check the existence of statistically significant differences (Fig. 8.6). It can be observed that in the case of women, when the generation of value is greater, their appropriation is lower, in contrast to the case for men.

The results of this first approach allow us to conclude that through statistical non-lineal models we can specify, regarding the production/direct consumption for this alimentary product, a concrete form of labour exploitation. This means that if we analyse reproduction in terms of production of human beings and their material conditions we can also study the concrete forms of exploitation of labour, and relate them to those discovered in the case of the production of goods.

Discussion

The results obtained by contrasting the ethnographic and archaeological sources of the same Fueguian societies allowed us to gain insights and some relevant conclusions about the essential features of the mode of production and reproduction and the social relations of hunter-gatherer societies materialised in the archaeological record.

1. *Ethnic group divisions are sometimes consequences of different intensities in social exchange and reproduction requests.* This case study has given us the opportunity to see the relations and contradictions between ethnography, anthropology and archaeology, including how the different cultures in the sources are not sustained in the archaeological record. Ultimately, the groups that were culturally defined in the texts could not be directly correlated with the conserved material records. Sometimes in the same text one finds descriptions of anatomical and language differences, but in other statements there are no boundaries, but a constant flow of people and items between different zones, as well as a command of multiple languages by some of the neighbouring people, who in addition shared fundamental rituals and beliefs (as reflected in ethnography, e.g. Hyades & Deniker 1891; Gusinde 1986). From these contradictions we can conclude that there was no real territorial exclusivity, and the problem that arises is how and why these language distinctions persisted over millennia when there were no political barriers and a constant flow of people, ideas and items. This leads us to consider the differences and relationships between some of the later hunter-gatherer societies and the early farmers who maintained exclusive rights over some parts of the territories they used for resource exploitation.

2. *Social relationships were less adaptive than subsistence strategies.* The Fueguian example shows that the social and economic systems among hunter-gatherer societies are subject to different and particular tolerance levels against external changes. They are resilient to external changes up to a point and within different limits, and these limits are dependent on the time scale involved. This implies that one must take account of and evaluate the influence of changes that are sudden and infrequent, for these may exceed the tolerance limits for change, resulting in catastrophic consequences on the whole system. Sometimes sudden extinction is produced, as in the collapse of the Yamana society. In this case, the introduction of new diseases caused the extinction of the whole society, because the social system

was structured to impose long-term restrictions on reproduction (see Estévez & Prieto, this volume).

3. *Social organisation is not synchronised with subsistence and therefore cannot be derived automatically from the evidence of the management of resources.* An ethnographic survey clearly revels that even if in most hunter-gatherer societies women do less food procurement, they do more weaving, basketry, pottery and cordage manufacture, house building, firewood collection, water hauling, leather working, camp moving and clothing (Waguespack 2005; Kelly 2013, 216). Most of these critical working activities are hardly visible archaeologically but require more effort and are more time-consuming (including low-return-rate food procurement) than others that are more visible and socially valued.

The proposal to calculate the real value generated for each social agent responsible for a work process and contrast this with the appropriated value generated by the same agent has been a first approach when trying to recognise the degree of inequality in a hunter-gatherer society through its material reflection. During this experimentation some serious inconsistencies could be observed between the sample of museum objects, ethnographic literature and areas documented by contemporary archaeology of settlements. Thus, for example, the work on the development of stone tools, including arrowheads was totally underestimated or even denied in the ethnographic literature, and was relatively underrepresented among the collections from the museums (only few points were made with stone, most were made from pieces of European glass), while on the other hand this has an important archaeological presence. Besides, we could observe the existence of a contradiction between the work investment made and the subjective assessment collected in the ethnography, both by native informants and the ethnographers.

To sum up, the contextualisation of all the information obtainable from archaeological material studies allows a better understanding than the purely ethnographic description. Regarding the use of resources, technical capabilities and work processes of that society, we were able to evaluate the explanatory power of the current archaeological methodology.

Perspectives for hunter-gatherer research

As CHAGS demonstrated, hunter-gatherer ethnoarchaeology, in its traditional sense is facing a paradox. On one hand, most non-capitalist societies have ceased to exist as such or were dramatically transformed before the 1930s. Even those societies that still have to some extent a hunter-gatherer lifeway (e.g. the Ju/'hoansi of Botswana and Namibia, the Ache of Eastern Paraguay, the Agta of Philippines) cannot escape the impact of industrial society. Furthermore, in many cases, researchers do not look at the historical development of these societies, which usually has impacts on changes in social and economic strategies. On the other hand, ethnoarchaeology in a wide sense – i.e. the study of ethnographic societies with an archaeological perspective – is essential in order to research the links between the form and content of material production and social organisation, and thus improve archaeological methodology.

We think that an extended use of ethnoarchaeological experimentation in as many ethnographic and archaeological contexts as possible should help to develop markers that would allow archaeologists to infer work processes invisible, or hard to see in the material record and even associate them with social agents (chemical analysis; intra-site analysis; markers of activity patterns etc). We have already begun to research the correlations between these specific social relations and their material manifestation in the organisation of space for the Yamana case (e.g. Dragicevic *et al.* 2012; Briz *et al.* 2013), and we are currently doing a comparative work with other ethnographic cases.

In the terrain of what Gándara has called 'substantive theory', that is, researching and formulating hypotheses about 'the model of a society and its dynamics' (1990, 74), current ethnographic knowledge offers a way to perform new lines of experimental research. Indeed, one question that emerged from research in Tierra del Fuego was the use of social norms as a mechanism to regulate the behaviour of individuals and social relations of reproduction: to what extent does the normative system of a hunter-gatherer society affect its reproductive capacity, by increasing, stabilising or decreasing it?

To try to answer this we have developed a realistic simulation of human societies with Multi-Agent Systems (MAS), in which 'the regulatory system is both the core and the main topic of research of simulation' (De la Cruz *et al.* 2010, 152). In the current phase of the project a general computer model of the social behaviour of a hunter-gatherer society has been developed without political institutions but with strict social norms; the social behaviour considered by default has been isolated (using death rates and fertility of the available contemporary hunter-gatherer societies). Social norms relating to the reproductive behaviour of four particular ethnographic societies (the Yamana and Selk'nam of Tierra del Fuego; the Coast Salish from the Canadian Northwest Coast; and the Yolngu of northeast Australia) have been selected, formulated into the standardised language and tested in MAS (Fig. 8.7). These societies have different environments and different subsistence strategies, but they share a strict sexual division and marked inequality between the sexes. The ultimate goal of this project is to see which social norms are crucial in regulating reproduction, to be able then to proceed with the investigation of its archaeological materialisation.

In short, within its limitations, this methodological approach allows us to test the theory about the importance of controlling reproduction for the survival of all hunter-gatherer societies, and experimentally explore the operation of those societies to deepen our understanding of social processes. In addition, we hope to raise new hypotheses that make us look at the archaeological record again.

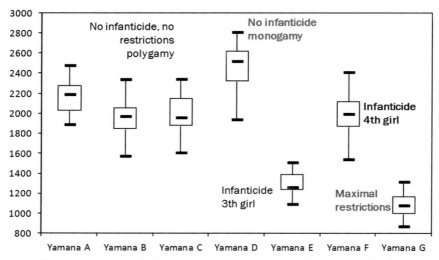

Figure 8.7. Total population attained after 100 years (Y axis) departing from 600 people after several test sets experimenting with Yamana norms. Box plots representing the variability resulting from 30 simulations each test set: A, B, C) Without infanticide and without other restrictions but with polygamy; D) No infanticide no other restrictions but with monogamy; E) Social norms with infanticide of 3rd girl; F) Social norms with infanticide just of 4th girl; G) Maximal restricting social norms.

Conclusions

The ethnoarchaeological experimentation in Tierra del Fuego has proved to be a useful approach in hunter-gatherer research. The combination of the study of ethnographic information of all hunter-gatherers, archaeological research itself, and the use of quantitative techniques or computational modeling is a way to increase and contrast the knowledge of historical and social dynamics of these groups. It is also an approach to test new methodologies and techniques that help us to build an interpretation of the archaeological record more successfully and completely.

Archaeology has to focus on deep methodological research to be able to reach a comprehensive knowledge of the development of any society and to formulate hypotheses to explain both changes and stability. This re-statement of our discipline must be done on the basis of a reflection of the theoretical bases from which we depart. The methods have to be calibrated; that is, to set up, evaluate and cleanse archaeological methodology, verifying at the same time explicative models or general laws of the hunter-gatherer mode of production.

References

Alvarez, M., Zurro, D., Briz, I., Madella, M., Osterrieth, M., & Borrelli, N. (2009) Análisis de los procesos productivos en las sociedades cazadoras-recolectoras-pescadoras de la costa norte del canal Beagle (Argentina) el sitio Lanashuaia. In M. Salemne, F. Santiago, M. Álvarez, E. Piaña, M.

Vázquez & E. Mansur (eds) *Arqueología de la Patagonia - Una mirada desde el último confín,* 903–917. Ushuaia, Editorial Utopías.

Argelés, T., Bonet, A., Clemente, I., Estévez, J., Gibaja, J., Lumbreras, L. G., Piqué, R., Ríos, M., Taulé, M. A., Terradas, X., Vila, A. & Wünsch, G. (1995) Teoría para una praxis: 'Splendor realitatis'. *Congreso de Arqueologia peninsular; Trabalhos de Antropologia e Etnologia,* 35(1), 501–507.

Barceló, J. A., Briz, I., Clemente, I., Estévez, J., Mameli, L., Maximiano, A., Moreno, F., Pijoan, J., Piqué, R., Terradas, X., Toselli, A., Verdún, E., Vila, A. & Zurro, D. (2006) Análisis etnoarqueológico del valor social del producto. In Departament d'Arqueologia i Antropologia Institució Milà i Fontanals & CSIC (eds), *Etnoarqueología de la Prehistoria: más allá de la analogía* 6, 189–207. Madrid, CSIC.

Begler, E. (1978) Sex, status, and authority in egalitarian society. *American Anthropologist* 80, 571–588.

Binford, L. (1978) *Nunamiut Ethnoarchaeology.* London, Academic Press.

Binford, L. R. (1980) Willow smoke and dogs' tails: hunter-gatherer settlement systems and archaeological site formation. *American Antiquity,* 45, 4–20.

Briz, I., Zurro, D., Álvarez, M. & Vila, A. (2013) The integrity of social space: hunters-gatherers at the end of the world. In M. Madella, G. Kovacs, I. Briz i Godino & B. Berzsenyi (eds), *The Archaeology of Household,* 23–43. Oxford, Oxbow Books.

De la Cruz, D., Estévez, J., Noriega, P., Pérez, M., Piqué, R., Sabater-Mir, J., Vila, A. & Villatoro, D. (2010) Normas en sociedades cazadoras-pescadoras-recolectoras. Argumentos para el uso de la simulación social basada en agentes. *Cuadernos de Prehistoria y Arqueología de la Universidad de Granada* 20, 149–161.

Dragicevic, I., Estévez, J., Piqué, R. & Vila, A. (2012) Gestión del espacio y organización social: ejemplos etnoarqueológicos de Tierra del Fuego. In G. Acosta Ochoa (ed.), *Arqueologías de la vida cotidiana: espacios domésticos y áreas de actividad en el México antiguo y otras zonas culturales,* 533–548. México, UNAM.

Endicott, K. M. & Endicott, K. L. (2012) *The Headman was a Woman: The Gender Egalitarian Batek of Malaysia.* Subang Jaya, Malaysia, Center for Orang Asli Concern.

Estévez, J. (2009) Ethnoarchaeology in the Uttermost Part of the Earth. *Arctic Anthropology.* 46, 132–143.

Estévez, J., Vila, A., Terradas, X., Piqué, R., Taulé, M., & Gibaja, J. (1998) Cazar o no cazar: ¿es ésta la cuestión? *Boletín de Antropología Americana* 33, 5–24.

Estévez, J. & Vila, A. (1995) Etnoarqueología: el nombre de la cosa. In J. Estévez & A. Vila (eds), *Encuentros en los conchales fueguinos,* 17–23. Treballs d'Etnoarqueologia 1. Bellaterra, CSIC-UAB.

Estévez, J. & Vila, A. (1998) Tierra del Fuego, lugar de encuentros. *Revista de Arqueología Americana* 15, 187–219.

Estévez, J. & Vila, A. (1999) *Piedra a Piedra. Historia de la construcción del Paleolítico en la en la Península Ibérica.* British Archaeological Report S 805. Oxford, British Archaeological Reports.

Estévez, J. & Vila, A. (2000) Estratigrafías en contexto. *Krei* 5, 29–61.

Estévez, J. & Vila, A. (2006) Colecciones de museos etnográficos en arqueología. In A. Vila-Mitjá & J. Estévez (eds), *Etnoarqueología de la Prehistoria: más allá de la analogía, Serie de Treballs d'Etnoarqueologia,* 13–23. Madrid, IMF-CSIC.

Estévez, J. & Vila, A. (2007) Twenty years of Ethnoarchaeological research in Tierra del Fuego: some thoughts for European Shell-Midden Archaeology. In N. Milner, O. E. Craig & G. N. Bailey (eds), *Shell Middens in Atlantic Europe,* 183–195. Oxford, Oxbow Books.

Estévez, J. & Vila, A. (2013a) Arqueología de 1800–1850: una mirada desde el otro lado de la frontera. *Vínculos de Historia* 2, 287–308.

Estévez, J. & Vila, A. (2013b) Fum als ulls: etnografia i arqueologia a la Terra del Foc. *Perifèria: revista de recerca i formació en antropologia* 18, 10–18.

Gándara, M. (1990) La analogía etnográfica como heurística: lógica muestreal, dominios ontológicos e historicidad. In Y. Sugiura, & M. C. Serra (eds), *Etnoarqueología: Coloquio Boch-Gimpera:[celebrado en México del día 22 al 26 de 1989],* 43–82. México, UNAM.

Gassiot Ballbè, E. & Estévez, J. (2006) Last foragers in coastal environments: a comparative study of the Cantabrian Mesolithic, Yamana of Tierra del Fuego and Archaic foragers of the Central American coast. In C. Grier, J. Kim & J. Uchiyama (eds), *Beyond Affluent Foragers: Rethinking Hunter-Gatherer Complexity*, 90–105. Oxford, Oxbow Books.

Gould, R. & Watson, P. (1982) A dialogue on the meaning and use of analogy in ethnoarchaeological reasoning. *Journal of Anthropological Archaeology* 1, 355–381.

Gusinde, M. (1986 [1937]) *Los Indios de Tierra del Fuego. Tomo 2, Los Yámana*. Buenos Aires, Centro Argentino de Etnología Americana, Consejo Nacional de Investigaciones Científicas y Técnicas.

Hardy, K. (ed.) (2010) *Archaeological Invisibility and Forgotten Knowledge: conference proceedings, Lódz, Poland, 5th-7th September 2007*. British Archaeological Report S2183. Oxford, Archaeopress.

Hyades, P. D. J. & Deniker, J. (1891) *Mission Scientifique du Cap Horn 1882-1883, Tome VII, Anthropologie, Ethnographie*. Paris, Gauthier-Villar et fils Imprimeurs-Libraires.

Kelly, L. R. (2013) *The Lifeways of Hunter-Gatherers. The Foraging Spectrum*. Cambridge, Cambridge University Press.

Legoupil, D. (2008) Les indiens de Patagonie entre science et romance. L'apport des recherches françaises. *Les Nouvelles de l'archéologie* 111/112, 27–32.

Martial, L., Hyades, P. & Deniker, J. (2007) *Etnografía De Los Indios Yaghan en La Misión Científica Del Cabo De Hornos 1882-1883*. Instituto Francés de Estudios Andinos. Punta Arenas, UMAG.

Orquera, L. A. & Piana, E. L. (1999a) *La vida material y social de los Yámana*. Buenos Aires, Instituto Fueguino de Investigaciones Científicas.

Orquera, L. & Piana, E. (1999b) *Arqueología de la región del Canal Beagle: Tierra del Fuego, República Argentina*. Buenos Aires, Sociedad Argentina de Antropología.

Orquera, L. & Piana, E. (2009) Sea nomads of the Beagle Channel in southernmost South America: over six thousand years of coastal adaptation and stability. *Journal of Island and Coastal Archaeology* 4, 61–81.

Orquera, L., Legoupil, D. & Piana, E. (2011) Littoral adaptation at the southern end of South America. *Quaternary International* 239, 61–69.

Pedraza Marín, D. (2014) Las ceremonias y el mundo simbólico en la producción y reproducción de las sociedades Yámana y Selk'nam de Tierra del Fuego. *RAMPAS Revista Atlántica-Mediterránea de Prehistoria y Arqueología Social* 15, 141–164.

Pennington, C. (2001) Hunter-Gatherer demography. In C. Panter-Brick, R. H. Layton & P. Rowley-Conwy. (eds), *Hunter-Gatherers: An Interdisciplinary Perspective*, 170–204. Cambridge, Cambridge University Press.

Piana, E., Vila, A., Orquera, L. & Estévez, J. (1992) Chronicles of 'Ona-Ashaga': archaeology in the Beagle Channel (Tierra del Fuego-Argentina) *Antiquity* 66, 771–783.

Prieto, A., Stern, C. & Estévez, J. (2013) The peopling of the Fuego-Patagonian fjords by littoral hunter-gatherers after the mid-Holocene H1 eruption of Hudson Volcano. *Quaternary International* 317, 3–13.

Reybrouck, D. V. (2012) *From Primitives to Primates. A History of Ethnographic and Primatological Analogies in the Study of Prehistory*. Leiden, Sidestone Press Dissertations.

Trigger, B. G. (1992) *Historia del pensamiento arqueológico*. Barcelona, Crítica.

Verdún, E., Briz, I., Camarós, E., Colonese, A., Estévez, J. & Zurro, D. (2010) Metodología de excavación y análisis de concheros: experiencias acumuladas después de 20 años de estudios etnoarqueológicos en la costa norte del Canal Beagle (Tierra del Fuego, Argentina). *Fervedes* 6, 25–32.

Vila, A. (2011) Es posible obtener una muestra etnográfica para trabajar en arqueología prehistórica. In E. Williams, M. García Sanchez, P. C. Weigand & M. Gándara (eds), *Mesoamérica. Debates y perspectivas*, 95–114. Zamora, Colegio de Michoacán.

Vila, A. & Estévez, J. (2010) *La excepción y la norma: las sociedades indígenas de la Costa Noroeste de Norteamérica desde la arqueología*. Treballs d'Etnoarqueologia 8. Madrid, CSIC.

Vila, A. & Ruiz, O. (2001) Información etnológica y análisis de la reproducción social. El caso Yamana. *Revista Española de Antropología Americana*, 31, 275–291.

Vila, A., Piqué, R. & Mansur, E., (2004) Etnoarqueología de rituales en sociedades cazadoras-recolectoras. In A. Luis & G. Dalla Corte (eds) *Catalunya-América. Fonts i documents de recerca*, 284–294. Barcelona, Institut Català de Cooperació Iberoamericana.

Vila, A., Casas, A. & Vicente, O. (2006) Mischiuen III, un contexto funerario singular en el Canal Beagle (Tierra del Fuego). *Revista Española de Antropología Americana*, 36(1), 47–61.

Vila, A. & Estévez, J. (1995) Encuentros en los conchales fueguinos. In J. Estévez & A. Vila (eds), *Encuentros en los conchales fueguinos*, 5–15 Treballs d'Etnoarqueologia 1. Bellaterra, CSIC-UAB.

Vila, A., Mameli, L., Terradas, X., Estevez, J., Moreno, F., Verdún, E., Zurro, D., Clemente, I., Piqué, R., Briz, I. & Barceló, J.A. (2007) Investigaciones etnoarqueológicas en Tierra del Fuego (1986–2006): reflexiones para la arqueología prehistórica europea. *Trabajos de Prehistoria* 64(2), 37–53.

Vila, A., Estévez, J., Villatoro, D. & Sabater-Mir, J. (2010) Archaeological materiality of social inequality among hunter-gatherer societies. In K. Hardy (ed.) *Archaeological Invisibility and Forgotten Knowledge*, 202–210. Oxford, Archaeopress.

Waguespack, N. M. (2005) The organization of male and female labor in foraging societies: Implications for early Paleoindian archaeology. *American Anthropologist*, 107(4), 666–676.

Wobst, H. (1978) The archaeo-ethnology of hunter-gatherers or the tyranny of the ethnographic record in archaeology. *American Antiquity* 43, 303–309.

Wylie, A. (1985) The reaction against analogy. *Advances in Archaeological Method and Theory* 8, 63–111.

Chapter 9

Strangers in a strange land? Intimate sociality and emergent creativity in Middle Palaeolithic Europe

Penny Spikins, Gail Hitchens and Andy Needham

Introduction

Europe in the Middle Palaeolithic would have been an unfamiliar world. The landscapes which we reconstruct for this period seem almost alien – often shrouded in ice, occupied by now-extinct fauna, such as mammoths and woolly rhinoceros, and moreover by people seen by many as 'not quite human'. Unlike in later periods such as the Mesolithic (see Warren this volume), analogies between modern foragers and *Neanderthals* are rare. Such comparisons have typically been restricted to generalised ecological models, rarely extending to the social and cultural lives of these *strangers in a strange land*. A blurring of the boundaries between Neanderthals and modern humans in recent years has encouraged the application of data derived from ethnographically documented societies in increasing frequency, and as an analogy to understand Neanderthal sociality. Such applications are not without risk as they can compress the very diversity we hope to understand. Even so, not only can modern foragers potentially provide much needed insight, but the distant lives lived by Neanderthals equally present us with a possibility of bringing something new to our understanding of hunter-gatherers.

Here we aim to rise to the challenge of including Neanderthals within the diversity of hunter-gatherer social existence without imposing a modern foraging adaptation on to their way of life. We review some of the difficulties with the direct application of analogies from contemporary hunter-gatherers, and explore alternative approaches to help us to understand the nature of Neanderthal sociality.

Changing perspectives on Neanderthals

Neanderthal's robust physique and apparent position outside of a ladder of progression to modernity has historically consigned them to being seen as different and primitive.

Despite a similar brain size to modern humans the shape of Neanderthal crania, for example, led William King in 1864 to conclude 'considering that the Neanderthal skull is eminently simial, both in its general and particular characters, I feel myself constrained to believe that the thoughts and desires which once dwelt within it never soared beyond those of a brute' (*King 1864*, 96, cited by Zilhão 2012, 35). Certain biases have been apparent in realms ranging from early technical drawings (Van Reybrouck 2002), popular reconstructions (Moser 1992) and literature (Hackett & Dennell 2003). Neanderthals have in turn been interpreted as unable to think in complex or creative ways, incapable of burying the dead, using language or symbolism and as having limited abilities to think innovatively. Neanderthals were defined by their extinction, with a default presumption of simplicity due to their failure to survive into the present (Zilhão 2014).

Over recent years there has been a notable change in thinking, with a growing tendency to include Neanderthals within narratives of increasingly complex hunting and gathering societies. This change has been fuelled by new evidence for social complexity in Neanderthals, including a diverse range of treatments of the dead (Hovers *et al.* 2000; Pettitt 2013) as well as an expanding range of art and/or symbolic material cultures (see for example Jaubert *et al.* 2016; Roebroeks *et al.* 2012; Peresani *et al.* 2013; Rodríguez-Vidal *et al.* 2014; Radovčić *et al.* 2015). Variability within Neanderthal cultures has also emerged, not only in changes through time, with the addition of novel production techniques and artefact forms after 60,000 BP (Djindjian 2012; Zilhão 2014), but also in regional cultural distinctions (Ruebens 2013). However, the main driving factor influencing changing approaches was the publication of the complete Neanderthal genome (Green *et al.* 2010), demonstrating a Neanderthal contribution to modern human genes. This has encouraged a rebranding of Neanderthals into something more recognisably similar to humans, rather than relegation to a distant side-branch.

Extending ethnographic analogies to an archaic past

Our new relationship with Neanderthals prompts us to extend the diversity of hunter-gatherers to include, rather than exclude, Neanderthal societies. However, this is not without problems. Syntheses of Neanderthal capacities tend to argue for Neanderthal complexity through similarity to what is familiar to us, extending the ethnographic record of modern foragers to Neanderthals (e.g. Burdukiewicz 2014; Hayden 2012; Zilhão 2014) and conflating differences as a means of most comfortably including Neanderthals within what we see as truly (and familiarly) 'human'. Emancipating Neanderthals from their inferior position can all too easily find us making them just another example of what we already know. Drawing on modern ethnographically documented societies, without simply replicating their existence to an ancient past, is a challenge.

Most obviously the archaeological evidence for lifestyles and behaviour is ever more impoverished in these distant time periods, particularly before the last glacial maximum. The loss of perishable items of material culture is ever more acute. Moreover unique glacial and pre-last-interglacial environments provide a further challenge, being unlike any occupied by contemporary hunter-gatherers. The Middle Palaeolithic adds yet a further complication: Neanderthals were biologically and physically distinct from modern humans, separated by at least 600,000 years of evolutionary change (Hublin 2009). Typical assumptions we make about the body might not apply given this evolutionary separation, with Neanderthals displaying notable anatomical differences to modern humans that cannot be assumed to be insignificant to accommodate a neat ethnographic analogy.

Generalisations which hold for modern small scale foragers might not be applicable to distant periods of prehistory (Kelly 2013). The modern foraging adaptation, recognisable in contemporary hunting and gathering societies, seems to have appeared only recently on an evolutionary timescale. Signs of familiar social patterns, documented ethnographically, such as large scale social networks which provide a social buffer in times of resource stress, cemented by social interactions, exchanges of non-utilitarian gifts and regular aggregations are absent prior to 100,000 BP and only begin to emerge sporadically and episodically after this time. For example, we find perforated and ochred shell beads in use at Taforalt in Morocco at 82,000 BP (Bouzouggar *et al.* 2007) and Blombos Cave in South Africa at 75,000 BP (d'Errico *et al.* 2005), but these developments disappear subsequently. It is only after 44,000 BP, with the typical San material culture found at Border Cave, that we see the material evidence which matches a recognisable and sustained modern foraging adaptation as we know it today (d'Errico *et al.* 2012). The implication is that we cannot take for granted what we feel to be familiar about the social structures of modern foragers when we deal with archaic populations or even those of much of the early Upper Palaeolithic. Even those commonalities with modern foragers which Kelly feels can confidently be extended into prehistory, i.e. group sizes of around 18–30 individuals and that men predominantly hunt and women predominantly gather (Kelly 2013, 274), are by no means certain in the Middle Palaeolithic.

It can be tempting to extend what we know of modern hunter-gatherer social structure into the Middle Palaeolithic in order to include Neanderthals within narratives of emerging complexity. Hayden for example presents Neanderthal societies as essentially modern foragers with sophisticated social groupings, personal and ethnic identities, collective rituals and large scale social connections (Hayden 2012). While a refreshing change from portrayals of Neanderthals as lacking social abilities, certain claims remain contentious. Hayden infers, for example, that Neanderthal group size was around 12–25 individuals, i.e. within the range of modern hunting and gathering groups, based on ethnographic generalisations from modern foragers backed up by a small selection of those archaeological sites where we see the greatest evidence of spatial structuring (Hayden 2012, 8). He likewise infers the presence of ethnic groups of around 80-300 individuals, with periodic aggregations, also based on the direct application of ethnographic models (Hayden 2012, 12).

While interpretations of a complex social behaviour in Neanderthals are welcome, inferences based on models derived from modern foragers fail to correlate well with estimates or interpretations using more direct sources of evidence. Churchill, considering the ecological and archaeological evidence, argues for much smaller groups, typically in the order of 8–10 individuals (Churchill 2014), a position also supported by genetics (Rosas *et al.* 2006). In reviewing evidence from the Swabian Alb, Conard *et al.* (2012) conclude that social groups would have consisted of a small number of close kin. While larger sites, such as Tor Faraj, Jordan, are known, they are much less common than small sites (Henry *et al.* 2004). In modern contexts, exceptionally small site sizes might be explained as an adaptation to ecological circumstance through the exploitation of small distributed resources by specialist groups. However, good evidence for the importance of the collaborative exploitation of game as large as mammoth in some regions contrasts with this pattern (Smith 2015; Sistiaga *et al.* 2014). The availability of game animals certainly seems an important influence on group size and mobility nonetheless (Delagnes & Rendu 2011). Whilst there must have been considerable variability in patterns of mobility across the time and space of Neanderthal occupation, a predominant feature of small groups, probably made up of close kin, seems to have been typical.

Inferring the existence of modern forager like aggregation sites is perhaps even more problematic. As Hayden notes, even modern foragers living at the lowest population densities, such as in the Western desert of Australia, identify with a larger ethnic and mating group and go to great efforts to organise aggregations (Hayden 2012, 10). This may not have been true of Neanderthals for whom there is little evidence of any sizeable aggregation. Hayden argues that the site of Mauran, France, with its large quantities of bison bones, might have been an aggregation site that could have supported 200 people. Interpolations on the basis of the bone densities in a 25 m² area, with approximately 137 individuals, have been used to infer at least 900 bison were killed there (Farizy 1994, 157). However, the excavators themselves interpret Mauran as a palimpsest, accumulated over many hundreds or even thousands of years of small scale kills of one to three bison, hunted into or herded off a large cliff (Farizy 1994). As at La Cotte de St Brelade, Jersey, and at similar sites where accumulations of the bones of large game are recovered, discrete episodes of accumulation are often the most probable explanation for apparently large accumulations (Scott *et al.* 2015). A repeated use of significant sites within the landscape, often distinctive features such as cliffs, suggests a certain tie to place amongst Neanderthals (Burke 2006) without necessarily implying any aggregation of several groups.

Sites which are potentially socially significant exist in Middle Palaeolithic Europe, but lack the scale of population concentration familiar to modern aggregations. Molodova I (level IV) in the Ukraine for example, shows good evidence for the hunting of several mammoths, a dwelling structure, potential meat storage and symbolic activity in the form of deliberate grooves on an ochred mammoth scapula and pelvis (Demay *et al.* 2012). Molodova I, as well as other notable sites such as Tor Faraj and

Abric Romaní, may be socially significant, or even represent places where parts or all of small neighbouring groups joined together, on a different scale from that seen in ethnographic contexts.

A distinctive Neanderthal sociality?

Archaeological evidence points to a distinct pattern of social groups, social movement and social connections in Middle Palaeolithic Europe, the character of which we risk losing if we expect social behaviour to comply with modern contexts. A certain *local focus* to Neanderthal settlement and social organisation seems inescapable. The great majority of flint artefacts found on Middle Palaeolithic sites in many regions are made of raw materials collected within *c.* 20 km of a site, and often within 5 km (Féblot-Augustins 2009). Within the Massif Central, for example, most raw material used for flint artefacts comes from within 5 km of where it is discarded, with over 20 km being exceptional (Fernandes *et al.* 2008). A similar pattern can be found in the Swabian Alb (Conard *et al.* 2012). Movements of raw materials over distances over 100 km occur but are rare (Marwick 2003; Féblot-Augustins 2009), making it unclear if these represent personal procurement or links with other social groups (see Féblot-Augustins 2009; Meignen *et al.* 2009). Greater extremes of long distance movements of a small percentage of artefacts within assemblages, as with pieces travelling over 400 km to Cap Grand in southwest France, involve just a few well-used artefacts (Slimak & Giraud 2007). Though we might reasonably infer that such movements imply social contacts between groups (Sykes 2012), it is still possible to explain these raw material transfers as no more than personal transport (Kuhn 2012). Only in unique circumstances such as in Salento, Italy where local raw materials were almost unworkable are greater proportions of raw material from non-local sources found (Spinapolice 2012). Patterns of lithic raw material procurement suggest that long distance movements and external social connections were uncommon (Djindjian 2012), contrasting with modern foragers where substantial material movements through fluid and dynamic fission and fusion over large regions is common.

Isotopic and genetic data supports the notion of restricted movements (Richards *et al.* 2008) and poorly connected groups (Sánchez-Quinto & Lalueza-Fox 2015), with mating between half siblings common (Prüfer *et al.* 2014).

As Kuhn (2012, 78) comments, 'the sheer difficulty of identifying consistent evidence for exchange of artefacts or raw materials in the Middle Palaeolithic of Eurasia suggests that strategies of social alliance formation were different from, or not as geographically ambitious, as they were among more recent foragers'.

We would be wrong to paint a picture of Neanderthals as living in isolated groups, but certainly both the frequency and the scale of large scale social interactions seems to be constrained and the scale of social relationships and social life predominantly an intimately focused one. Social dynamics based on small groups often made up of close kin, infrequent social connection and a lack of large scale aggregations may be a common feature of archaic humans, and potentially a response to particular ecological contexts (Djindjian 2012). Nonetheless Middle Palaeolithic Europe perhaps provides us with the best opportunities for understanding the ramifications of such a social strategy.

The intimate scale of Neanderthal sociality in context

The behavioural ecology of Middle Palaeolithic communities provides an obvious explanation for distinctions with modern populations (see O'Connell 2006), and for the intimate scale of their sociality. Neanderthal's robust body shape offered greater protection from cold, enabled a high level of physical endurance and even physical strength advantages. However, robusticity also comes at a cost. Neanderthals needed significant extra energy to power their robust physiques, and though estimates vary, their average estimated extra calorific requirement is of the order of 2000 calories a day more than an equivalent modern Inuit (Churchill 2014, 326). Population densities will have necessarily been low given the greater 'energetic footprint' of each individual. Most significantly, travelling to maintain large scale connections would have been as much as 20–24% more energetically expensive (Froehle *et al.* 2013, 318). Furthermore whilst Neanderthal distal limb morphology made them better suited to travelling over complex terrain (Higgins & Ruff 2011) within which they may have been remarkably agile (de los Terreros *et al.* 2014) a distinct heel morphology also made them inefficient in certain gaits, potentially also affecting long distance travel (Raichlen *et al.* 2011).

Modern foragers depend on travelling great distances to support large scale networks. The Jo/huansi, for example, maintain their hxaro network by spending a third of their time travelling to visit distant friends (Wiessner 2002). In ecological terms, the costs of such travel for modern foragers is more than recouped through the benefits of a support network reducing risk in times of need. Such expenditure would have been far less energetically feasible by contrast for Neanderthals (see Verpoorte 2006, Pearce & Moutsiou 2014).

It is the implications of a distinctive local focus to social structures, influenced by biology, which is perhaps the most interesting. Here the responses of modern ethnographically documented societies to the opportunities and constraints which they face in their physical and social environments can provide some insights.

Small group sizes, low population densities and infrequent large scale social contacts have often been interpreted as evidence of Neanderthal simplicity. Low population density for example has been argued, on the basis of agent based models, to lead to a lack of innovation in Neanderthal societies, with low populations and a lack of contacts hampering the spread of ideas (Powell *et al.* 2009). Understanding the principles and constraints under which modern foragers act (Kelly 2013, 273) can however help us to move away from seeing Neanderthals as less social (and less open to new ideas) than their modern counterparts, and towards a better understanding of how such societies might have functioned.

Distinctions are frequently made between how ideas emerge and are spread between Middle and Upper Palaeolithic communities, with the latter seen as quicker to adopt new ideas. The limited and varied evidence for Middle Palaeolithic personal ornamentation has been seen as simple and sporadic for example compared with that of Upper Palaeolithic societies entering Europe (characterised by their ubiquitous, identically produced and rapidly evolving types of artefacts). However our knowledge of modern foragers argues that explanations for what has been seen as a lack of spread of new ideas may be a more complex and more cultural phenomenon than it appears. Cross cultural ethnographic comparisons illustrate for example that any observable relationship between population density and innovation is lacking (Collard *et al.* 2013). It may be an intimate sociality, rather than population density *per se*, that encouraged a focus on local culture and resistance to external ideas. What has been seen as an inability to adopt new ideas might be better understood as a cultural strength in local distinctiveness and a certain 'cultural resilience' (Fortier 2009).

Clearly, if we move beyond a progressivist narrative we can begin to appreciate that infrequent social contact and a markedly local focus to sociality may lead to the emergence of ideas and meanings which are *different* but *not necessarily simpler* than in more connected societies. Infrequent large scale social connection brings with it a freedom to develop external ideas, concepts and material culture negotiated within a local social context, inspired but not constrained by external views and through this a certain emergent creativity. The use of bottle glass from colonial encounters to make arrowheads in societies in Tierra del Fuego is one example (McEwan *et al.* 2014). In the same regions gifts of clothing from colonists, carefully torn apart and re-distributed as pieces, subverts the concept of protection from cold into an affirmation of equality and sharing is another (Hazlewood 2000). Turnbull likewise records metal tubing subverted for use in sacred ritual performance amongst the Mbuti (Turnbull 1961). Such novel adaptations of a wider concept are creative innovations in themselves.

The cultural resilience seen in intimately focused societies extends to examples beyond modern foragers. In a historical context the island occupants of St Kilda, Scotland, numbering less than 200 individuals until the 19th century, lived several days journey by boat from mainland Scotland and thus were exposed only infrequently to Christianity. As such they developed their own ritual practices, for example involving built stone circles (Macaulay 1764). Mellars (Mellars 1999, 360) used so-called Melanesian 'cargo cults' as an analogy for Châtelperronian artefacts in a derogatory sense to imply that Neanderthals copied modern human ornamentation without understanding (Zilhão 2012, 6). However this type of creative use of novel material goods is now viewed not as a lack of understanding of their 'proper use' but a sophisticated social manipulation of concepts, sometimes lost in western notions of

Table 9.1. *Locally unique forms of personal ornamentation and personal expression in Neanderthals*

Form	Site/Region	Date approximate years ago	Reference
Eight white tailed eagle talons, with modifications consistent with mounting as personal ornamentation	Krapina, Croatia	c. 130,000	Radovčić *et al.* 2015
Decorated (personal?) bone fragment found with La Ferrassie I burial	La Ferrassie, France	60–75,000	Zilhão 2012
Ochred and perforated shell (*Pecten maximus*) (transported at least 60 km)	Cueva Antón, S Spain	c. 50,000	Zilhão *et al.* 2010
Perforated shells (*Acanthocardia tuberculata* and *Glycymeris insubrica*)	Cueva de los Aviones, S Spain	c. 50,000	Zilhão *et al.* 2010
Marine shell which has travelled over 500 km (as personal item?)	Lezetxiki, N Spain	c. 55–48,000	Arrizabalaga 2009
Ochred marine shell	Fumane Cave, N Italy	48,000	Peresani *et al.* 2013
Use of bird feathers for personal decoration	Fumane Cave, N Italy	c. 44,000	Peresani *et al.* 2011
Red disc and hand print, potentially created by Neanderthals	El Castillo Cave, N Spain	41–37,000	Pike *et al.* 2012
Incised (rather than perforated) tooth pendants	Grotte du Renne, S France	c. 45–40,000	Zilhão 2012; Caron *et al.* 2011
Perforated wolf canine	La Grande Roche de la Plématrie, S France	c. 45–40,000	Zilhão 2012
Spindle shaped bone pendant	Bacho Kiro Cave, Bulgaria	c. 45–40,000	Kozłowski & Ginter 1982; Zilhão 2012

'primitive' (Otto 2009). To negotiate and recreate external social and material concepts, whether those of other Neanderthal groups or newcomers, within an intimately focused social setting is more 'creative' than any wholesale adoption of imposed ideas.

An understanding of the emergent creativity, which infrequent exposure to outside influence generates, allows us to reflect anew on the local and unique character of Neanderthal symbolic material culture and personal ornamentation (Table 9.1). Within the context of what appears to have been a wider European practice of personal expression, observable through the widespread use of ochre, we see the emergence of unique local signatures of art. Many expressions of personal ornamentation are entirely unique, such as animal teeth or a marine shell with incisions (rather than perforations) for suspension, eagle talons hung as ornaments, or the use of feathers (Fig. 9.1). Other entirely unique forms of symbolic expression also emerge in Neanderthal contexts, such as annular structures made of stalagmites at Bruniquel Cave in Southwest France (Jaubert *et al.* 2106). Within each context, meanings must have emerged creatively and been distinct. From this perspective the rigid imposition of an inflexible idea seen in the imposed similarity of Aurignacian shell beads, or split-based bone points, across Europe by supposedly more complex moderns appears

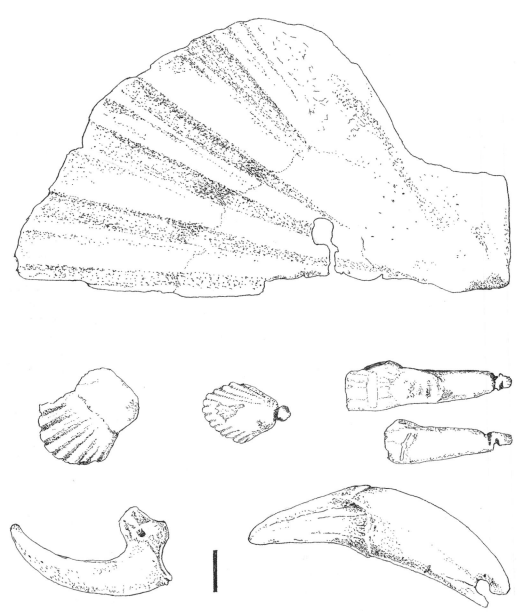

Figure 9.1. Examples of local creativity in Neanderthal personal expression. From left to right: Perforated and ochred pecten shell from Cueva Antón (Pecten maximus), incised teeth from Grotte du Renne, incised shell from Grotte du Renne, perforated wolf canine from La Grande Roche de la Plématrie, eagle claw from Grotta di Fumane, perforated shell from Cueva de los Aviones (Acanthocardia tuberculata). Redrawn by P. S. after Zilhão et al. (2010); Zilhão (2012); Radovčić et al. (2015).

to be lacking in creative or novel engagement. Early Upper Palaeolithic groups could rather be viewed as more simple, with more frequent fission and fusion leading to less internal cohesion, reduced cultural resilience and subsequently a more marked wholesale adoption of external ideas.

Intimate sociality and Neanderthal childhood experience

The childhood experience of modern hunter-gatherers can also provide us with insights into how Neanderthal cultural resilience might have been constructed and maintained.

A distinctive intimate and local focus on sociality and social emotions would have had a subtle influence on the experience of being a child, in turn directing the flavour of adult Neanderthal sociality and culture (Spikins *et al.* 2014). Mutual support within a highly cohesive social system is certainly evidenced by high rates of care for the vulnerable amongst Neanderthals (Spikins *et al.* 2010; Spikins 2015), including attention to infants and children (Spikins *et al.* 2014). In terms of emotional development, the constancy of adult relationships with children, in contrast to the fission-fusion seen in modern foragers, may well have been a factor increasing infant security (Tottenham 2012), self-control and collaborative motivations (Mikulincer & Shaver 2010). It may be from this intimate basis for social life, allowing Neanderthals to develop collaborative and caring motivations (Gilbert 2015), that societies could develop their resilience to the adoption of external ideas or ways of doing things.

An intimate focus and concern with the well-being of children is reflected in Neanderthal burial. Currently over 20 burials of children have been discovered, with many showing signs of great care being taken. For example, the burial of a 2-year-old child at Dederiyeh Cave in Syria (Akazawa *et al.* 1999) was laid out on its back, with arms extended and legs flexed, with a triangular flint placed upon its chest and a stone slab beside its head. Further, a 10-month-old infant recovered from Amud Cave in Israel, was found with a complete maxilla of red deer (*Cervus elaphus*) lying on its pelvis (Hovers *et al.* 1995). A number of sites have also produced multiple child burials, most notably La Ferrassie, France. Here, in addition to two adults, five children were discovered. This included a new-born found within an oval depression with three flint scrapers (La Ferrassie 5), and a 3-year-old child with three stone tools and a limestone block with cupules above the grave (La Ferrassie 6) (Capitan & Peyrony 1912; Delporte 1976). Within the context of an inwardly focussed society, we have previously argued this evidence represents a social and potentially symbolic focus on the young (Spikins *et al.* 2014).

Whilst our modern western attitudes tend to assume that children are taught and given instruction, ethnographic research illustrates the remarkable autonomy of children in hunter-gatherer societies, who instead learn from exposure and personal exploration (Terashima 2013; Hewlett 2013). Neanderthal children are likely to have learnt in the same way through being exposed to new experiences. Within an intimate scale of social life, secure relationships to constant carers and a familiar social environment will have fostered emotional development and learning. There is good evidence for learning through exploration in novice knapping debris at sites such as Maastricht-Belvedere and Rhenen for example (Stapert 2007). As well as learning how to manage emotions and be part of the close knit group, children were clearly being exposed to skills such as flint knapping, and given opportunities and support to learn.

An intimate scale to sociality can of course also bring constraints. Limited exposure to novel landscapes might discourage distant exploration and encourage a firmer tie to local landscapes, for example. Firstly, Neanderthal biology made opportunities for children to travel *simply to explore* relatively costly, potentially limiting the scale at which exploration beyond the camp took place. Secondly, the particular exposures to risk which children faced when exploring farther from camp may also play a role. Blurton-Jones *et al.* (1994), for example, illustrate the significance of relative exposure to risk in explaining why Hadza children forage frequently and successfully well beyond the camp, whilst Ju/'hoansi children forage very little and do not venture far. The Hadza environment is much easier to navigate, as well as there being foraging opportunities very close to camp and far more shade available to avoid dehydration. In contrast, for a Ju/'hoansi adult to achieve the same as a 5–10 year old Hadza child, they must travel 5.5–6 km in a landscape that is not only lacking in shade to avoid dehydration but also 'oddly featureless' (Blurton-Jones *et al.* 1994, 197) and thus difficult to navigate in. This difference in environment has important implications, with Hadza children able to explore, but Ju/'hoansi children more constrained to staying near to a camp. As well as biological constraints on mobility, and a cultural focus on the local, Neanderthal children may well have faced particular risks beyond those experienced by modern foragers or many Upper Palaeolithic populations. Significant risks to individuals, the young in particular, were posed by predation in the Pleistocene for example (Camarós *et al.* 2015). Such predation risks might have been particularly significant for Neanderthal children for whom smaller group sizes implied a reduced number of peers who might travel together. Only in the Upper Palaeolithic might childhood patterns of landscape exploration have become much safer through larger group sizes, projectile technology and later even the domestication of wolves (Shipman 2010; Morey 2010). The need to ensure that Neanderthal children felt and were safe from harm may have kept them relatively focused on landscapes close to camp, further reinforcing an intimate tie to place (Burke 2006), and in turn a marked cultural resilience to imposed ideas.

An understanding of modern ethnographically documented societies may not be directly applicable to any single Neanderthal context. However such insights do allow us to speculate that neither biology, ecology, nor culture alone but a mutually reinforcing relationship between these factors may have maintained a certain intimate and culturally resilient sociality to life as a Neanderthal.

Conclusions

Here we argue that the large scale social structure characteristic of modern foraging societies may not be applicable in its entirety to communities in Middle Palaeolithic Europe. Familiar features of a modern foraging adaptation such as extended networks of large scale social interactions, large scale exchanges of non-utilitarian items and regular aggregations of a 'macroband' may not be there to be found. Instead, a smaller scale, local sociality might have been more typical. Sociality on an intimate scale is no less sophisticated however, and the particular creativity and resilience which emerges in such situations, and is reflected in and through childhood experience, may help explain the notable local novelty seen in Neanderthal personal ornamentation and artistic expression.

The landscapes and peoples of the European Middle Palaeolithic might seem alien, but these communities were not *strangers*. They were societies and cultures responding to unusual constraints and opportunities in ways that nonetheless resonate with our understanding of adaptations in small scale societies. If we move beyond looking for modern foragers in the past to developing a more subtle understanding of how different experiences in modern ethnographically documented contexts influence sociality and culture, we can open up new insights in Middle Palaeolithic communities, and from this greater insights into hunter-gatherer diversity.

References

Akazawa, T., Muhesen, S., Ishida, H., Kondo, O. & Griggo, C. (1999) New discovery of a Neanderthal child burial from the Dederiyeh Cave in Syria. *Paléorient* 25, 129–142.

Blurton-Jones, N., Hawkes, K. & Draper, P. (1994) Differences between Hadza and !Kung children's work: affluence or practical reason? In E. S. Bursch Jr & L. J. Ellanna (eds), *Key Issues in Hunter-gatherer Research,* 189–215. Oxford, Berg.

Bouzouggar, A., Barton, N., Vanhaeren, M., d'Errico, F., Collcutt, S., Higham, T., Hodge, E., Parfitt, S., Rhodes, E., Schwenninger, J.-L., Stringer, C., Turner, E., Ward, S., Moutmir, A. & Stambouli, A. (2007) 82,000-year-old shell beads from North Africa and implications for the origins of modern human behavior. *Proceedings of the National Academy of Sciences* 104, 9964–9969.

Burdukiewicz, J. (2014) The origin of symbolic behavior of Middle Palaeolithic humans: Recent controversies. *Quaternary international* 326–327, 398–405.

Burke, A. (2006) Neanderthal settlement patterns in Crimea: A landscape approach. *Journal of Anthropological Archaeology* 25, 510–523.

Camarós, E., Cueto, C., Lorenzo, C., Villaverde, V., and Rivals, F. (2015) Large carnivore attacks on hominins during the Pleistocene: a forensic approach with a Neanderthal example. *Archaeological and Anthropological Sciences,* 1–12.

Caron, F., d'Errico, F., Del Moral, P., Santos, F. & Zilhão, J. (2011) The reality of Neandertal symbolic behavior at the Grotte du Renne, Arcy-sur-Cure, France. *PLoS one* 6, e21545.

Churchill, S. (2014) *Thin on the ground: Neandertal biology, archeology and ecology,* Oxford, Wiley.

Collard, M., Buchanan, B. & O'Brien, M. (2013) Population size as an explanation for patterns in the paleolithic archaeological record. *Current Anthropology* 54, S388–S396.

Conard, N., Bolus, M. & Münzel, S. (2012) Middle Paleolithic land use, spatial organization and settlement intensity in the Swabian Jura, southwestern Germany. *Quaternary International* 27, 236–245.

Delagnes, A. & Rendu, W. (2011) Shifts in Neandertal mobility, technology and subsistence strategies in western France. *Journal of Archaeological Science* 38, 1771–1783.

Delporte, H., 1976. Les sépultures moustériennes de La Ferrassie. In B. Vandermeersch, ed. *Les Sépultures Néanderthaliennes*, 8–11. Nice, Union Internationale des Sciences Préhistoriques et Protohistoriques IXe Congrès.

Demay, L., Péan, S. & Patou-Mathis, M. (2012) Mammoths used as food and building resources by Neanderthals: Zooarchaeological study applied to layer 4, Molodova I (Ukraine). *Quaternary International* 276–277, 212–226.

Djindjian, F. (2012) Is the MP-EUP transition also an economic and social revolution? *Quaternary International* 259, 72–77.

d'Errico, F., Henshilwood, C., Vanhaeren, M. & van Niekerk, K. (2005) Nassarius kraussianus shell beads from Blombos Cave: evidence for symbolic behaviour in the Middle Stone Age. *Journal of Human Evolution* 48, 3–24.

d'Errico, F., Backwell, L., Villa, P., Degano, I., Lucejko, J.J., Bamford, M.K., Higham, T.F.G., Colombini, M.P. & Beaumont, P.B. (2012) Early evidence of San material culture represented by organic artifacts from Border Cave, South Africa. *Proceedings of the National Academy of Sciences* 109, 13214–13219.

Farizy, C. (1994) Spatial Patterning of Middle Paleolithic Sites. *Journal of Anthropological Archaeology* 13, 153–160.

Féblot-Augustins, J. (2009) Revisiting European Upper Paleolithic raw material transfers: the demise of the cultural ecological paradigm? In B. Adams & B. S. Blades (eds), *Lithic Materials and Paleolithic Societies,* 25–46. Oxford, Wiley-Blackwell.

Fernandes, P., Raynal, J-P. & Moncel, M-H. (2008) Middle Palaeolithic raw material gathering territories and human mobility in the southern Massif Central, France: first results from a petro-archaeological study on flint. *Journal of Archaeological Science* 35, 2357–2370.

Fortier, J. (2009) *Kings of the Forest: the Cultural Resilience of Himalayan Hunter-gatherers*, Honolulu, University of Hawaii Press.

Froehle, A.W., Yokley, T. R. & Churchill, S. E. 2013. Energetics and the origin of modern humans. In F. H. Smith & J. C. M. Ahern (eds), *The Origins of Modern Humans: Biology Reconsidered*, 2nd edition, 285–320. Chichester, Wiley-Blackwell.

Gilbert, P. (2015) The evolution and social dynamics of compassion. *Social and Personality Psychology Compass* 9, 239–254.

Green, R. E., Krause, J., Briggs, A.W., Maricic, T., Stenzel, U., Kircher, M., Patterson, N., Li, H., Zhai, W., Fritz, M.H.-Y., Hansen, N.F., Durand, E.Y., Malaspinas, A.-S., Jensen, J.D., Marques-Bonet, T., Alkan, C., Prüfer, K., Meyer, M., Burbano, H.A. (2010) A draft sequence of the Neandertal genome. *Science* 328, 710–722.

Hackett, A. & Dennell, R. (2003) Neanderthals as fiction in archaeological narrative. *Antiquity* 77, 816–827.

Hayden, B. (2012) Neandertal social structure? *Oxford Journal of Archaeology* 31, 1–26.

Hazlewood, N. (2000) *Savage: the Life and Times of Jemmy Button*. New York: Thomas Dunne Books.

Henry, D.O., Hietala, H.J. & Rosen, A.M. (2004) Human behavioral organization in the Middle Paleolithic: were Neanderthals different? *American Anthropologist* 106, 17–31.

Hewlett, B., 2013. 'Ekeloko' the spirit to create: innovation and social learning among Aka adolescents of the central African rainforest. In T. Akazawa, Y. Nishiaki & K. Aoki (eds), *Dynamics of Learning in Neanderthals and Modern Humans Volume 1: Cultural Perspectives*, 187–195. Tokyo, Springer Japan.

Higgins, R. & Ruff, B. (2011) The effects of distal limb segment shortening on locomotor efficiency in sloped terrain: implications for Neandertal locomotor behavior. *American Journal of Physical Anthropology* 146, 336–345.

Hovers, E., Rak, Y., Lavi, R. & Kimbel, W.H. (1995) Hominid remains from Amud Cave in the context of the Levantine Middle Paleolithic. *Paléorient* 21, 47–61.

Hovers, E., Kimbel, W.H. & Rak, Y. (2000) The Amud 7 skeleton – still a burial. Response to Gargett. *Journal of Human Evolution* 39, 253–260.

Hublin, J. J. (2009) The origin of Neandertals. *Proceedings of the National Academy of Sciences* 106, 16022–16027.

Jaubert, J., Verheyden, S., Genty, D., Soulier, M., Cheng, H., Blamart, D., Burlet, C., Camus, H., Delaby, S., Deldicque, D., Lawrence Edwards, R., Ferrier, C., Lacrampe-Cuyaubère, F., Lévêque, F., Maksud, F., Mora, P., Muth, X., Régnier, É., Rouzaud, J.-N., (2016) Early Neanderthal constructions deep in Bruniquel Cave in southwestern France. Letter to *Nature*, published online May 25th 2016. Available at: http://dx.doi.org/10.1038/nature18291

Kelly, R. (2013) *The Lifeways of Hunter-gatherers: the Foraging Spectrum*. Cambridge, Cambridge University Press.

King, W. (1864) The reputed fossil man of the Neanderthal. *Quarterly Journal of Science, Literature, and the Arts* 1, 88–97.

Kuhn, S. (2012) Emergent patterns of creativity and innovation in early technologies. In S. Elias (ed.), *Origins of Human Innovation and Creativity*, 69–87. London, Elsevier.

Macaulay, K. (1764) *The History of St. Kilda*. London, printed for T. Becket and P. A. de Hondt, in the Strand.

Marwick, B. (2003) Pleistocene exchange networks as evidence for the evolution of language. *Cambridge Archaeological Journal* 13, 67–81.

McEwan, C., Borrero, L. A. & Prieto, A. (2014) *Patagonia: Natural History, Prehistory, and Ethnography at the Uttermost End of the Earth*. Princeton, Princeton University Press.

Meignen, L., Delagnes, A. & Bourguignon, L. 2009. Patterns of lithic material procurement and transformation during the Middle Paleolithic in Western Europe. In B. Adams & B. Blades (eds), *Lithic Materials and Paleolithic Societies*, 15–24. Chichester, Wiley-Blackwell.

Mellars, P. (1999) The Neanderthal problem continued. *Current Anthropology* 40, 341–364.

Mikulincer, M. & Shaver, P. (2010) *Attachment in Adulthood: Structure, Dynamics, and Change*. London, Guildford Press.

Morey, D. (2010). *Dogs: Domestication and the Development of a Social Bond*. Cambridge, Cambridge University Press.

Moser, S. (1992) The visual language of archaeology: a case study of the Neanderthals. *Antiquity* 66, 831–844.

O'Connell, J. (2006) How did modern humans displace Neanderthals? Insights from hunter-gatherer ethnography and archaeology. In N. Conard. (ed.), *When Neanderthals and Modern Humans Met*, 43–64. Tübingen, Kerns.

Otto, T. (2009) What happened to cargo cults? Material religions in Melanesia and the West. *Social Analysis* 53, 82–102.

Pearce, E. & Moutsiou, T. (2014) Using obsidian transfer distances to explore social network maintenance in late Pleistocene hunter-gatherers. *Journal of Anthropological Archaeology* 36, 12–20.

Peresani, M., Vanhaeren, M., Quaggiotto, E., Queffelec, A. & d'Errico, F. (2013) An ochered fossil marine shell from the Mousterian of Fumane Cave, Italy. *PloS one* 8, e68572.

Pettitt, P. (2013) *The Palaeolithic Origins of Human Burial*. London, Routledge.

Powell, A., Shennan, S. & Thomas, M. (2009) Late Pleistocene demography and the appearance of modern human behavior. *Science* 324, 1298–1301.

Prüfer, K., Racimo, F., Patterson, N., Jay, F., Sankararaman, S., Sawyer, S., Heinze, A., Renaud, G., Sudmant, P.H., de Filippo, C., Li, H., Mallick, S., Dannemann, M., Fu, Q., Kircher, M., Kuhlwilm, M., Lachmann, M., Meyer, M., Ongyerth, M. (2014) The complete genome sequence of a Neanderthal from the Altai Mountains. *Nature* 505, 43–49.

Radovčić, D.D., Sršen, A.O., Radovčić, J. & Frayer, D.W. (2015) Evidence for neandertal jewellery: modified white-tailed eagle claws at Krapina. *PloS one* 10, e0119802.

Raichlen, D., Armstrong, H. & Lieberman, D. (2011) Calcaneus length determines running economy: implications for endurance running performance in modern humans and Neandertals. *Journal of Human Evolution* 60, 299–308.

Richards, M., Harvati, K., Grimes, V., Smith, C., Smith, T., Hublin, J.-J., Karkanas, P. & Panagopoulou, E. (2008) Strontium isotope evidence of Neanderthal mobility at the site of Lakonis, Greece using laser-ablation PIMMS. *Journal of Archaeological Science* 35, 1251–1256.

Rodríguez-Vidal, J., d'Errico, F., Giles Pacheco, F., Blasco, R., Rosell, J., Jennings, R.P., Queffelec, A., Finlayson, G., Fa, D.A., Gutiérrez López, J.M., Carrión, J.S., Negro, J.J., Finlayson, S., Cáceres, L.M., Bernal, M.A., Fernández Jiménez, S. & Finlayson, C. (2014) A rock engraving made by Neanderthals in Gibraltar. *Proceedings of the National Academy of Sciences* 111, 13301–13306.

Roebroeks, W., Sier, M.J., Nielsen, T.K., De Loecker, D., Parés, J.M., Arps, C.E.S. & Mücher, H.J. (2012) Use of red ochre by early Neandertals. *Proceedings of the National Academy of Sciences* 109, 1889–1894.

Rosas, A. *et al.* (2006) Paleobiology and comparative morphology of a late Neandertal sample from El Sidron, Asturias, Spain. *Proceedings of the National Academy of Sciences* 103, 19266–19271.

Ruebens, K. (2013) Regional behaviour among late Neanderthal groups in Western Europe: a comparative assessment of late Middle Palaeolithic bifacial tool variability. *Journal of Human Evolution* 65, 341–362.

Sánchez-Quinto, F. & Lalueza-Fox, C. (2015) Almost 20 years of Neanderthal palaeogenetics: adaptation, admixture, diversity, demography and extinction. *Philosophical Transactions of the Royal Society of London. Series B, Biological Sciences* 370 (1660), 20130374.

Scott, B., Bates, M., Bates, R., Conneller, C., Pope, M., Shaw, A. & Smith, G. (2015) A new view from La Cotte de St Brelade, Jersey. *Antiquity* 88, 13–29.

Shipman, P. (2010) The Animal Connection and Human Evolution. *Current Anthropology* 51, 519–538.

Sistiaga, A., Mallol, C., Galván, B. & Summons, R.E. (2014) The Neanderthal meal: a new perspective using faecal biomarkers. *PloS one* 9, e101045.

Slimak, L. & Giraud, Y. (2007) Circulations sur plusieurs centaines de kilomètres durant le Paléolithique moyen. Contribution à la connaissance des sociétés néandertaliennes. *C. R. Palevol* 6, 359–368.

Smith, G. (2015) Neanderthal megafaunal exploitation in Western Europe and its dietary implications: a contextual reassessment of La Cotte de St Brelade (Jersey). *Journal of Human Evolution* 78, 181–201.

Spikins, P. (2015) *How Compassion Made Us Human: The Evolutionary Origins of Tenderness, Trust and Morality*, Barnsley, Pen and Sword.

Spikins, P., Hitchens, G., Needham, A. & Rutherford, H. (2014) The cradle of thought: growth, learning, play and attachment in Neanderthal children. *Oxford Journal of Archaeology* 33, 111–134.

Spikins, P., Rutherford, H. & Needham, A. (2010) From homininity to humanity: compassion from the earliest archaics to modern humans. *Time and Mind* 3, 303–325.

Spinapolice, E. (2012) Raw material economy in Salento (Apulia, Italy): new perspectives on Neanderthal mobility patterns. *Journal of Archaeological Science* 39, 680–689.

Stapert, D. (2007) Neanderthal children and their flints. *PalArch's Journal of Archaeology of Northwest Europe* 1, 16–39.

Sykes, R. M. W. (2012) Neanderthals 2.0? Evidence for expanded social networks, ethnic diversity and encultured landscapes in the Late Middle Palaeolithic. In K. Ruebens, I. Romanowska, & R. Bynoe (eds), *Unravelling the Palaeolithic - 10 Years of Research at the Centre for the Archaeology of Human Origins (CAHO, University of Southampton)*, 73–84. British Archaeological Report S2400. Oxford, Archaeopress.

Terashima, H. (2013) The evolutionary development of learning and teaching strategies in human societies. In T. Akazawa, Y. Nishiaki & K. Aoki (eds), *Dynamics of Learning in Neanderthals and Modern Humans: Volume 1, Cultural Perspectives,* 141–150. Tokyo, Springer Japan.

de los Terreros, J. & Gómez-Castanedo, A. (2014) Specialised hunting of Iberian ibex during Neanderthal occupation at El Esquilleu Cave, northern Spain. *Antiquity* 88, 1035–1049.

Tottenham, N. (2012) Human amygdala development in the absence of species-expected caregiving. *Developmental psychobiology* 54, 598–611.

Turnbull, C. (1961) *The Forest People: A Study of the Pygmies of the Congo.* New York, Simon & Schuster.

Van Reybrouck, D. (2002) Boule's error: on the social context of scientific knowledge. *Antiquity* 76, 158–164.

Verpoorte, A. (2006) Neanderthal energetics and spatial behaviour. *Before Farming* 2006(3), 1–6.

Wiessner, P. (2002) Taking the risk out of risky transactions: a forager's dilemma. In F. Salter (ed.), *Risky Transactions: Trust, Kinship, and Ethnicity,* 21–43. Oxford, Berghahn Books.

Zilhão, J. (2012) Personal ornaments and symbolism among the Neanderthals. *Developments in Quaternary Science* 16, 35–49.

Zilhão, J. (2014) The Neanderthals, evolution, palaeoecology and extinction. In V. Cummings, P. Jordan & M. Zvelebil (eds). *The Oxford Handbook of the Archaeology and Anthropology of Hunter-gatherers,* 191–213. Oxford, Oxford University Press.

Zilhão, J., Angelucci, D.E., Badal-García, E., d'Errico, F., Daniel, F., Dayet, L., Douka, K., Higham, T.F.G., Martínez-Sánchez, M.J., Montes-Bernárdez, R., Murcia-Mascarós, S., Pérez-Sirvent, C., Roldán-García, C., Vanhaeren, M., Villaverde, V., Wood, R. & Zapata, J. (2010) Symbolic use of marine shells and mineral pigments by Iberian Neandertals. *Proceedings of the National Academy of Sciences of the United States of America* 107, 1023–1028.

Chapter 10

Making the familiar past: northwest European hunter-gatherers, analogies and comparisons

Graeme Warren

Introduction

This paper focuses on the hunter-gatherers who (re)colonised north-western Europe after the Late Glacial Maximum (LGM, *c.* 15,000 cal BP, all dates presented in calendar years) and considers the role of analogies and comparisons in our constructions of their lives. Regional terminologies and chronologies proliferate for the groups under discussion, but they include archaeological cultures falling into the Late Glacial and early Holocene, or the Final/Terminal/Upper Palaeolithic and the Mesolithic periods, with agriculture, and the Neolithic, appearing in the area in the centuries surrounding 6000 cal BP (Bailey & Spikins 2008).

The aim of the paper is twofold. On the one hand, I will outline how scholars of this period and especially the Mesolithic are approaching the use of ethnographic analogies and comparative frameworks in constructing their narratives of the period. My argument will be that analogy has, perhaps surprisingly, dropped from explicit analytical consideration, and that as a consequence of this, there is a danger of assuming the timelessness and universality of some of our analytical categories, thus rendering the past in a very familiar sense and reducing our awareness of the diversity of hunter-gatherer lives. As a counterpoint to this, in the second half of the paper I will highlight some alternative facets of hunter-gatherer diversity as manifest in the archaeology of the Mesolithic. This will include consideration of the (re)colonisation of the area after the Late Glacial Maximum, and the meeting and interaction of different peoples and ideas throughout the Mesolithic. This sketch of the 'unfamiliar' Mesolithic is of necessity impressionistic. The intention here is not to argue that these developments are unique to the Mesolithic of Europe, but to suggest that they have received less attention than they perhaps deserve – especially at the level of synthesis. This in turn means that our overall understanding of the causes and character of diversity in hunter-gatherer behaviour is impoverished.

The epistemological nature of analogies and the ways in they draw upon specific criteria for success have been extensively debated (Wylie 1985). I do not wish to revisit these debates, and my use of the term analogy here is deliberately loose: including general comparative frameworks that have been developed from ethnographic fieldwork or comparative analysis as well as consideration of direct comparisons to specific ethnographically observed examples.

Familiar themes: analogy and the Mesolithic of Europe

The role of ethnographic analogy in constructing archaeological interpretations of hunter-gatherer lives during the Mesolithic in Europe has flickered in and out of explicit focus in British and European scholarship over the last 20 years (or broadly, since the development of a more avowedly interpretative archaeology of the period). Whilst analogy and ethnoarchaeology were discussed strongly in the early 2000s (Jordan 2003; Zvelebil 1997) this has become less common recently. For example, a seminar (in 2004) and subsequent publication (Conneller & Warren 2006) exploring 'New Approaches' to the Mesolithic in Britain and Ireland included an important contribution focusing entirely on analogy, arguing that 'a reliance on a narrow range of ethnographic analogies have brought us to the present impasse' (Jordan 2006, 99) and that careful and creative use of ethnography would be 'crucial' (100) to the development of Mesolithic studies. A follow up conference session was held 10 years later (TAG2014, Manchester), exploring how Mesolithic archaeology had developed since the 2004 meeting and publication. This did not include a specific contribution focusing on analogy, and analogy was rarely discussed – although frequently used. It is interesting to note that during this period the role of analogy in constructing models of Neolithic society saw significant debate, with critiques of the 'Pacification' of the European Neolithic including debates about the influence of global historical processes on the source side of the analogies (Roscoe 2009; Spriggs 2008).

In order to demonstrate these claims, I present two different analyses of two landmark Mesolithic publications. The 2005 meeting of the Mesolithic in Europe conference in Belfast was published in 2009 as *Mesolithic Horizons* (McCartan *et al.* 2009) and includes a range of short papers covering all aspects of Mesolithic research from across Europe. I am grateful to Oxbow Books for providing an electronic copy of *Mesolithic Horizons*, which has facilitated quantitative analyses. The second volume, *Mesolithic Europe* (Bailey & Spikins 2008), is a collection of papers summarising the Mesolithic in different parts of Europe with in depth reviews covering common themes. This has been analysed thematically.

Mesolithic Horizons was examined for frequency of use of key terms (Table 10.1). Using basic word counts is a fairly crude mechanism for assessing the significance of a concept, but it is interesting to note that *analogy/ies, analogous, analogues* are used a total of 33 times. By way of comparison, *phenomenology* was used 35 times. It is hard to avoid the conclusion that analogy is not really a central concern for Mesolithic

Table 10.1. Frequency of use of a selection of terms in Mesolithic Horizons (McCartan et al 2009)

total word count	564,271		
analogies	11	hazelnuts	110
analogous	7	hunter-gatherer	290
analogues	4	hunter-gatherers	271
analogy	11	lithic	731
anthropological	86	Mesolithic	4270
archaeology	789	microlith	33
Binford	82	microlithic	29
ethnoarchaeology	15	phenomenology	35
ethnographic	82	quartz	411
ethnographically	9	radiocarbon	397

Table 10.2. Frequency of use of analogy and related words in specific chapters of Mesolithic Horizons (McCartan et al 2009). Authors name on top row

	Bamforth	Carlsson	Cobb	Conneller	Domańska & Waş	Englestad (intro)	Englestad	Grimaldi	Hardy	Hardy et al	Little	Mansrud	Riede	Rizner	Schulting	Takala	Zvelebil	Total
analogous				2	1				1	1	1					*1*		7
analogues											3	1						4
analogy	5		*1*				1	*1*					1	1	1			11
analogies	2	4		1	2	1											1	11
Total	7	4	1	3	3	1	1	1	1	1	4	1	1	1	1	1	1	

scholarship. *Ethnoarchaeology* is used 15 times, which initially appears promising, but 14 of these uses are only in the references, mainly to Binford's *Nunamuit ethnoarchaeology* (Binford 1978). *Ethnoarchaeology* was also used once as a keyword, although ironically it was not present in the chapter that followed. Ethnographic/ally and anthropological are both used more frequently, which might suggest that analogies or comparisons are being used – but not explicitly and with a lack of epistemological clarity and rigour. It is interesting to note that Richard Bradley's acute observation from nearly 40 years ago that Mesolithic people have ecological relationships with hazelnuts rather than social relations with each other (Bradley 1978) is possibly offered further support by the fact that word *hazelnuts* is used more frequently than either ethnographic or anthropological.

The word analogy is used in 17 contributions to the volume (11.8% of the 144 papers), and is only used more than once in five chapters (3.4%) (Table 10.2). The most frequent and explicit use is by Bamforth, who offers an explicitly 'Americanist approach' to studying hunter-gatherer mobility, and does not at any stage discuss the European Mesolithic (Bamforth 2009). Carlsson (Carlsson 2009) uses analogies in general discussions of theory and to caution about uncritical use of analogies. Conneller (Conneller 2009) discusses analogous body parts in different species and analogies to other archaeological sites. Domańska and Waş (2009) use analogy/ies to describe relationships to other archaeological sites. Little (Little 2009) is critical of aspects of the use of ethnographic analogies and discusses analogues between modern and ancient fish behaviour.

The overwhelming impression from this analysis of *Mesolithic Horizons* is therefore that analogy is not a major subject of concern for Mesolithic researchers. Some warnings are given about the improper use of analogical reasoning, but for the vast majority of the papers analogy is not a major subject of critical reflection. Ethnoarchaeology is rarely discussed, but some insights from this are utilised. Notwithstanding this absence of discussion, analogies of different kinds, of course, continue to be used in the construction of interpretations, but not at a very explicit level.

Mesolithic Europe (Bailey & Spikins 2008) offers a further opportunity to assess the role analogy plays in building our narratives of the Mesolithic. An electronic version of the text was not available, so quantifications are not used in this analysis. Some papers are very narrowly focused and descriptive in characterising the archaeological evidence, but alongside definitions of site types and lithic typologies, most offer interpretations of subsistence, key social and historical processes etc. These broader discussions all rely on analogies to some extents. One of the most interesting aspects of the use of these comparative frameworks is the different level of support through references the authors provide for key concepts: put simply, some analogies appear to be accepted as received wisdom and therefore are not perceived to be in need of justification. Bonsall, for example, cites unspecified 'ethnographic studies' that show a connection between the treatment of the body and the status of the individual (Bonsall 2008, 259). Tolan-Smith states that 'the high status of boat owning and handling is well known among hunter-gatherers in the ethnographic record' (Tolan-Smith 2008, 152) also without reference. It is important to note that as these papers appear in edited volumes, it would appear that the editors (and referees) also shared the acceptance of these concepts without the need for detailed reference.

A more widespread example of this lies in the consideration of mobility strategies. The papers frequently use terms such as base-camp, residential camp, or hunting station. Whilst there is a common-sense aspect to these definitions, these uses are often combined with explicit consideration of the role of logistical or residential mobility with no explanation (e.g. Jochim 2008, 216; Pluciennik 2008, 340). These terms are clearly being treated as accepted wisdom and are not often supported by references. Binford's distinction between models of residential and logistical mobility (Binford 1980) have been hugely influential in hunter-gatherer archaeology, but are not unproblematic. As Binford recognised, idealised mobility systems would be difficult to identify archaeologically, given that most hunter-gatherer systems incorporated both strategies.

More problematically, many papers make reference to an accepted combination of evidence which is considered to indicate developing social complexity, often making links between particular classes of archaeological evidence and particular social characteristics. Bjerck, for example, discusses '... more residential stability, stronger regional ties, the establishment of socially defined territories, increased social complexity and probably social formations that may be labelled as ethnic groups' (Bjerck 2008, 105). Tolan-Smith suggests that the development of delayed-return systems led to social differentiation and population growth (Tolan-Smith 2008, 152). Bonsall suggests that it is 'thought by archaeologists' that cemeteries are associated with sedentism (Bonsall 2008, 258), and that sedentism and storage are prominent in ethnographic accounts of complexity (Bonsall 2008, 275). No references or explicit discussions of these analogies are provided. There is some irony that Spikins' introduction to the volume argues that '(a)cross Mesolithic Europe the relationship among "delayed return" economies, "complexity" discernible in evidence of increased sedentism, exchange relationships, and defined stratification in burial *is often unclear*' (Spikins 2008, 9, my emphasis) – as the assumptions that these are linked drive many of the accounts that follow. It is important to be clear here – the recognition of 'complex' or 'transegalitarian' foragers has been a very significant development in our understanding of hunter-gatherer diversity. But using these concepts without critique or consideration runs a very real risk of imposing a particular model onto the past reality. Sassaman, for example, argues that '... the archaeological record will be rife with examples of non-egalitarian hunter-gatherers, potentially including organisation forms with no known ethnographic parallel' (Sassaman 2004, 265). In a rare attempt to critique the general models of the Mesolithic, Zvelebil's contribution to *Mesolithic Europe* argues that many of the archaeologically observed cultures in northern Europe are actually *more* hierarchical than those observed by ethnography (Zvelebil 2008, 41).

Outside of Europe, many accounts are increasingly focusing on the *emergence* of complexity amongst hunter-gatherer groups and the need to understand social variation and specific historical trajectories rather than general processes in order to account for this (Sassaman 2004; Arnold 1996; Moss 2011; Prentiss 2011). It is also important to note that it has been demonstrated that we cannot assume that simple or egalitarian hunter-gatherers are the origin point from which complexity develops (Moss 2011, 29; Sassaman 2004, 238). Different factors are seen as being significant in the development of different trajectories of emergent complexity, including the importance of households, storage, surplus as well as productive environments. Few of these factors have been demonstrated to be significant in the archaeology of Mesolithic Europe, where discussions focus more on using a small number of material signifiers for the presence of complex hunter-gatherers, rather than specific trajectories that led to the emergence or decline of complexity or inequality. Given the variation within the Mesolithic record outlined above, this imposition of a simplistic so-called 'type' of hunter-gatherer behaviour is clearly problematic in terms of understanding potential hunter-gatherer diversity.

Returning to *Mesolithic Europe,* analogy is considered more explicitly where the argument being made does not have the status of received or accepted wisdom. Some of these analogies are specific links, and are backed up by specific references to particular studies: this includes Jochim's use of comparative ethnographic perspectives on late weaning of hunter-gatherer children in a group with a highly carnivorous diet (Jochim 2008, 209), Bonsall's (Bonsall 2008, 260) use of Binford and Kelly's arguments that plant use is likely among hunter-gatherers in temperate environments, and Pluciennik's comparative perspectives on demography and kinship (Pluciennik 2008, 352, 354). Such explicit discussions include clear recognition of the dangers of analogies: Jochim, for example, is critical of any reliance on ethnographic analogies to interpret exchange/mobility in the past because of the highly varied character of ethnographic information on exchange and mobility (Jochim 2008, 216).

Analogies are discussed most explicitly when a new model or approach is being introduced as a subject for archaeological attention. There are two main examples of this in *Mesolithic Europe.* Firstly Spikins introduces a wide variety of ethnographically and comparatively grounded 'social-psychological' perspectives on the interplay of prestige and dominance in hunter-gatherer contexts as a way of understanding 'prestige-based' social dynamics in Mesolithic society (Spikins 2008, 15). There is, at times, a slight deference to the ethnographic material here, when she suggests that '(n)aturally, ethnographic evidence may provide the main source for suggestions as to how material culture may reflect societies governed by prestige' especially as societies based on prestige are considered unlikely to mark this in material forms. But the approach highlights new potentials for archaeological analysis of social relationships in prehistory.

The most explicit discussions of analogy, however, surround the argument that hunter-gatherer 'belief', 'cosmology' or 'ideology' is a subject for archaeological analysis. Spikins (Spikins 2008, 11) argues that analogies and ethnography place belief and cosmology 'at heart' of understanding hunter-gatherers (this is not borne out in most of the chapters that follow). Zvelebil (Zvelebil 2008) provides a compelling argument for the centrality of worldviews in structuring the archaeological record of hunter-gatherers and the significance of analogy in understanding this. This contribution is by far the most substantial consideration of the basis of, and role of, analogy in archaeological reasoning in *Mesolithic Europe.* These themes, of course, are not unique to the Mesolithic of Europe, with a wide range of scholarship stressing the importance of considering the thoughts and practices of past hunter-gatherers, not simply their so-called adaptation to particular environments (Sassaman & Holly 2011a; Cannon 2011).

Analogy, it appears, has not gone away, but is not always being used explicitly. It is not a subject of much critical reflection by scholars of the Mesolithic in Europe, but remains vital to much of our work, especially as soon as we move beyond description of archaeological materials. Analogy and perspectives from ethnography are being used explicitly to argue for the identification of new subjects of archaeological enquiry.

At the same time, and more problematically, some comparative frameworks which are based on analogies appear to have obtained the status of received wisdom in Mesolithic scholarship. I do not mean to be dismissive of these hard-won understandings about forms of hunter-gatherer social organisation and adaptation, and there is clearly merit in understanding the hunter-gatherer settlement of Europe in such terms. But this is potentially problematic if we are to understand the diversity of hunter-gatherer behaviour across space and time as there is some risk that the familiar dominates, especially where data sets are often thin and overarching models sometimes based on comparatively weak foundations. General rules are good, but we must beware the potential dangers of doing 'ethnography with a shovel' (Wobst 1978, 303). As Binford observed long ago (Binford 1967), one of the aims of using analogies and making comparisons is to provoke new questions about the nature of the order and structure of the archaeological record of past human activity when the analogies don't seem to work. Rejecting, or being cautious, about familiar generalisations does not mean claiming that the Mesolithic of Europe was unique, but there is some value in highlighting the less familiar aspects of the period.

Unfamiliar worlds

Arguing that Mesolithic scholarship has been somewhat beholden to familiar models of hunter-gatherer organisation and behaviour is straightforward. Identifying and developing convincing models of Mesolithic Europe that are not as familiar, whilst remaining suitably grounded in well justified and epistemologically rigorous analogies is far less easy. These discussions do not pretend to be exhaustive, but will highlight some features of the period that may be of broader interest and are perhaps not receiving the attention they might. Focusing on what may be distinctive features is not to suggest that these are necessarily the most characteristic of the period, but simply to argue that particular forms of practice were present at this time and place, and that these may be of wider interest to students of hunter-gatherer behaviour. In this sense, focusing on the distinctive emphasizes the historically contingent (Sassaman & Holly 2011b). Some of the distinctive aspects of the Mesolithic in Europe are patterns seen across the long term temporally and large scale spatially. As such, their relationship to general theories of hunter-gatherer behaviour founded on ethnographic observations based on shorter periods of time is problematic (Bailey 2007, 2008; Murray 2008). Put simply, the forms of behaviour that have archaeological visibility at a temporal scale of millennia may not be the same as the forms of behaviour that have ethnographic visibility.

My first example here focuses on the timing and character of the (re)colonisation of Northern Europe following the LGM. This can be understood in a number of ways. The expansion of small groups of hunter-gatherers into northern latitudes is clearly related to climate and environmental changes, and can be seen exemplifying human reactions to such changes at different scales. These expansions can be rapid, as for example with the movement of Creswellian/Late Magdalenian groups into central England *c.* 14,600 cal BP (Jacobi & Higham 2011). This was part of a broader and longer term European process of spread from population refugia in southern Europe which happened near synchronously across Northern Europe, but can also be seen as a very sudden reaction to climate amelioration. Notably, the radiocarbon evidence places the movement of people into at least two regions of England *before* climate amelioration at the onset of the Bølling interstadial (GI-1) is identified in the GISP-2 core in Greenland (Jacobi & Higham 2011, 243). Climate change at this time is considered to be time transgressive, with warming in Europe earlier than in Greenland, but the expansion of hunter-gatherer settlement is clearly rapid.

More broadly, approaches to colonisation have often seen rapid human movement into new areas as a key facet of humanity – a universal human drive for exploration, and the speed of colonisation at a global level is often considered significant. It is interesting to note that the belief in the 'opportunism' of hunting and gathering communities at this time has sometimes been called into question: McCannon for example reverses some aspects of our narratives, suggesting that the climate change of this period forced movements of people who followed their habitats as these ecosystems moved northwards, rather than providing opportunities:

> 'Some were crowded out of more desireable ecozones by accelerating population growth. Others had their skills and folkways rendered obsolete by changes to their habitat. Many were refugees, fleeing environmental shocks and stresses.' (McCannon 2012, 40)

It is well-recognised that very few ethnographic parallels exist for the processes involved in colonisation at this scale. Meltzer, for example, reviewing the North American situation suggests that 'the process of hunter-gatherers learning a wholly new landscape has rarely, if ever, been recorded' (Meltzer 2009, 211). A variety of archaeological approaches have been developed, with mutually incompatible terminology, but often stressing the very low, or very different, archaeological visibility of pioneering groups or small-scale exploration in comparison to more substantial forms of settlement. The very low visibility of evidence for colonisation is especially significant given the very large scale of landscape change in Northern Europe and the difficulty of identifying early shorelines in particular (Warren 2014). Taken at face value, however the European data combines evidence of rapid responses to climate change and delays before the movement into new environments. These in turn provide some broader perspectives on learning new landscapes.

In western and northern Norway, for example, a rich maritime landscape was available for settlement for some 1000 years, and had human populations living in close proximity to it, before a rapid, and almost synchronous development of settlement across the area *c.* 11,500 cal BP (Bjerck 1995; 2009). This delay in settlement is often considered as a consequence of the delayed timing of development of the technological system of skin boats that facilitated the exploitation of these rich, but difficult to access ecosystems. Indeed, Bjerck argues that the preservation of shore lines of this period in Northern Scandinavia is unusual, and therefore the study of this period provides a very rare opportunity to examine 'the roots of specialised, marine adaptations' amongst hunter-gatherers (Bjerck 2008, 85). There is also a delay in settlement of large islands such as Ireland, which has no evidence of substantial activity until *c.* 10,000 cal BP, long after settlement was established in Britain, and long after advanced marine technologies were developed elsewhere in Europe. In this case, the delay is not considered to relate to technological processes – the sea crossings are short – and the lag in colonisation is ascribed to generalisations about common delays in humans occupying large islands combined with an assumption that the absence of most large mammals from the Irish fauna, including red deer, aurochs and probably wild boar, meant that it was not attractive for early settlement (Woodman 2003).

Such approaches downplay key aspects of human behaviour and important features of the archaeological record. Woodman, for example, suggests that 'colonisation is not an automatic process, as it requires a combination of climate and environment as well as the appropriate technology' (Woodman 2009, 2). These factors are of course important, but there is also a critical need to consider human motivation (Finlayson 1999) and colonisation must be understood in the context of particular histories of hunter-gatherer individuals and communities making decisions about the best course of action in uncertain worlds. Hunter-gatherer worlds were constituted by human and non-human agencies, and, at the risk of some simplification, it seems that large game played a key subsistence and symbolic role for many terrestrial hunter-gatherers of the Late Glacial/early Holocene period. In a Scandinavian context, for example, Fuglestvedt suggests that reindeer 'played a central role not only in terms of subsistence, but also in the Late Upper Palaeolithic and Early Mesolithic pantheon of spirits' (Fuglestvedt 2011, 38). In this sense, Fuglestvedt suggests that the movement of human groups North was an attempt to maintain this key relationship as the animals themselves moved north. This is seen not just as a technological or environmental decision, but as having 'existential value' (Fuglestvedt 2012, 21). Bjerck's discussion of the lag between the availability of marine resources and the development of suitable technology also highlights issues of belief and practice, stressing that there was an ontological challenge to developing such a new way of life and that '(t)his may have been a threshold that the Late Glacial hunters lacked the motivation to cross' (Bjerck 2008, 86). Returning to the case of Ireland, it may be that the absence of large game from the island was a deterrent to colonisation not so-much because of an absence of suitable alternative resources, but because an island without key animals was not imaginable as an appropriate location for human settlement (Warren 2017).

The northern European situation in the Late Glacial provides valuable perspectives on the role of world-view, belief and agency in structuring hunter-gatherer colonisation of 'new' landscapes. This suggests that we must beware any technological or environmental determinism in this context, where the Late Glacial hunter-gatherers provide valuable alternative perspectives on hunter-gatherer behaviour and diversity.

The other 'unfamiliar' aspect of the European Mesolithic I want to highlight is meetings between hunter-gatherers and other groups of people, as a long-term and pervasive characteristic of the period. The Mesolithic period sees evidence of meetings of different hunting and gathering groups and the outcome of long processes of interaction between them. This includes different groups who meet during the colonisation of empty landscapes, for example, the colonisation of northern Scandinavia sees the meeting of traditions from the Atlantic coast and from the East with different technical traditions and subsistence strategies. The 'conical core pressure blade' concept appears to have arrived from eastern Europe, associated with hunter-gatherer groups adapted to the exploitation of elk and beaver in taiga landscapes (Blankholm 2009; Sørensen *et al.* 2013). In northern Scandinavia this tradition comes into contact with settlers moving up the north Atlantic coasts 'deriving from the European western final Palaeolithic tradition (who) seem to have had a maritime focus, employing boats in their migrations' (Sørensen *et al.* 2013, 28). These communities appear to have had very different mobility and subsistence strategies. Although less frequently commented on, it is likely that these groups were also arriving from different European refugia after the LGM and might therefore have had different genetic and linguistic backgrounds.

These meetings of traditions and ideas – and presumably different groups of people – happen at large scales throughout the Mesolithic, not just at its outset. For example, the general European shift in a 'trapeze' projectile point technology and blade production (in French typologies, from the Première to Seconde Mésolithique) took place over many centuries (from *c.* 9000–7300 cal BP) and spread from the Mediterranean to Northern Europe (Marchand 2014; Perrin *et al.* 2009). Perrin and colleagues highlight that we are seeing 'mainly the "stone" expression of a major historical phenomenon affecting the European continent' (Perrin *et al.* 2009, 178) but commentators are still unclear about the origins of the new technologies and whether their spread indicates population change (including possible genetic and linguistic change), social or economic change, or technology and/or knowledge transfer. Importantly, some areas of Europe such as Britain and Ireland are in contact with these new traditions of behaviour, but choose not to accept them whilst adopting other European practices instead (Warren 2015; Elliott 2015): the nature of these interactions between hunter-gatherer groups is varied across time and space.

Many scholars have commented on the significance of contact between different groups at the end of the Mesolithic in Europe – that is to say on the meetings of hunter-gatherers and farmers and the need to generate ethnographic frameworks for understanding such interactions (Lane 2014, 139). But the same dynamic in solely Mesolithic hunter-gatherer contexts has received much less attention. This is unfortunate, partly because it makes our analysis of the process of hunter-gatherer/farmer interaction problematic by casting it as something new and different from on-going processes within hunting and gathering societies. Our neglect of these processes, and the replacement of these narratives with generalised accounts of particular kinds of hunter-gatherers and their supposed response to environmental changes, renders hunter-gatherers of the Mesolithic static until contact with farmers. Given the level of variation within the European Mesolithic, it is also important to note that contact between hunting and gathering communities could also mean contact between communities with very different social and economic structures: at the risk of using generalised terminology, between egalitarian and non-egalitarian groups. Indeed, Burch has argued that theorists have 'failed to address' the question of how 'world-systems' operated in a world populated entirely by hunter-gatherers (Burch 2005, 2).

More importantly, the long term relationship between cultural, genetic and linguistic transmission cannot be documented ethnographically and has been underexplored in European hunter-gatherer archaeology, although not in other areas (Pitblado 2011). There is great potential for this data set to inform us about long-term interaction and trajectories of change. This is important for a number of reasons. The increasing use of ancient DNA as evidence for the movement of peoples in the Mesolithic (Olalde *et al.* 2014; Skoglund *et al.* 2014) raises significant challenges for our understanding of the relationship between genetic and archaeological inheritance especially as there remains a tendency to consider hunter-gatherer social worlds as static and unchanging, thus facilitating the use of small sample sizes to make large claims about historical process. Emphasising the historical variability of hunter-gatherers is significant in this regard. It is important to note, for example, that claims that Stone Age hunting and gathering communities had low genetic diversity and lived at low population densities (Skoglund *et al.* 2014) is at some odds with aspects of the archaeological interpretations. Evidence from linguistics is less frequently included in discussion of the European Mesolithic, although claims have been made about the role of post Ice Age colonisers in spreading particular language groups (Vennemann 1994; Baldi & Page 2006). Increased attention to the interplay of cultural, genetic and linguistic transmission amongst hunter-gatherers is an important, and challenging, area for future research. As noted above, understanding the relationships between the different kinds of data is critical here: the DNA of a Mesolithic individual tells us important things about the ancestry of that individual, things that the style of stone tools they used do not. But the stone tools tell us things that the DNA does not. This is not to say that one form of data is better than the other. Simply that they are different.

Finally in this regard, it is important to note that some overviews are pessimistic about the history of human interaction with other human groups, with Fernández-Armesto, for example, commenting on 'people's inability to conceive of strangers in the same terms as themselves' (Fernández-Armesto 2015, 47). Without downplaying the evidence for conflict and violence within hunter-gatherer Europe (Roksandic 2004), the provision of longer-term perspectives on the ways in which these meetings of new people and new ideas develop into different social and cultural forms over archaeological time scales is an important contribution for the wider field of hunter-gatherer studies.

Discussion

> 'In an imperfect world, such analogies are sometimes the best available – although in many cases their proponents could do more to highlight their limitations rather than just their applications.' (Lane 2014, 138)

In this paper, I have argued that the study of the north European Mesolithic, in common with many regional histories of hunter-gatherers, has relied on a comparatively small number of significant generalisations about hunter-gatherer behaviour. These models have been very influential, but at times are not widely questioned or explicitly acknowleged. They are part of a shared intellectual heritage, a pedagogical and research tradition that most scholars of the Mesolithic have developed their thought within. They have been valuable, and have generated significant knowledge. At the same time, their very familiarity means that we are often less than clear about the epistemological basis of these analogies and explicit questioning of the fit of the data to the model is comparatively rare. As such, we account for the past in rather familiar terms. This is potentially problematic on a number of levels, not least our overall understanding of hunter-gatherer diversity.

In contrast to these models, my acounts of the history of the post Late Glacial Maximum hunter-gatherer settlement of northern Europe, highlight a number of themes which are less clear in the general literature, and for which our general models are somewhat underdeveloped. Aspects of the recolonisation of the region and the meeting of different groups have been highlighted here. My contention is that these less-familiar aspects of hunter-gatherer behaviour in this region are of some potential in our attempts to understand hunter-gatherer diversity at a global scale. Developing mechanisms for dealing with these problems will raise important issues about the integration of different types of data and their ability to contribute to key questions about hunter-gatherer diversity.

Acknowledgements

My thanks to participants in the CHAGS session for discussion and questions. I would like to thank Julie Gardiner for facilitating access to an electronic copy of *Mesolithic Horizons*. I am grateful to Bill Finlayson for helpful comments on an earlier draft of this paper, and for ongoing discussions about analogies and comparisons. Any errors of fact or interpretation are my responsibility.

References

Arnold, J. E. (1996) The archaeology of complex hunter-gatherers. *Journal of Archaeological Method and Theory* 3, 77–126.

Bailey, G. (2007) Time perspectives, palimpsests and the archaeology of time. *Journal of Anthropological Archaeology* 26, 198–223.

Bailey, G. (2008) Time perspectivism: origins and consequences. In S. Holdaway & L. Wandsnider (eds), *Time in Archaeology: Time Perspectivism Revisited*, 13–30. Salt Lake City, University of Utah Press.

Bailey, G. & Spikins, P. (eds) (2008) *Mesolithic Europe*. Cambridge, Cambridge University Press.

Baldi P. & Page, B. R. (2006) Europa Vasconica-Europa Semitica: Theo Vennemann, Gen. Nierfeld. In: Patrizia Noel Aziz Hanna (ed.), Trends in Linguistics, Studies and Monographs 138, Mouton de Gruyter, Berlin, 2003, pp. xxii + 977 (Review Article). *Lingua* 116: 2183–2220.

Bamforth, D. B. (2009) Top-down or bottom-up?: Americanist approaches to the study of hunter-gatherer mobility. In S. McCartan, R. Schulting, G. Warren & P. Woodman (eds), *Mesolithic Horizons: Papers presented at the Seventh International Conference on the Mesolithic in Europe, Belfast 2005*, 80–89. Oxford, Oxbow Books.

Binford, L. (1980) Willow smoke and dog's tails: hunter-gatherer settlement systems and archaeological site formation. *American Antiquity* 45, 4–20.

Binford, L. R. (1967) Smudge pits and hide smoking: the use of analogy in archaeological reasoning. *American Antiquity* 32, 1–12.

Binford, L. R. (1978) *Nunamiut Ethnoarchaeology*. London, Academic Press.

Bjerck, H. B. (1995) The North Sea continent and the pioneer settlement of Norway. In A. Fischer (ed.), *Man and Sea in the Mesolithic: Coastal Settlement Above and Below Present Sea Level*. 131–144. Oxford, Oxbow Books.

Bjerck, H. B. (2008) Norwegian Mesolithic trends: a review. In G. Bailey & P. Spikins (eds), *Mesolithic Europe*, 60–106. Cambridge, Cambridge University Press.

Bjerck, H. B. (2009) Colonizing seascapes: comparative perspectives on the development of maritime relations in Scandinavia and Patagonia. *Arctic Anthropology* 46, 118–131.

Blankholm, H. P. (2009) *Målsnes 1: an Early Post-Glacial Coastal Site in Northern Norway*. Oxford, Oxbow Books.

Bonsall, C. (2008) The Mesolithic of the Iron Gates. In G. Bailey & P. Spikins (eds), *Mesolithic Europe*, 238–279. Cambridge, Cambridge University Press.

Bradley, R. (1978) *The Prehistoric Settlement of Britain*. London, Routledge.

Burch, E. S. Jr (2005) *Alliance and Conflict: the World System of the Iñupiaq Eskimos*. London, University of Nebraska Press.

Cannon, A. (ed.) (2011) *Structured Worlds: The Archaeology of Hunter-Gatherer Thought and Action*. Sheffield, Equinox Publishing.

Carlsson, T. (2009) Two houses and 186,000 artefacts. Spatial organization at the Late Mesolithic site of Strandvägen, Sweden. In S. McCartan R. Schulting, G. Warren & P. Woodman (eds), *Mesolithic Horizons: Papers presented at the Seventh International Conference on the Mesolithic in Europe, Belfast 2005*, 430–435. Oxford, Oxbow Books.

Conneller, C. (2009) Transforming bodies: mortuary practices in Mesolithic Britain. In S. McCartan R. Schulting, G. Warren & P. Woodman (eds), *Mesolithic Horizons: Papers presented at the Seventh International Conference on the Mesolithic in Europe, Belfast 2005*, 690–697. Oxford, Oxbow Books.

Conneller, C. & Warren, G. M. (eds) (2006) *Mesolithic Britain and Ireland: New Approaches*. Stroud, Tempus.

Domańska, L. & Wąs, M. (2009) Dąprowa Bikupia 71: a specialised camp from the Maglemose culture. In S. McCartan R. Schulting, G. Warren & P. Woodman (eds), *Mesolithic Horizons: Papers presented at the Seventh International Conference on the Mesolithic in Europe, Belfast 2005*, 261–269. Oxford, Oxbow Books.

Elliott, B. (2015) Facing the chop: Redefining British antler mattocks to consider larger-scale maritime networks in the early fifth millennium cal BC. *European Journal of Archaeology* 18, 222–244.

Fernández-Armesto, F. (2015) *A Foot in the River: Why Our Lives Change and the Limits of Evolution*. Oxford, Oxford University Press.

Finlayson, B. (1999) Understanding the initial colonisation of Scotland. *Antiquity* 73, 879–883.

Fuglestvedt, I. (2011) Humans, material culture and landscape: outline to an understanding of developments in worldviews on the Scandinavia Peninsula, ca. 10,000–4500 BP. In A. Cannon (ed.), *Structured Worlds: The Archaeology of Hunter-Gatherer Thought and Action*, 32–53. Sheffield, Equinox Publishing.

Fuglestvedt, I. (2012) The pioneer condition on the Scandinavian Peninsula: the last frontier of a 'Palaeolithic Way' in Europe. *Norwegian Archaeological Review* 45, 1–29.

Jacobi, R. & Higham, T. (2011) The Later Upper Palaeolithic recolonisation of Britain: new results from AMS Radiocarbon Dating. In N. Ashton, S. G. Lewis & C. Stringer (eds), *Developments in Quaternary Sciences* 14, 223–247. http://www.sciencedirect.com/science/bookseries/15710866/14.

Jochim, M. A. (2008) The Mesolithic of the Upper Danube and Upper Rhine. In G. Bailey & P. Spikins (eds) *Mesolithic Europe*, 203–220. Cambridge, Cambridge University Press.

Jordan, P. (2003) *Material Culture and Sacred Landscape: the Anthropology of the Siberian Khanty*. London, Alta Mira.

Jordan, P. (2006) Analogy. In C. Conneller & G.M. Warren (eds), *Mesolithic Britain and Ireland: New Approaches*, 83–100. Stroud, Tempus.

Lane, P. J. (2014) Hunter-gatherer-fishers, ethnoarchaeology and analogical reasoning. In V. Cummings, P. Jordan & M. Zvelebil (eds) *The Oxford Handbook of the Archaeology and Anthropology of Hunter-gatherers*, 104–150. Oxford, Oxford University Press.

Little, A. (2009) Fishy settlement patterns and their social significance: a case study from the northern midlands of Ireland. In S. McCartan R. Schulting, G. Warren & P. Woodman (eds), *Mesolithic Horizons: Papers presented at the Seventh International Conference on the Mesolithic in Europe, Belfast 2005*, 698–705. Oxford, Oxbow Books.

Marchand, G. (2014) Beyond the technological distinction between the Early and Late Mesolithic. In A. Henry, B. Marquebielle, L. Chesnaux, L. & S. Michel (eds) *Techniques and Territories: New Insights into Mesolithic Cultures, Proceedings of the Round table, November 22-23 2012, Maison de la recherche, Toulouse (France)*, Vol. 6, 9–22. Palethnology. Toulouse, Palethnologie association.

McCannon, J. (2012) *A History of the Arctic: Nature, Exploration and Exploitation*. London, Reaktion.

McCartan, S., Schulting, R., Warren, G. & Woodman, P. (eds) (2009) *Mesolithic Horizons: Papers presented at the Seventh International Conference on the Mesolithic in Europe, Belfast 2005*. Oxford, Oxbow Books.

Meltzer, D. J. (2009) *First Peoples in a New World: Colonizing Ice Age America*. London, University of California Press.

Moss, M. L. (2011) *Northwest Coast: Archaeology as Deep History*. Washington DC, Society for American Archaeology.

Murray, T. (2008) Paradigms and metaphysics, or 'Is this the end of archaeology as we know it?'. In S. Holdaway & L. Wandsnider (eds), *Time in Archaeology: Time Perspectivism Revisited*, 170–180. Salt Lake City, University of Utah Press.

Olalde, I., Allentoft, M. E., Sanchez-Quinto, F., Santpere, G., Chiang, C. W. K., DeGiorgio, M., Prado-Martinez, J., Rodriguez, J. A., Rasmussen, S., Quilez, J., Ramirez, O., Marigorta, U. M., Fernandez-Callejo, M., Prada, M. E., Encinas, J. M. V., Nielsen, R., Netea, M. G., Novembre, J., Sturm, R. A., Sabeti, P., Marques-Bonet, T., Navarro, A., Willerslev, E. & Lalueza-Fox, C. (2014) Derived immune and ancestral pigmentation alleles in a 7,000-year-old Mesolithic European. *Nature* 507, 225–228.

Perrin, T., Marchand, G., Allard, P., Binder, D., Collina, C., Garcia-Puchol, O. & Valdeyron, N (2009) Le second Mésolithique d'Europe occidentale: origine et gradient chronologique (the late Mesolithic of Western Europe: origins and chronological stages). *Annales de la Fondation Fyssen* 24, 160–177.

Pitblado, B. (2011) A tale of two migrations: reconciling recent biological and archaeological evidence for the Pleistocene peopling of the Americas. *Journal of Archaeological Research* 19, 327–375.

Pluciennik, M. (2008) The coastal Mesolithic of the European Mediterranean. In G. Bailey & P. Spikins (eds), *Mesolithic Europe*, 328–356. Cambridge, Cambridge University Press.

Prentiss, A. M. (2011) Social histories of complex hunter-gatherers: Pacific Northwest prehistory in a macroevolutionary framework. In K. E. Sassaman & D. H. Holly (eds), *Hunter-Gatherer Archaeology as Historical Process*, 19–33. Tucson, University of Arizona Press.

Roksandic, M. (ed.) (2004) *Violent Interactions in the Mesolithic*. British Archaeological Report S1237. Oxford, Archaeopress.

Roscoe, P. (2009) On the 'pacification' of the European Neolithic: ethnographic analogy and the neglect of history. *World Archaeology* 41, 578–588.

Sassaman, K. E. (2004) Complex hunter–gatherers in evolution and history: a North American perspective. *Journal of Archaeological Research* 12, 227–280.

Sassaman, K. E. & Holly, D. H. (eds) (2011a) *Hunter-Gatherer Archaeology as Historical Process*. Tucson, University of Arizona Press.

Sassaman, K. E. & Holly D. H. (2011b) Transformative hunter-gatherer archaeology in North America. In K. E. Sassaman & D. H. Holly (eds) *Hunter-Gatherer Archaeology as Historical Process*, 1–13. Tucson, University of Arizona Press.

Skoglund, P., Malmström, H., Omrak, A., Raghavan, M., Valdiosera, C., Günther, T., Hall, P., Tambets, K., Parik, J., Sjögren, K., Apel, J., Willerslev, E., Storå, J., Götherström, A. & Jakobsson, M. (2014) Genomic diversity and admixture differs for stone-age Scandinavian foragers and farmers. *Science* 344, 747–750.

Sørensen, M., Rankama, T., Kankaanpää, J., Knutsson, K., Knutsson, H., Melvold, S., Eriksen, B. V. & Glørstad, H. (2013) The first eastern migrations of people and knowledge into Scandinavia: evidence from studies of Mesolithic technology, 9th–8th millennium BC. *Norwegian Archaeological Review* 46, 1–38.

Spikins, P. (2008) Mesolithic Europe: glimpses of another world. In G. Bailey & P. Spikins (eds), *Mesolithic Europe*, 1–17. Cambridge, Cambridge University Press.

Spriggs, M. (2008) Ethnographic parallels and the denial of history. *World Archaeology* 40, 538–552.

Tolan-Smith, C. (2008) Mesolithic Britain. In G. Bailey & P. Spikins (eds), *Mesolithic Europe*, 132–157. Cambridge, Cambridge University Press.

Vennemann, T. (1994) Linguistic reconstruction in the context of European prehistory. *Transactions of the Philological Society* 92, 215–284.

Warren, G. M. (2014) Transformations? The Mesolithic of north-west Europe. In V. Cummings, P. Jordan & M. Zvelebil (eds) *The Oxford Handbook of the Archaeology and Anthropology of Hunter-gatherers*, 537–555. Oxford, Oxford University Press. DOI: 10.1093/oxfordhb/9780199551224.013.060

Warren, G. M. (2015) Britain and Ireland inside Mesolithic Europe. In H. Anderson-Whymark, D. Garrow & F. Sturt (eds), *Continental Connections: Exploring Cross-Channel Relationships from the Mesolithic to the Iron Age*, 43–58. Oxford, Oxbow Books.

Warren, G. M. (2017) The Human Colonisation of Ireland in Northwest European Context. In P. Coxon, S. McCarron, & F. Mitchell (eds), *Advances in Irish Quaternary Studies* 293–316. Paris, Atlantis Press.

Wobst, H. M. (1978) The archaeo-ethnology of hunter-gatherers or the tyranny of the ethnographic record in archaeology. *American Antiquity* 43, 303–309.

Woodman, P. C. (2003) Colonising the edge of Europe: Ireland as a case study. In L. Larsson, H. Kindgren, K. Knulsson, D. Loeffler & A. Akerlund (eds), *Mesolithic on the Move*, 57–61. Oxford, Oxbow Books.

Woodman, P. C. (2009) Introduction: New lands. In S. McCartan R. Schulting, G. Warren & P. Woodman (eds), *Mesolithic Horizons: Papers Presented at the Seventh International Conference on the Mesolithic in Europe, Belfast 2005*, 1–2. Oxford, Oxbow Books.

Wylie, A. (1985) The reaction against analogy. *Advances in Archaeological Method and Theory* 8, 63–111.

Zvelebil, M. (1997) Hunter-gatherer ritual landscapes: spatial organisation, social structure and ideology among hunter-gatherers of northern Europe and western Siberia. In A. van Gijn & M. Zvelebil (eds), *Ideology and Social Structure of Hunting, Gathering and Farming Communities in Stone Age Europe*, 33–50. Leiden, *Analecta Praehistorica Leidensia* 29.

Zvelebil, M. (2008) Innovating hunter-gatherers: the Mesolithic in the Baltic. In G. Bailey & P. Spikins (eds), *Mesolithic Europe*, 18–59. Cambridge, Cambridge University Press.

Chapter 11

Hunter-gatherers in sub-tropical Asia: valid and invalid comparisons

Jana Fortier and Paul S. Goldstein

Introduction

Archaeologists often find themselves with some tantalising artefact, perhaps a figurine, a well-preserved serving bowl or some delicate shell beads. Whether 'symbols of excellence' (Clark 1986) or more prosaic material culture, these pose a question of interpretation: how are prehistoric materials which were once imbued with cultural meaning to be interpreted? More broadly, how might we increase the validity of our interpretations about these precious and everyday materials? We stand on the shoulders of many scholars who have asked similar questions, some who have written entire books on the subject of the valid interpretation of the past. In this essay, we offer one answer by way of a diachronic cross-cultural comparison of contemporary versus Mesolithic hunter-gatherer societies. Overall, we find that despite a relatively poor track record for such analogies, a culturally grounded and materially informed ethnographic analogy can contribute to that which, at the 2015 CHAGS conference Paul Lane called 'a genuinely reciprocal anthropology', in order to better know the archaeological unknowns (*cf. also* Lane 2014).

Specifically, components of the material culture of the Raute[1], a modern foraging people who hunt local forest fauna and dig wild yams for subsistence, are compared with regional archaeological site materials from the early Holocene. The area under discussion is located in the Raute's foraging territory in the Nepal Siwaliks, an area of hilly subtropical forests in the southernmost and geologically youngest east–west mountain chain of the Himalayas. The region is a humid subtropical highland (1000–2500 m) with hot, wet summers and mild winters similar to those along the entire southern Himalayan range and into parts of east Asia and Taiwan (Kottek *et al.* 2006). One of our primary goals is to outline how a multivariate method can strengthen diachronic comparisons of artefacts used by Neolithic and Mesolithic food collecting societies with portable objects used by modern hunter-gatherers. Our comparisons and comments will speak to the debate over the validity, legitimacy and ethics of asking modern foraging peoples to contribute in the interpretation of their own ancestral history, as well as that of others.

Scholars from all archaeological schools of thought explicitly or implicitly use contemporary foragers as analogies for pre-historic hunter-gatherer lifeways. For example, following Binford, processualists have used the continuum between 'homology' and 'analogy' to illustrate both the potential and the pitfalls of ethnographic analogy. The Binford school favours the use of homology and historical continuity when available over analogical reasoning. In the use of homology, present foraging practices and peoples are compared with their own geographical region's past, based on the assumption that there is a tighter 'fit' between foragers in present and past circumstances if they come from the same region (Binford 2001). Here we will consider the proposition that descendent communities who occupy roughly similar physical environments and speak daughter languages of a mother tongue can offer up detailed interpretations of the past. Sometimes these culturally informed interpretations contain surprisingly subtle interpretations about technologies that may otherwise not be available to archaeologists.

Even the most positivist of processualists admits that perfect homology is rare, however. Analogy proves the next best thing, and processualists can carefully document correlations in key features shared by present cultures, such as styles of housing, tools and utensils, or distances from key resources, to infer common behaviour and meaning in past cultures. Following Binford again, as scientists, processualists usually temper their analogic interpretations with the caveat that the validity of their interpretations would directly correlate with the 'closeness' of the two cultures in time, distance, environment and certainty of relationship.

On the other hand, post-processual schools of thought are more sceptical about privileging interpretation using either ethnographic analogy or homology. On methodological grounds, archaeologists such as Christopher Tilley have found such interpretations to be relativist, and based on the point of view of the researcher open to multiple and equally valid, or invalid, interpretations (Tilley 2014). Some scholars express discontent with the idea of using or even exploiting modern foraging peoples to serve the interests, both political and theoretical, of archaeologists who are interpreting deep history (i.e. Tilley 1989; Wylie 2002). Partly this may stem from the fact that all recent and contemporary foraging societies in Native North America have been subject to varying impacts of colonialism. In an era of decolonisation, we hope that members of foraging communities might contribute to interpretations of their own and cultural others' pasts through dialogue, pioneering new work in archaeology and experimental archaeology recreating tools and testing their uses.

Diversity in hunter-gatherer diachronic analogies

One of the key questions posed in this book involves diversity: what is the role of diverse hunter-gatherer behaviours and technologies across space and time? And further, how is such diversity manifested in the archaeological record? We agree that historians and archaeologists often draw on an overly stereotypical set of hunter-gatherer features. Many hunter-gatherer societies today are characterised as egalitarian, animistic, technologically simple and organised into patrilineal bands. And it is true that the Raute of Nepal fit these features. Yet we also know that each hunter-gatherer society also features important differences from the stereotype. The Raute, for example, have one of the most widely ranging nomadic lifetime territories as they move every week or two to new camps within a range of *c.* 20,000 km^2. In addition, their subsistence is based on medium-sized prey of primarily langur and macaque monkeys, with occasional opportunistic supplimentary resources such as porcupine, otter and wild boar (Fig. 11.1). Monkey hunts are carried out 2–4 times per week and constitute a uniform density throughout the seasons (Fortier 2012).

Figure 11.1. Raute woman rests after netting a juvinile boar (Sus scrofa). Nets like this one are made from various textiles. This net appears to be made from Himalayan nettle, Giardinia diversifolia, for the netting and Camel's foot climber, Phanera vahlii (=Bauhinia vahlii), for the ties.

These hunting prey choices, territories and tool technologies are just a few of the features that make Rautes distinct from other modern hunter-gatherers (Binford 2001; Kelly 2013).

In our approach, we argue that consciously or not, archaeologists use modern hunter-gatherers as exemplars for the interpretation of prehistoric behaviours. Given this situation, we feel that homologies, meaning direct relationships over time between cultures operating in similar environments, allow the most productive comparisons of subsistence and settlement systems (Lane 2014; Stahl 1993; Gould 1989; Gould & Watson 1982). As Binford suggested, since we use them anyway, we might as well be rigorous and explicit about our comparisons of past and present foraging societies (2001, 5). We thus advocate for comparative research which draws on the same regions and the same climates.

However, homologies are not always practical. For example, there are no modern European hunter-gatherer societies which can help make homologous comparisons with Mesolithic Europe. In addition, intracultural variations exist within hunter-gatherer societies themselves. Even though the Raute mainly use nets and axes for hunting, their neighbours known as the Indian Raji mainly use spears while hunting (Fortier 2009). For practical reasons, nets work best among Rautes with their dense forest surroundings and extensive meat sharing practices while spears work better for Indian Raji who often hunt porcupine. While both live in the same climate and speak the same mother tongue, they've adapted distinct hunting techniques (Fortier 2012). So while comparisons based on environmental constraints are likely to produce useful analogies, they run some risk of environmental determinism that overlooks the diversity of cultural choices.

What we propose is the addition of a linguistic dimension of comparison to gauge the closeness of analogues. When people speak, the way they produce sounds is tightly patterned. Using similar phonological and morphological patterns, comparative language study and historical linguistics allow us to trace language changes over time, such as the spread of prefixes or vowel inflections. Linguistic patterns enable us to know that the speakers of a reconstructed Proto-Indo-European language, for example, used a similar lexicon which included words for chariots, wagons and wheels. Even if such objects aren't found at a site from *c.* 4000 years ago in Europe, it is likely that people then and there had knowledge of such technology (Anthony 2010). In another language-based example from east-central Mexico, researchers compared the words for useful plants used by two different Mixe speaking societies. These cultures, separated for about 2000 years, have cognates for medicinal plant names, suggesting a Proto-Mixe society that also used similar medicinal plants (Leontí *et al.* 2003).

Yet linkages between facts, artefacts and material culture on the one hand, and the interpretation of the evidence on the other, involve sifting out all sorts of human agency and biases. Considering symbolic meanings, for example, what significance might an object that is the colour red have had for those who used it to enrich their lives thousands of years ago? We find it helpful if the interpreter (archaeologist, historian, *et al.*) begins with identifying their own standpoint. They need to sift through issues about how their research training and dominant questions of the day affect interpretation; how their own contemporary political agendas influence interpretation of artefacts, cultural features and habitation sites. We need to acknowledge our own social roles and consider how these affect our interpretation of the material past (Wylie 2003).

Background

While prehistoric sites do not reveal the language of culture bearers, we might know the protolanguages spoken in a given region. For example, in the case presented here, there are over 100 indigenous Tibeto-Burman languages spoken in the region (Lewis *et al.* 2016). Their parent languages are part of the Tibeto-Burman language family and Proto-Tibeto-Burman (PTB) is the hypothesised 'parent language' spoken as early as 4–5000 years ago. Proto-Tibeto-Burman, even further back in prehistory, is the daughter of a parent language which provisionally is related to the Sinitic languages such as Mandarin. This reconstructed protolanguage, or mother tongue, is called Proto-Sino-Tibetan (PST); it is the theoretical parent language of Tibetan, Burmese, Mandarin and about 350 more languages spoken throughout Asia (Handel 2008).

PST is being reconstructed using lexical correlations of its daughter languages and there are now about 560 accepted word items which would have been spoken sometime near the beginning of the Neolithic revolution/expansion. Lexicographers have reconstructed words in PST for singularly Neolithic items such as *enclosure, fence, village, masonry, sheep, yak, cattle, onion, bean, grain, rice, wine/liquor, soup, servant, war, weave* and possibly *iron* and *harvest* (Matisoff 2016). PST may have been spoken by pioneer groups of both foragers and farmers as they spread slowly across and down different river watersheds. The prehistoric date given for when the hypothetical language of PST is reconstructed is uncertain; tentatively between 6000 and 9000 years ago (Handel 2008; Thurgood & LaPolla 2003). The reconstructed PST is a linguistic construct and we don't know how close it is to the actual prehistoric spoken PST language. Similarly, we really don't know what the 'PST' society was like, but they probably were incipient farmers, and included communities of nomadic pastoralists and hunter-gatherers. We can, at this point, only examine the evidence through archaeology, historical linguistics, environmental studies and the culture of descendent communities like the Raute.

One of the ethnolinguistic descendants in the Sino-Tibetan language family are a small society known to the outside world as the Raute of Nepal. Raute call themselves Moutow [mọ.thọ́ː] 'Descendants'; *Baṛola* 'People of the Sun,' and *Horka G'rung* 'Born of God.' They live within and north of the Nepal Siwaliks in territory characterised as humid subtropical (Cwa) with a subtropical highland variety (Cwb) with hot, humid summers and cool winters (Kottek *et al.* 2006). This environment produces lush vegetation and rich and diverse biota.[2] While humid and lush, the region is not favourable for intensive farming due to the mountainous terrain. Horticulture of pigs, goats, sheep, rice, millets and garden yams, however, has been prevalent in the area for over 2000 years. Only in the last 100 years has rain-fed terracing and canal-based valley bottom farming been introduced to feed growing populations.

The Raute hunter-gatherers have a food economy based on 1) protein from hunting; 2) vitamins and carbohydrates from gathering wild fruits and vegetables (*Dioscorea* yams in particular) and 3) carbohydrates from grains obtained from farmers. Rautes probably also depended on wild grains in previous generations, but domesticated grains have become ubiquitous with the influx of farmers over the last century. Rautes are not fond of fishing or nut gathering, so their protein mostly derives from hunting. The nomadic Raute do not farm, raise livestock, nor work for farmers. Other 'settled' Raute communities, however, have been persuaded to do subsistence farming and raise livestock. Politically, the Raute groups are led by consensus of opinion and have no political power over other groups. The kinship system holds the band together through bilateral marriage, meaning that a family prefers to give their daughter in marriage to a reciprocal family, so that the receiving family in turn, and through delayed reciprocity, gives back their own daughter to the donor family during the next marriage cycle or the next generation.[3] This means that a person's aunt or uncle (FZ/MZ and FB/MB) is usually also one's parent's sibling's spouse (FZ = MBW; MZ = FBW; FB = MZH; MB = FZH), making for a very tight 'double helix' marriage system.

Although their total population is small at about 150 people, the Raute have exogamous patriclans, meaning a set of kin whose members believe themselves to be descended from a common ancestor, linked through male descent, but along a lineage that becomes untraceable and may verge on the supernatural (Ember & Ember 2015, 267). Raute patriclans have their own Sino-Tibetan family names but these are kept secret and rarely revealed to outsiders (and won't be named here as well). Rautes instead use Nepalese high caste family names in conversation with outsiders, giving themselves surnames such as *Raskoti, Shah, Samal, Shobangsi* and *Kalyal*. These are all names befitting old elite farming families of western Nepal, a practice of impression management like that described by Fredrik Barth in his work among coastal Sámi of Norway and also among subordinated tribes of Afghanistan (Barth 1969). Similar to other dominant and subordinate ethnic groups who engage in a 'pseudo-agreement' about communication in public, the Raute too have private social norms but supply Indic norms (including Indic family names) to others when asked. Rautes designate others using the 'on-stage' script, calling farmers *Pahāḍi* 'hills-people' or '*kisān* 'farmers'. But off-stage and in private, they have their own Sino-Tibetan family names, using private 'otherising' ethnic names for social others, such as *B'ley* 'the people who trade', *B'ling* 'the people who farm' and *Bhwa* 'the Tharu ethnic people'.

We have various kinds of evidence that can elucidate the culture of people living in the geographic area under discussion. One might trace history through archaeological excavations and surveys. Presently, however, there are only a few studies concerning pre-Neolithic societies in the central Himalayas. Perhaps the most relevant is by

Gudrun Corvinus which focuses on about 50 sites along the Babai River valley in Dang District, Nepal (Corvinus 2007). This is coincidently the vicinity where the nomadic Raute spent most of the year 2014 (as they moved from camp to camp). The Dang District area is frequented by the contemporary Raute hunter-gatherers about every ten years as part of their lifetime territory; a few of the Kusunda people, who are recently hunter-gatherers, also reside in Dang District.

The prehistoric material culture at the Dang valley sites features in-situ deposits and surface scatters of lithics including handaxes; levallois-like blades, microliths, scrapers and points. Both Neolithic and Mesolithic sites are found. As we are concerned with foraging cultural sites, we are focused on sites that include polished stone axes, adzes, chisels and beads, but not necessarily evidence of agriculture. In the Dang District region, Corvinus found a recent Neolithic site with polished stone axes and cord-marked pottery associated with a date of *c.* 1600 BP (*c.* AD 350). Mesolithic sites are found in Dang District as well, with a nearby site from the Patu industry, located 120 km east of Dang District. The site, with stone adzes, choppers, core-scrapers and flakes, has been dated using thermoluminescence (TL), with dates ranging from Middle Pleistocene to Neolithic (Kadereit *et al.* 2007). During the early/mid-Holocene period *c.* 7000 BP, there existed a unique Mesolithic culture which used macrolithic rather than earlier microlithic tools (Corvinus 1987; 1989; 2007, 284). It is described as similar to the Hoabinhian of Southeast Asia and dissimilar compared to Mesolithic sites in penninsular India. Based on a sequence of Patu site industries, Corvinus provisionally named a 'chopper-chopping tool culture' dating to the early Holocene and an earlier 'handaxe culture' dating to 20–24,000 BP (Corvinus 1987; 1989). Earlier Soanian and Acheulian Palaeolithic cultural materials have also been described for this area as well (Chauhan 2009). There are also a series of relevant studies of interest in the Gangetic plains that are concerned with hunter-gatherer communities living 6–10,000 years ago. These involve sedentary Mesolithic communities with cemeteries along the Ganges (e.g. James & Petraglia 2005; Lukacs & Pal 1993; Pandey 2013; Sharma 1983) and paleoethnobotanical studies of Neolithic Gangetic communities (Fuller 2006).

Within the territory of the Indian Raji of Kumaun, a region of central Himalayan India which borders Nepal, there are numerous petroglyphs, rock art images and cupoles. The Indian Raji inter-marry with the settled Raute in Nepal and are also recent foragers who were forcibly settled by the Indian government in the 1980s. They are now part-time foragers, supplementing hunting and gathering with wage labour and horticulture. While Raji have extensive knowledge of the local limestone cave system, and frequently hunt bats and porcupines inside the caves, they aren't known to practise rock art. Despite their lack of rock art activities, we should consider how the Indian Raji maintain extensive indigenous knowledge of limestone caves (Pandey 2008). While interviewing among them in 2004–5, one youngster who was hunting bats boasted that he and his friends could slip inside the cave holes and make their way to the top of the mountain without getting lost. Their ethnographic example may provide comparison for how pre-Neolithic communities used these systems of caves in the Kumaun area.

Comparing modern and ancient hunter-gatherer tool traditions

What shall we compare? The Raute use a few tool materials of note, the major ones being metals, stone, wood and other plant-based materials such as nettles (*Giardinia diversifolia*). Since plant-based materials survive poorly over time, we'll first look at the Raute's most characteristic tools which include metal axes and adzes. The Rautes carve the handles for these objects but they obtain the iron parts in trade from ironsmiths. Metal is further featured in Raute jewellery and women sport numerous iron bangles, rings, earrings and necklaces (Figs 11.2 and 11.5). Metal is also used for tin/bronze alloy patches on their 50 gallon soup and alcohol storage containers known as *dzyum*. Because carving large containers from hard woods, such as mountain ebony (*Bauhinia variegata*), is rather labour intensive, such items are patched rather than thrown away.

The materials listed in Table 11.1 represent a few items used by the Raute that have linguistic derivations from proto-languages within the Sino-Tibetan language family discussed in this essay. They represent material items which were also named and presumed to be used by ancestral speech communities in PTB and/or PST speaking communities in the mid- to early Holocene.

Comparisons of modern and early Neolithic tools might be limited to the morphology and functions of these tools, given that axes and, adzes have common physical shapes and uses. We might also consider how modern Rautes talk about tools, including how they perceive gendered uses, distribution of tools in camp, times of use, etc. For example, we might compare the Raute *goro* 'axe' with ground stone axes from early Neolithic sites in Nepal. The Raute axe could be described as long-faced, flat edged and generally shaped like a splitting axe or wood maul. By comparison, Corvinus describes 'small polished' Neolithic stone axes that resemble the Babai River Neolithic (BRN) axes described in Table 11.2 (Corvinus 2004:38).

The Raute name *goro* 'axe' provisionally derives from PST **giər* 'axe' (Starostin n.d.), which implies that ancestral speech communities used axes for similar functions. While some sort of **giər* 'axes' were used by ST ancestral groups, upon close inspection, the functions and meanings of the Raute *goro* 'axes' are significantly different from early Neolithic axes. For example, compare a modern Raute axe with early Neolithic ground stone axe heads from sites near the Babai River, Dang District, Nepal (Banerjee & Sharma 1969:54; Corvinus 1996, 40). Differences in all features of the Raute versus Neolithic axes are indicators that the tools were handled differently and probably had different purposes. In the Neolithic examples, most composite axes were hafted and one had a perforation for a handle in the butt end (Banerjee & Sharma 1969, 57; Corvinus 1996, 40). All Neolithic examples were notably smaller than modern Raute axes. Our conclusion is that modern Raute metal objects can be compared with Neolithic and more recent cultural periods but provide only broad analogies with

Table 11.1. Vocabulary for Raute material culture terms

Material class	Raute	Word Root (√) and provisional proto-form	Selected other language correlates
iron, wood	goro(w) 'axe'	√gor, PST *giǎr 'axe'	Tibetan (written) gzhor 'hoe, grubbling-hoe, pick-axe'; Thulung Rai kho 'axe'. cf. also PIE *kerw- 'axe, sickle, sword, spear; PTB *klaw 'dig out' weed' hoe'
iron, wood	1. leʔɦan; 2. liphan 'chisel'	√leʔɦan, PTB *lwan 'bore, pierce'	PTB *pan 'braid, plait, interweave'; WB phan 'weave'; WB phan 'make, create'; WB lwan 'gimlet, bore with a gimlet'. OC *bian 'braid, plait'
iron, wood	tohraya ~ toʁaya 'adze, mallet-chisel'	√to-, cf. PTB *tow 'hammer' √hray~ʁay, cf. PTB *m-dzəy 'chisel'	PTB *s/m-t(w)a ~ tu 'hammer, strike, slap'; PKC *hray 'axe, adze.' OC *twan 'to hammer; forge, refine; strike'; Tibetan (Lhasa) thō 'hammer'
plant fiber	dzi-na 'cape-sack'	√dzi, PTB *dzyīp 'shut, close'	Lisu dzi 'close; closely knit'; Ao (Naga) tʃhi' 'closed'; OC nˤaŋ 'sack, bag'; Tangut (Xixia) no 'bag, sack'
plant fiber	tshi-d'rūŋ 'net'	√rūŋ, cf. PTB *ruŋ 'hole, orifice, ear'	Bodo doróŋ 'net (kind of)'; Bokar a ruŋ 'trap, pitfall'; Apatani da-re 'trap (rock)'
plant stem	g'rǎy 'scratcher, comb (hair)'	√gǎray, PTB *m-kryat 'scratch, scrape'	OC *kriat 'notch, engrave'; Chamling Rai khrəyd 'claw, scratch (tiger)'
plant stem, leaf	l̥apa 'leafy enclosure'	√lap, PST *lap 'boundary, enclosure; leafy part'	PTB *s-lap 'leaf, leaflike part'; OC *sə-ləp 'additional robe, repeat'
plant stem, leaf, wood	nāw 'dwelling, home'	√na, PTB *na 'stay, rest, dwell, be, live'	Tibetan (written) naŋ 'dwelling, domicile, house'
stone	bara 'mortar'	√bar, PTB *b-rak 'rock, stone'	PTani *par 'mortar'; Yamphu o'braek 'big flat rock on which grain is dried'
stone	hwā-bara 'hearth stone'	√hwa, PTB *hwa(l/r) 'fire, shine'+ √bar, PTB *b-rak 'rock, stone'	PKC *wāy 'husk, chaff'
wood	dzyum 'pot (large, for liquids)'	√yum, PTB *yam 'pot, gourd' or PTB *yu(w) 'liquor'	Tibetan (written) rdza ma 'pot, jar, tin'; Tibetan (Lhasa dialect) tchu təm 'pot, jar, tin (water)'; Jingpho jam 'vat, jar'

Key to Proto-Language acronyms: " * " indicates a word that is a generally accepted reconstruction. A reconstructed word item is a hypothesized prehistoric word which has been posited using words and sound rules of documented languages that are related to the reconstructed (proto-) language. Reconstructed proto-languages here include PST = Proto-Sino-Tibetan; PTB = Proto-Tibeto-Burman; PKC = Proto-Kuki-Chin; PTani = Proto-Tani; OC = Old Chinese; and PIE = Proto-Indo-European. The etymologies are constructed with reference to the Sino-Tibetan Etymological Dictionary and Thesaurus database (STEDT) (Matisoff 2016). STEDT contains a source bibliography and a compilation of about 300 dictionaries and wordlists from nine branches of the ST languages. Non-English sounds in the Table are written in the international phonetic alphabet (IPA) which readers are encouraged to consult online. ɦ = a voiced "h" sound; ʔ = a paused sound as in 'uh--oh'; ā = a long vowel as in English 'pot' rather than 'putt'; ʁ = a voiced uvular fricative as in French rester 'to rest'; ʕ = a pharyngeal fricative sound similar to French pret; tʃ = a tight sibilant sound as in English 'niche'; ǎ and ə = short and regular schwa sounds as in the sound of the 'a' in 'Rosa's'; l̥ = an 'l' pronounced as a breathless greeting, 'hullo.'

Table 11.2. Compositional Comparison of Raute (RT) axe vs. Babai River Neolithic (BRN) Axe

Artefact trait	RT & BRN similarity	RT & BRN difference
1. Butt		RT flat, BRN curved
2. Edge corners		RT sharp, BRN curved
3. Edge slope		RT 10–15°, BRN 30° slope from side to center of cutting edge
4. Hold	handled	
5. Insertion of handle		RT 90° into bottom of axe face, BRN flush/direct into axe face
6. Length		RT 'long' ~240 mm., BRN 'short' ~190 mm.
7. Material		iron vs phyllite
Usewear notes		BRN axe's chamfered edge plus handle insertion on the flat side of the axe indicates it was used as an adze and might properly be called an "axe-adze"; RT axe not used to dig tubers

Comparison using 'textbook specimen of Neolithic ground stone axe' in Banerjee & Sharma (1969, 57, fig. 9).

stone axes and adzes. For a host of reasons – differences in use-wear, durability, source of materials, etc – iron objects are hard to compare with their stone counterparts. From the names and general properties, however, it is clear that both modern and prehistoric axes were used to cut wood materials.

Nonetheless, from ethnographic observation, we know that one of the most important aspects of tool use among the Raute involves using tools for *multiple* purposes. Since the human body has a limited carrying capacity, nomadic peoples like the Raute have relatively few tools. Axes are one of the most important multipurpose tools in Raute society. Aside from woodworking, axes are used in hunting for dispatching game animals, along with capture nets and poles. Further, all Raute men and women have equal access to axes which can be used not only for hunting animals, but for personal defense or even to threaten other people. As James Woodburn noted, the ability to have equal access to weapons is one of the features of immediate-return based, egalitarian foraging societies as it acts like an equaliser, and in reverse, the lack of equal access to weapons is featured in socially stratified societies (Woodburn 1982, 436).

One of the interesting multiple purposes of Raute axes is the use of axes as grinding tools rather than having a separate pestle, mallet or hammer in the Raute toolkit. One day in March 2015, I sat with a young Raute woman as she began to prepare a meal. She walked over to the river nearby, selected a flat grinding stone, and walked back to her hearth. After collecting some garlic scapes (*allium sativa*), salt and red pepper, she grabbed an iron axe, flipped it upside down and began hammering the spices using the flat butt of the axe (Fig. 11.2). In addition, axe butts are used to tap carved wood into place, to tap tent poles in place and for other hammer-like purposes.

In the archaeological record, hammering or pounding with the butt of an axe or an adze is rarely flagged as a functional use (see Figs 11.2 & 11.3). Judging from

Figure 11.2. A young woman grinds spices using the butt of an axe (goro) as a pestle. She picked up the mortar (bara) from the nearby river bank. A large wooden jar (dzyum) sits in the background and is used to store soups and ferment alcohol.

descriptions of axes and adzes in the archaeological literature in general, there is not an association between a cleaving instrument and hammering action. However, in conversation with an archaeologist studying use-wear of stone tool materials in late Paleolithic to Neolithic sites in East Asia, she confirmed that axe butts tended to have use-wear indicative of hammer/pounding actions (Liu, pers. comm. May 16, 2016; cf. also Liu *et al.* 2014). Yet other researchers in the region often base their analyses on analogies from historical circumstances using iron tools. Use-wear studies of battering on the butt of an axe are thus not available (Bennett 2010, 55). In addition, Rautes often use the butt of their tool called a 'mallet-adze' (*tohraya*) for hammering actions. They regularly flip the mallet-adze over and pound wooden pegs into boxes; pound

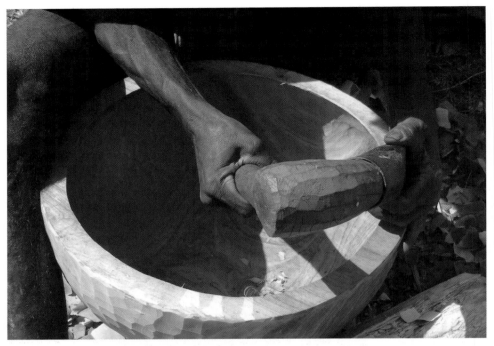

Figure 11.3. View of an adze (tohraya) being used to smooth the top inner edge of a trade bowl. The 'hammer' side of the adze is used to tap chisels, pound tent pegs into the ground, fit wood pieces together, etc.

tiny wood chips into faults in bowls to patch them; and tap chisels when completing woodwork projects. Indeed, the tool's name is the best descriptor because the word derives from a compound PTB *to 'hammer'+hray 'adze.'

Other tools, such as grinding stones, may be opportunistic and left relatively unworked. Further, grinding slabs or stones normally only show a superficial wear pattern on their surface. Raute users discard such stones when moving camp, which occurs after anywhere from a week to a month. Since several people borrow flat stone slabs from each other, they might get up to 50 uses before being discarded, leaving pulp and minor hammer marks from repeated pounding and grinding. Otherwise, such utilised river cobbles might only be recognisable archaeologically as manuports; they are hard to identify since the habitation sites are located anywhere from c. 20 m to a kilometre's distance from rivers.

Along with axes and adzes, chisels are some of the most common tools used by the Raute. Chisels, for example, are used for bowl and box detail work (Fig. 11.4). Coincidently, chisels and burins are also frequent stone tool categories from the Mesolithic and Neolithic archaeological sites in Asia. But in the archaeological record, the uses of chisels and burins are often left undescribed, partly because wood materials preserve poorly and partly because scientists cannot physically encounter

Figure 11.4. Chisels (leʔɦan and liphan) are used to create a tight fit on the edges of bowl and box lids (dzapa 'lid', photo top center). Chisels are also used to fashion box edges and to gouge holes for wooden pegs which secure box edges together.

a workshop or see a worker using chisels. Thus archaeological reports often focus on describing chisels' shapes, material compositions, frequencies, distributions at sites, etc (Stocks 2013). Although chisels and burins have been interpreted as being used for cleaning animal skins, drilling holes and other scraping functions, among Rautes, chisels are primarily woodworking tools. Wood bowls are carved both for Rautes' own cuisine-wares and as a form of indigenous commodity for exchange with villages for grain, cloth, etc. The chisels are unusually long (see Fig. 11.4), being from 236–373 mm length of iron plus 152 mm of the wooden handle, giving a total length of *c.* 400–520 mm.

How woodworking tools were used during Neolithic and Mesolithic eras can be difficult to reconstruct for archaeologists since most wooden objects disintegrate over time. This makes comparisons with Raute material culture particularly helpful since a large part of their material culture involves making items out of wood. Further, Rautes don't use ceramic materials; their use of wood in the sub-tropical Asian context can provide further analogies given the importance of bamboo and hardwoods such as *Michelia, Phanera* and *Bauhinia* (for a list of construction woods, cf. Fortier 2012, 183). Although wooden objects are absent from most prehistoric regional sites, it is probable that bamboo and hardwoods were important materials in ancient Asian cultures. Thus Raute use of wood is important for helping in reconstruction of the uses and meanings of prehistoric wooden materials. Their repertoire, including distinct types of wooden bowls and wooden pots and boxes; handles for tools; digging sticks; and carved tent poles plus wooden mesh framing of shelters, give us some idea of what we may be missing and shows the potential complexity of material culture in ancient hunter-gatherer societies.

Discussion

What is a valid ethnoarchaeological comparison? A direct homology between Rautes and ancestral groups is lacking, and analogies between modern and prehistoric foraging material cultures are tenuous, leaving interpretation to the standpoint of the interpreter. We propose that diachronic analogies between modern hunter-gatherer materials and prehistoric hunter-gatherer excavated materials might usefully be compared along a *continuum* of validity. In this continuum, multiple factors are weighed, generating support for interpretive consensus.

For such comparative work, we employ the term 'correlation'. By *correlation* we mean that ancient and present-day items that feature a positive set of physical, design, functional and semantic features conform to a generally recognised pattern. We are using the term 'correlation' in a specific fashion for specific objects and activities, and not as correlation of large-scale comparables (e.g. spread of agriculture with spread of a language family) or as correlations for dating (e.g. the use of pollen to date and correlate population movements).

1. *Direct correlations.* By a direct correlation is meant that more than 50% of a comparable set of materials have physical and linguistic attributes that match. The most direct correlations of modern Raute to people living in early Holocene subtropical areas of South and Southeast Asia involve directly relatable objects which also have PTB or ST lexical items. This direct correlation of past and present suggests we may project concepts that the Raute themselves would offer about materials, customs and beliefs that are part of their own core culture and that they believe extend in some form from the time of their ancestors. For example, when people say that their original ancestor, Old Grandfather (*Pu Gin*), created yams for food,[4] they are connecting their current culinary choices to their own ancestry. Wild yams continue to be a staple and there is also evidence for their consumption in Asia since the Pleistocene (Barton *et al.* 2007). It is reasonable to infer that *Dioscorea* yams have been used as a source of carbohydrates for thousands of years because: a) yams were abundant in areal sub-tropical forests; b) Raute *koy* 'yam' derives from PTB * *kywəy* 'yam'; and c) cultural myths of an original ancestor using yams as food exist.

2. *Structural correlations.* In some comparisons, there may be cogent correlations, but there are no direct ties between a cultural present and past archaeological material. There may be several traits in common between present and past materials, such as similar materials, parallel functions and analogous cultural significance of particular materials. But with structural correlations, there are no direct links or similarities of materials, forms, names of items or cultural meanings over time. Nevertheless, structural correlations can be important for broad comparisons when they enable our interpretations to be more plausible in some way. For example, in Nepal, cowrie (*kauṛi*) has been used for exchange into the twentieth century but was eventually replaced by paper and metal money. Today cowries continue to be used by rural Nepalese men and women as gambling dice, which is related to an earlier use in divination. These uses have been documented in the ethnographic literature, but there has been no documentation of how cowrie shells are used or regarded among the Raute to date.

Among Rautes, maidens wear shell bead necklaces featuring cowrie shells (*Monetaria moneta* or *M. annulus*) (Fig 11.2 & 11.5). They believe the shell beads are especially lovely and only young maidens (about ages 14–18) wear the cowrie, implying the beads are symbols of excellence (Clark 1986) but also symbols of fertility. These necklaces are passed down to a woman's younger sister after a woman marries and has children. Young women also sometimes wear cowrie shell hair braids which are woven into their hair. Although cowries have these two specific meanings among the Raute, among other South Asian societies cowrie shell has additional cultural uses and meanings, as dance jingles, gambling dice, jacket decorations and magic charms (Elwin 1942). Additionally, one Raute maiden said that she was wearing a *pāisa-ko gātha*, a Nepali phrase for 'a string of money'. At the time cowrie was first documented as money in Nepal, *c.* AD 500 during the Licchavi Era, 80 cowrie equalled one copper coin (Cunningham 1891; Walsh 1908). As time passed, metal currencies prevailed and cowries became used for local trade. As one writer put it, cowrie was a humble currency, the coinage of the masses (Gregory 1997, 256). Among Rautes, the idea of adornment and value intersect, as the cowrie shell has signified value through fertility and beauty, though not as a form of money.

In broad perspective, shell beads have been found in Asia since the late Pleistocene. Some of the earliest beads, from sites 700 km away in Patna, Bihar State, India are also made of *Oliva* marine shell (Bednarik 1993; Francis 1981). Originating in the Indian ocean, cowries have been used in trade throughout southern Asia and northward along ancient silk road caravan routes. Broadly, arts depicting notable women in prehistory[5] contain enormous numbers of cowrie shells. The tomb of Lady Hao, who was the Shang dynasty king's wife *c.* 3400 years ago (early 12th century BC) had stores of wealth in her funeral chamber including about 7000 cowrie shells which reflected her enormous political power. As archaeologist Grahame Clark noted, the cowrie shell is one 'symbol of excellence' which often relates to gendered ideals of femininity and beauty (1986, 23). This is also true in the case of Raute, whose use of

Figure 11.5. Raute maiden of about 14 years old wears bead necklace of cowrie shell.

cowrie may be of interest for comparison with how pre-historic cultural groups may have valued cowrie shells. Comparatively, Rautes use of cowries signals value as a symbol of excellence yet it is not on the grand scale as in state societies. In addition, before cowries were used as money, they were used for gift exchange. According to inscriptions in various Shang-Zhou era bronze articles, cowries were the most frequently recorded gift. In some cases, more than 1000 cowries were given as gifts (Yang 2011, 5 citing *Zhongguo Huobi Shi*).

However, in comparative perspective, cowries are used by Raute women for gifting but they're not put in burials, not sewn onto jackets, nor thrown for divination or gambling. Among Rautes, cowries have generalised exchange value only. Further, in keeping with their communal rather than individual ownership, shell beads are not considered to be 'possessions' of one individual. Compared to Raute ideals, cowrie in burials elsewhere often signify a different set of cultural meanings such as elite social status at late hunter-gatherer to early Neolithic sites in Thailand (Higham *et al.* 2011, 534–538). Further, southern Asian cowrie shells have been used as a form of money and as evidence of ultimate exchange networks with coastal groups. Raute are thus not some isolated hunter-gatherer society, but are ultimately actively participating in long distance trading networks through trade of their woodenwares in exchange for shell beads. Broadly, we can say that there are *structural correlations or affinities* between modern and prehistoric hunter-gatherer uses of shell beads, but the meaning of cowrie shells needs to be a culturally mediated interpretation.

3. *Low-level correlations.* Finally at a low-level or minimal range of comparison, we can say that there are broad, low-level correlations between modern hunter-gatherers and prehistoric hunter-gatherer communities. These occur when there are physical features in common suggesting common functions of tools. Since 'form follows function', differences in shape, size or materials are important evidence of differences in tool functions. It follows that materials' cultural meanings also vary in important ways. For example, a low-level correlation involves the Raute's use of *bara* 'mortar stone,' and *hwa bara* 'hearthside stone mortar'. As a low-level correlation, we might watch how men and women procure their mortar stones and how they grind foods on them. If we are doing ethnoarchaeological studies, we might record the scatter of stones after a group migrates away from their camp to a new camp. During one interview session a girl named Daya was grinding some onions, salt and pepper for dinner preparations. She got her mortar stone from the river just a minute before she started preparing her spices (Fig. 11.2). Opportunistic sourcing for stone and other materials happens frequently since the Raute are nomadic and don't carry heavy objects from camp to camp during their periodic moves every 3–35 days. Rather, women take the opportunity to gather grinding-size stones from nearby rivers or hillsides. Grinding stones then are left *in situ* when its time to move to a new site.

The Rautes' heaviest portable object is another type of mortar, made of hardwood and measuring about 50 cm³. It looks like a portable wooden block with a deep grooved hole in the middle of it, but may weigh over 20 kg. Local ones used by farmers generally also are made of wood (the Nepali *okhal* 'threshing mortar'). However, wooden mortars and pounders usually have disintegrated in early Holocene archaeological sites. Since wooden items are difficult to recover in sub-tropical archaeological contexts, comparisons of Raute mortars to stone Neolithic or Mesolithic mortars are particularly useful. Further, comparing the lexical items of Raute with ancient PTB and PST may shed light on the nature of grinders and early grain grinding practices. It is likely that Mesolithic hunter-gatherer communities also used some portable wooden grinders as well. One working hypothesis is that if similar words (Table 11.1) were used 6000–9000 years ago, similar material objects would have existed as well. For example, at the 7000–9000 BP Jiahu archaeological site, which is part of the Peiligang culture in central China, the excavators note that wooden grain pounders may have been an important component in early grain processing (Liu *et al.* 2010).

Conclusions

In the end, we revisit the question of whether modern hunter-gatherers such as the Raute make for good comparison with prehistoric foraging populations. We find that Raute material culture overall does not provide direct correlations with prehistoric foraging populations through homologies or direct links with ancestral populations of the region. However, their tools and language may provide some mid-range or broad correlations that can be used to form more meaningful analogies with prehistoric cultures from the region. The Raute material culture might be most helpful with comparisons of subtropical hunter-gatherer societies that were egalitarian, nomadic and used wood-based materials for cuisine-wares, containers and house construction. However, they would not be a good candidate for comparison with sedentary societies living outside sub-tropical climates and/or using pottery, long-term storage or domestic buildings such as subterranean pit-houses, mud-dried or baked brick dwellings.

Rautes themselves recognise their ties to their 'oldest Grandfather' named Pu-Gin; it was he who created yams and their other essential subsistence foods. They themselves recognise and honour their ancestors by preserving their language and culture. People also express feelings of being morally satisfied with comparisons to their oldest (prehistoric) grandfathers and grandmothers. But what about comparisons with ancient cultural others? In keeping with Raute moral ethics, others (archaeologists, for example) are free to do as they wish as long as it doesn't affect Raute families in any way, positively or negatively. In this case, our archaeological comparative theory-making as a kind of 'thought-experiment' is thus ethical from an anthropological standpoint.

As our 'thought experiment', we suggest that there was almost certainly a greater variety of hunter-gatherer lifestyles than there is today among modern and recent hunter-gatherers of the region. Modern hunter-gatherers like the Raute conform to the stereotypes of being egalitarian and nomadic, albeit with forcibly settled compatriots, the Indian Raji and settled Raute. But prehistoric hunter-gatherer societies were able to spread into lush river valleys and other areas now controlled by farming communities. Ironically, we may erroneously think of modern hunter-gatherers as simple 'stone-age' people yet hunter-gatherer adaptations of simplicity may be a kind of modern adaptation, a result of needing to be nomadic due to fewer forest resources than in the early Holocene. It is entirely possible that modern foragers put more emphasis on being egalitarian and nomadic than was the case in pre-Neolithic time periods.

The ancestors of the Raute may not have had elite-commoner social stratification. There is little modern linguistic evidence of stratification in the form of honorific pronouns or other markers of social stratification except for a word *daling* 'leader, elder, head of a clan'. Instead, cultural in-group versus strangers are linguistically marked using verb agreement systems and pronouns such as 'we (not you/exclusive)' from 'we (you too/inclusive)'. In–out intergroup distinctions are marked through various other linguistic cues as well. Thus Rautes may serve as exemplars for strong in group–out group social boundaries, but they do not serve as exemplars for stratified or sedentary societies in prehistory. In the Ganges watershed area, for example, evidence of habitation sites with cemeteries indicates that Mesolithic communities (e.g. at Sarai Nahar Rai, Mahadaha and Damdama) were sedentary hunter-gatherers and thus we can't compare subsistence, funerary styles, settlement patterns etc. (Pandey 2013).

In summary, we compared modern foragers, the Raute of Nepal, with an early Holocene period around 6000–9000 years ago. We chose the comparative method because we have 1) hunting/gathering subsistence strategies from both time periods; 2) similar climates in both cases; 3) comparable tool materials from both cultural periods and 4) linguistic evidence of Proto-Sino-Tibetan language materials from this time period. For all of these reasons, modern Raute are usefully compared with pre-Neolithic hunter-gatherer archaeological sites within Sino-Tibetan language areas and within sub-tropical climates. This Sino-Tibetan and sub-tropical region includes large areas of mainland Asia. From modern Raute society, we can gain further appreciation of similar objects from pre-Neolithic sites, especially when we use a suite of carefully correlated material, environmental and linguistic evidence.

Notes

1. Authors contributed equally to article writing with JF responsible for ethnographic and linguistic data and PSG responsible for archaeological material. For ethnography of the Raute and Raji, see Fortier 2012; Pandey 2008; Reinhard 1974; 1976. For an overview of hunter-gatherer (HG) societies in South Asia, see Fortier 2009; for HG societies in Southeast Asia, see Fortier 2013. For a summary of Raute and Raji cultural geography and languages, see Lewis *et al.* 2016 under the names *Raute* (coded as *rau*); *Rawat* (*jnl*); and *Raji* (*rji*). The Indian Raji and settled Raute speak *Rawat*; the nomadic Raute speak *Raute*, and the Raji of Nepal speak *Raji*, which are closely related languages. Field research (JF) consisted of ethnographic interviews with Rautes in Jajarkot District, Nepal for four months in 1997 and a follow-up visit for a week in Achham District in 2015. JF also worked with the Indian Raji or Rawat in Pithoragarh District for three months in 2004–5 with a revisit for a week in 2015. JF interviewed the sedentary Raute in Dadeldhura District and two Raji settlements in Kanchanpur District for three weeks in 2015. This field research among foraging-based communities was carried out after spending 18 months of doctoral dissertation field research in 1986–87, 1989–90 and 1993 among Nepalese farming households.
2. Annual precipitation varies according to altitude, sites along high wind valleys, closeness to bluffs and mountain ranges. In Dailekh District reported annual precipitation is 1580 mm rainfall per year. At Chisapani, the nearest weather station, annual rainfall is 2156 mm per year. In the northern range of Raute territory, rainfall in Jumla District is 665 mm per year (Bishop 1990, 37). The climate is somewhat similar to that of Pensacola, Florida and places along the Gulf of Mexico; in Europe along the Adriatic coastal area of Montenegro.
3. The Raute marriage system is significantly different from that of surrounding farming families. Among Nepali speaking Hindu caste families, primarily *Kanyādān* 'the gift of a maiden' is practised. In this marriage form, no marriage reciprocity takes place due to the slightly lower social status of the wife giver's family.

4. The exact quote: *Pu-Gín, Jíjyu bɛlɛ, githya dzā-o khay-ma*, 'Old Grandfather, in the ancestral time, created yam food.'

5. By 'prehistory' generally is meant 'before written records'. The term is problematic in South Asia however because the Indus Valley civilization circa 2,400–1,800 BCE used writing but the Indus script is not deciphered. Therefore, the regional 'prehistory' dates to 3rd century BC with religious documents, royal records and edicts such as the Ashokan pillars (Falk 2006).

References

Anthony, D. W. (2010) *The Horse, the Wheel, and Language: how Bronze-Age Riders from the Eurasian Steppes Shaped the Modern World*. Princeton, Princeton University Press.

Banerjee, N. R. & Sharma, J. L. (1969) Neolithic tools from Nepal. *Ancient Nepal* 75, 1–12.

Barth, F. (1969) *Ethnic Groups and Boundaries: the Social Organization of Cultural Differences*. Boston, Little & Brown.

Barton, H. & Paz, V. 2007. Subterranean diets in the tropical rainforests of Sarawak, Malaysia. In T. Denham, J. Iriarte & L. Vrydaghs (eds), *Rethinking Agriculture: Archaeological and Ethnoarchaeological Perspectives*, 50–77. Walnut Creek, Left Coast Press.

Bednarik, R. G. (1993) About Palaeolithic ostrich eggshell in India. *Bulletin of the Indo-Pacific Prehistory Association* 13, 34–43.

Bennett, G. (2010) Stone tools and style in Chinese archaeology: Zhongba lithic artifacts and cultural interaction in the Yangzi River Valley. In Y. Wang (ed.), *Style and Material in Bronze-Age China*, 51–75. Newcastle-upon-Tyne, Cambridge Scholars Press.

Binford, L. R. (2001) *Constructing Frames of Reference: an Analytical Method for Archaeological Theory Building using Ethnographic and Environmental Data Sets*. Berkeley, University of California Press.

Bishop, B. C. (1990) *Karnali under Stress: Livelihood Strategies and Seasonal Rhythms in a Changing Nepal Himalaya*. Chicago, University of Chicago Press.

Chauhan, P. R. (2009) The South Asian paleolithic record and its potential for transitions studies. In M. Camps & P. Chauhan (eds), *Sourcebook of Paleolithic Transitions*, 121–139. New York, Springer.

Clark, G. (1986) *Symbols of Excellence: Precious Materials as Expressions of Status*. Cambridge, Cambridge University Press.

Corvinus, G. (1987) Patu, a new stone age site of a jungle habitat in Nepal. *Quartär* 37/38, 135–187.

Corvinus, G. (1989) The Patu industry in its environment in the Siwaliks in eastern Nepal. *Quartär* 39/40, 95–123.

Corvinus, G. (1996) The prehistory of Nepal after 10 years of research. *Bulletin of the Indo-Pacific Prehistory Association* 14, 43–55.

Corvinus, G. (2004) The prehistory of Nepal. *Ancient Nepal* 154, 33–53.

Corvinus, G. (2007) *Prehistoric Cultures in Nepal: From the Early Palaeolithic to the Neolithic and the Quaternary Geology of the Dang-Deokhuri Dun Valleys*. Wiesbaden, Harrassowitz.

Elwin, V. (1942) The use of cowries in Bastar State, India. *Man* 42, 121–124.

Ember, C. & Ember, M. (2015) *Cultural Anthropology*. Boston, Pearson.

Falk, H. (2006) *Aśokan Sites and Artefacts: A Source-book with Bibliography*. Mainz am Rhein, Philipp von Zabern.

Fortier, J. (2009) The ethnography of South Asian foragers. *Annual Review of Anthropology* 38, 99–114.

Fortier, J. (2012) *Kings of the Forest: The Cultural Resilience of Himalayan Hunter-gatherers*. Kathmandu, Mandala (2009, Honolulu, University of Hawaii Press).

Fortier, J. (2014) Regional hunter-gatherer traditions in South-East Asia. In V. Cummings, P. Jordan & M. Zvelebil (eds), *The Oxford Handbook of the Archaeology and Anthropology of Hunter-gatherers*, 1010–1031. Oxford, Oxford University Press.

Francis, P. (1981) Early human adorement [*sic*] in India part I: the Upper Palaeolithic. *Bulletin of the Deccan College Research Institute* 40, 137–144.

Fuller, D. Q. (2006) Agricultural origins and frontiers in South Asia: a working synthesis. *Journal of World Prehistory* 20, 1–86.

Gould, R. A. (1989) Ethnoarchaeology and the past. *Fennoscandia archaeologica* 6, 3–22.

Gould, R. A.,& Watson, P. J. (1982) A dialogue on the meaning and use of analogy in ethnoarchaeological reasoning. *Journal of Anthropological Archaeology* 1, 355–381.

Gregory, C. A. (1997) *Savage Money: the Anthropology and Politics of Commodity Exchange*. Abingdon, Taylor & Francis.

Handel, Z. (2008) What is Sino-Tibetan? Snapshot of a field and a language family in flux. *Language and Linguistics Compass* 2, 422–441.

Higham, C. F. W., Guangmao, X. & Qiang, L. (2011) The prehistory of a friction zone: first farmers and hunters-gatherers in Southeast Asia. *Antiquity* 85, 529–43.

James, H. A. & Petraglia, M. (2005) Modern human origins and the evolution of behavior in the later Pleistocene record of South Asia. *Current Anthropology* 46, S3–S27.

Kadereit, A., Wagner, G. A. & Corvinus, G. (2007) OSL/IRSL fine-grain dating: a preliminary chronology of Quaternary slopewash and alluvial deposits from the Dun Valleys of Dang and Deokhuri in western Nepal (appendix II). In G. Corvinus (ed.), *Prehistoric Cultures in Nepal*, 372–379. Wiesbaden, Harrassowitz.

Kelly, R. L. (2013) *The Lifeways of Hunter-gatherers: The Foraging Spectrum*. Cambridge, Cambridge University Press.

Kottek, M., Grieser, J., Beck, C., Rudolf, B., & Rubel, F. (2006) World map of the Köppen-Geiger climate classification updated. *Meteorologische Zeitschrift* 15(3), 259–263.

Lane, P. (2014) Hunter-gatherer-fishers, ethnoarchaeology, and analogical reasoning. In V. Cummings, P. Jordan & M. Zvelebil (eds), *The Oxford Handbook of the Archaeology and Anthropology of Hunter-Gatherers*, 104–150. Oxford, Oxford University Press.

Lewis, M. P., Simons, G. F. & Fennig, C. D. (eds) (2015) *Ethnologue: Languages of the World*, 18th edition. Dallas, SIL International.

Liu, L., Field, J., Fullagar, R., Bestel, S., Chen, X. & Ma, X. (2010) What did grinding stones grind? New light on Early Neolithic subsistence economy in the Middle Yellow River Valley, China. *Antiquity* 84, 816–833.

Liu, L., Kealhofer, L., Chen, X. & Ji, P. (2014) A broad-spectrum subsistence economy in Neolithic Inner Mongolia, China: evidence from grinding stones. *Holocene* 24, 726–742.

Lukacs, J. R. & Pal, J. N. (1993) Mesolithic subsistence in north India: inferences from dental attributes. *Current Anthropology*, 745–765.

Matisoff, J. A. (2016) *Sino-Tibetan Etymological Dictionary and Thesaurus (STEDT)*. Berkeley, Sino-Tibetan Etymological Dictionary and Thesaurus Project, Centers for South and Southeast Asia Studies, Univwesity of California. Elec. access: http://stedt.berkeley.edu/

Pandey, P. (2008) Raji: A tribe of Uttarakhand approach to tribal welfare. *Indian Journal of Political Science* 69, 381–391.

Pandey, N. (2013) Beliefs, rituals, and myth: a study of Mesolithic Culture in Indian sub-continent. *International Journal of Religion & Spirituality in Society* 3, 31–36.

Reinhard, J. (1974) The Raute: notes on a nomadic hunting and gathering tribe of Nepal. *Kailash* 2, 233–271.

Reinhard, J. (1976) Shamanism among the Raji of Southwest Nepal. In R. L. Jones (ed.), *Spirit Possession in the Nepal Himalayas*, 263–292. New Delhi, Vikas Publishing House.

Sharma, J. L. (1983) Neolithic tools from Nepal. *Ancient Nepal* 75, 1–12.

Stahl, A. B. (1993) Concepts of time and approaches to analogical reasoning in historical perspective. *American Antiquity* 58, 235–260.

Starostin, G. S. (n.d.) The Tower of Babel: An etymological database Project. http://starling.rinet. ru/cgi-bin/main.cgi?root=config&morpho=0. Accessed 2015.

Stocks, D. A. (2013) *Experiments in Egyptian Archaeology: Stoneworking Technology in Ancient Egypt.* New York, Routledge.

Thurgood, G., & LaPolla, R. J. (eds) (2003) *The Sino-Tibetan Languages.* London, Routledge.

Tilley, C. (1990) On modernity and archaeological discourse. In I. Bapty & T. Yates (eds), *Archaeology after Structuralism: Post-Structuralism and the Practice of Archaeology,* 128–152. London, Routledge.

Tilley, C. (2014) *Material Culture and Text: The Art of Ambiguity.* New York, Routledge.

Walsh, E. H. (1908) The coinage of Nepal. *Journal of the Royal Asiatic Society* 40, 669–759.

Woodburn, J. (1982) Egalitarian societies. *Man* 43, 14–51.

Wylie, A. (2002) *Thinking from Things: Essays in the Philosophy of Archaeology.* Berkeley, University of California Press.

Wylie, A. (2003) Why standpoint matters. In R. Figueroa & S. Harding (eds), *Science and Other Cultures: Issues in Philosophies of Science and Technology,* 26–48. New York, Routledge.

Yang, B. (2011) The rise and fall of Cowrie shells: the Asian story. *Journal of World History* 22, 1–25.

Chapter 12

Archaeological dimensions of past and present hunter-fisher-gatherer diversity

Paul J. Lane

Introduction

The *Eleventh Conference on Hunting and Gathering Societies* (CHaGS11) session 'The Diversity of Hunter-Gatherer Pasts', on which this book is based, brought together a range of speakers from different disciplinary backgrounds and academic traditions for the purposes of examining various lines of argument concerning the diversity of hunter-fisher-gatherers (HFGs) in the past and present. As a whole, the papers presented at that session, and the chapters offered here, worked/work both individually and collectively to destabilise the concepts 'hunter-fisher-gatherer' and 'forager', especially as commonly deployed within archaeological narratives. In some cases this objective is clearly intended by the author/s, in others this intent is less overt but nevertheless is a discernible outcome. Multiple kinds of sources are deployed to achieve this destabilisation – archaeological, ethnographic, ethnohistoric, historical linguistic, ethnoarchaeological and archival. The intersection of these different kinds of sources, the dissonance that may exist between them, and their combination in different ways so as to build more robust frameworks for interpreting archaeological records of HFGs are all central concerns of the different contributors, although they often differ in terms of emphasis, theoretical orientation and framing of their argument.

A particularly welcome feature of these chapters is that the individual authors take the need to historicise HFGs seriously. Archaeological studies of HFGs when taken collectively do, of course, highlight significant transformations over the long-term in HFG material culture, settlement dynamics and mobility, resource use, hunting tactics, social relations, exchange networks and a host of other features. Individual studies may also explore which of these transformations occurred in a particular geographical area, and how and when they happened. Yet there is still, also, a common tendency in the discipline to conceptualise the drivers of change among HFGs, particularly those of the more distant past, as being somehow qualitatively different from those factors that have shaped the course of history for the rest of humanity. Thus, for example, while it is common to refer to different HFG societies as lying at different points along a continuum between 'simple' and 'complex' (with the latter now increasingly attracting archaeological attention, e.g. Fitzhugh 2003; Prentiss & Kuijt 2004; Sassaman 2004; Cannon 2014), it is rare to encounter a similar categorisation of herding or farming societies, let alone for such terms to be used to distinguish between different mercantile, industrialised, maritime or urban communities, for instance. In effect, even though more recent studies are at pains to qualify what is meant by the terms 'simple' and 'complex' when applied to HFGs, and some scholars are rightly especially critical of singular and unilineal models of the emergence of 'complexity' among HFGs (e.g. Arnold *et al.* 2016), there remains a tendency within the wider discipline to regard HFG 'complexity' as distinct from 'complexity' in other settings and kinds of society. Part of the reason for this may emanate from the view that 'hunter-gatherers are quintessentially anthropological, *the subject matter* that separates anthropology from its separate sister social science disciplines: psychology, sociology, economics, and political science' (Bettinger *et al.* 2015, v, emphasis added), which tends to place HFGs despite all the claims to the contrary, outside of 'history'. The assumed 'egalitarianism' of HFGs may be another contributory factor, especially since the emergence of 'complexity' among HFGs is commonly associated with the demise of egalitarianism which, given the inherent logic of a simple-complex binary, seems to imply that maintaining egalitarian social conditions is a 'simple' matter, even though this may not be intended by the scholars who use these terms. However, as the chapters here illustrate, once the specifics of history begin to be taken into account, far more complex and diverse trajectories start to become apparent (and see also McCall & Widerquist 2015).

Diversity in context

As might be expected in a book aimed at emphasising the diversity of HFGs over the *longue durée* of human/hominin history, the importance of context in shaping HFG practices and societal dynamics, alongside externalities such as ecological parameters, climate changes and demographic conditions, is given considerable emphasis by the majority of contributors. By and large, this concern with context is not simply (if at all) some kind of 'Johnny-come-lately' recognition of post-processual critiques of the universalising narratives of optimal foraging theory or the equally universalising arguments of evolutionary anthropology. Instead, contributors approach the link between 'context' and 'diversity' from a number of different perspectives and with rather different objectives in mind. Broadly speaking, these can be grouped into four categories.

The first of these concerns the context in which the HFGs themselves lived out their lives. Thus, there are chapters that concern time periods ranging from the European

Upper Palaeolithic (Spikins, Hitchens and Needham) to the Late Pleistocene/Early Holocene (Finlayson, Warren) when hunting, gathering, fishing (and presumably, perhaps also scavenging) were the only means by which humans/hominins procured their food either globally or at least regionally (such as during the British Mesolithic). In other words, these papers address the context of a world without farmers, herders, merchants, political specialists and a host of other livelihood strategies, and in the case of the chapter by Penny Spikins and colleagues, also deals with the world of a different species – *Homo neanderthalensis*. They beg the questions, therefore, just how different were HFGs prior to the development of food production and might analogies with contemporary and historic HFGs do more interpretive harm than good, especially when dealing with the archaeological traces of a different species of *Homo*? As Colin Grier notes in the introduction to his chapter, we must always bear in mind when developing models of HFG society and material practice that HFG diversity 'has been significantly narrowed by western colonial expansion over the last 500 years', and was presumably also potentially significantly narrowed by millennia of global and regional expansions of non-HFGs prior to that.

While some chapters consider contexts when hunting, fishing and gathering were the only means of procuring food, others deal with contexts and time periods that post-date the emergence of food production, although many of these also deal with HFG worlds that appear to have had limited, if any, direct contact with food producers (e.g. Grier, Carracedo-Recasens and García-Piquer). Mark Hudson, on the other hand, explores the archaeological expressions of a group of maritime hunter-gatherers (the Okhotsk) in 1st millennium and early 2nd millennium AD Japan, and their relationship to the Epi-Jōmon and the Kofun state, while Jana Fortier and Paul Goldstein compare and contrast HFG practices and materiality in contexts prior to and following the emergence of agriculture in Nepal. Both papers highlight the importance of embedding HFGs within wider regional historical trajectories in a manner that acknowledges HFG agency and control over their preference for a particular livelihood strategy. A novel variant to this kind of analysis is provided by Kathryn de Luna, whose paper goes against the normal grain of hunter-gatherer studies by examining hunting, fishing and gathering *within* the context of farming society and the social value and esteem that could accrue from choosing to pursue these livelihoods.

The second kind of contextual issue explored by all of the contributors, albeit some more explicitly than others, relates to the context of research and especially its academic underpinnings. As Reinhard Blumauer's paper reminds us, this is not a new concern, and recognition of HFG diversity has re-surfaced periodically at least since the formalisation of archaeology and anthropology as distinct disciplines. For instance, during the first few decades of the twentieth century proponents of the Vienna School of Ethnology (the focus of Blumauer's chapter), and especially its key figure Father Wilhelm Schmidt, were particularly interested in explaining the causes of diversity among living HFGs, and although his explanatory frames now seem outmoded, Father Schmidt's models challenged the linear notions of sociocultural progress that dominated anthropology at the time (and to some extent still dominate).

As is evident from several studies (see, e.g., Pluciennik 2004; Barnard 2014 and references therein) the history of research on and contact with both individual HFG societies and with HFGs collectively, frequently changes the ontological position of hunter-gatherers within the academy. Jordi Estévez and Alfredo Prieto's chapter also makes this clear. In it, they draw a number of analytical insights from their long-term research on the archaeology, history and ethnography of the HFG societies of Tierra Del Fuego, and compare and contrast these data sets with evidence from the Pacific coast of Northwest America. We may recall, for example, that when the young Charles Darwin first encountered Tierra del Fuegans he was perplexed by them, describing them as 'wild savages', with coarse, black and entangled hair, 'widely different ... from any thing (*sic*.)' he 'had ever beheld' (Darwin 1839, 227), and seemingly unlike other humans in both appearance and behaviour:

> 'These poor wretches were stunted in their growth, their hideous faces bedaubed with white paint, their skins filthy and greasy, their hair entangled, their voices discordant, their gestures violent and without dignity. Viewing such men, one can hardly make oneself believe they are fellow-creatures, and inhabitants of the same world.' (Darwin 1839, 235, Dec 1832)

Today, as the chapters by Estévez and Prieto and by Carracedo-Recasens and García-Piquer make clear, the former inhabitants of this particular 'uttermost end of the Earth', as with other such localities elsewhere around the globe (Gamble 1992, 710–711), now seem central to understanding some of the causes of diversity among HFGs more generally. Estévez and Prieto note in particular the need to distinguish different levels of causal relationships – those that are dominant, those that are determinant and those that have a triggering effect – and that what matters most in explaining the direction of change is the nature of the relationships between all three levels. They go on to posit that after the mastering of fire, the dominant factor for human societies around the world became the relationship between population growth and the development of technology, raising the possibility that these could overrun resource reproduction and so threaten the sustainability of a particular HFG strategy. The manner in which individual HFGs societies resolved this dilemma, as they illustrate with reference to their case studies, can vary significantly however, and as a consequence may have rather different triggering causal effects on other dimensions of HFG society and behaviour.

This third aspect of context – that is the context of change and the causal factors behind it – is also explored in several other contributions, among them the chapter by Colin Grier, which also considers the example of 'complex' HFGs on the Northwest Coast of North America, and particularly the Coast Salish societies. As noted above, Grier cautions against using ethnographic accounts as the sole baseline against which to judge the range of diversity among HFGs globally, noting also that far from offering static 'snapshots' of HFG livelihoods and social relations the ethnographic sources, when read critically, may in fact document considerable change. Alongside this history of change and adaptation, especially within contexts of colonial encounters, it is nonetheless generally possible to identify some significant long-term continuities in HFG material practices – what Grier refers to as 'core principles'. Among Coast Salish societies these have been (1) physical and long-term construction of place, (2) ownership and maintenance of resource diversity, (3) proprietorship and (4) local autonomy. Since most of these also characterise other 'complex' HFGs it would be easy to regard them as universal features of a particular stage in the evolution of hunting-gathering-fishing. Grier, however, is rightly critical of such thinking, arguing that the persistence of these features within Coast Salish (or for that matter any other HFG society among whom they are found) needs to be explained and not just documented. This is an important point that has much wider implications for archaeological research on HFGs. Specifically, archaeological explanations of the emergence of diversity among HFGs and the existence of divergent practices tend to focus on the possible drivers of change, while neglecting to account for why some things stayed the same. This is an interpretive problem that is not restricted to hunter-gatherer studies, but is especially common in HFG archaeology and needs to be guarded against for the simple reason that, by neglecting to account for continuities unexamined assumptions about the universal, primordial and essentialist nature of particular practices are left unexamined and unchallenged. As Grier's paper and several others in this volume (e.g. Hudson, Finlayson, Fortier and Goldstein) make clear, change almost always takes place against a context of continuity, and it behoves archaeologists to pay more consideration to explaining why some things do not change among HFGs while others do. Mark Hudson's observation that the drivers of diversity among HFGs may change over time, and that ecological, demographic, economic and political forces come to the fore differentially makes a somewhat similar point. It also underlines why it is important to take histories of the particular trajectories of HFGs seriously, as his Japanese case study ably illustrates.

Analogy and homology

A consideration of context also features prominently in many of the chapters where authors discuss the nature and role of analogy, especially ethnographic/ethnoarchaeological analogy. Perhaps more than any other category of archaeological subject matter, the interpretation of the material traces of past HFGs is replete with the use of analogy, sometimes explicitly spelled out and contextualised but oftentimes either overly generalised from a very limited ethnographic data set or simply just derived from implicit assumptions about what HFG society is like.

A case in point is eastern Africa where, at the time of European expansion into the region in the mid-nineteenth century, an HFG presence was recorded in many different areas (Huntingford 1931; Kusimba, 2005). These included various groups typically found in forested highland areas along the margins of the Central Rift in Kenya and northern Tanzania and often referred to collectively by the Maasai term as 'Dorobo', who included clusters of Southern Nilotic speaking Okiek (Kratz 1999), as well as Eastern Cushitic speaking Yaaku (now Mukogodo; e.g. Cronk 2004), Eastern Nilotic speaking Akie (sometimes called Mosíro; e.g. Kaare 1995) and Southern Cushitic speaking Aasax (Bernsten 1976); peoples such as the Wataa, Boni and Degere whose territories were centred on the dry hinterland inland from the Indian Ocean coast (Stiles 1982; Walsh 1990; Kassam 1986); the Kilii (also known as Aweer) and Eyle hunter-gatherers who ranged across the arid lands of southern Somalia (Stiles 1981); forest-dwelling Batwa in Uganda and Rwanda (Lewis 2000); and the Sandawe (Newman 1970) and Hadzabe (or Hadza as they have been commonly named in the scholarly literature) (Woodburn 1968; 1970; Marlowe 2010) click-language speakers of northern central Tanzania. Yet there has been little sustained cross-disciplinary research on the majority of these groups or their possible connections to earlier HFGs documented in the archaeological record, with the notable exception of the Hadzabe (Marlowe 2002; Mabulla 2007), the Kenya Okiek (Blackburn 1974; Zwanenburg 1976; Kratz 1980; Distefano 1990; Ambrose 1986; Dale *et al.* 2004) and to a lesser extent the Mukogodo (Mutundu 1999) and Sandawe (ten Raa 1969; Newman 1991/2). Even more problematic, given such evident regional diversity in HFG practices, is the manner in which the Hadzabe have come to be regarded within the wider discipline as archetypal hunter-gatherers for much of tropical Africa, and as offering the best scope for developing analytically robust analogies for interpreting the fossil record of early hominins (e.g. Domínguez-Rodrigo 2002, see Lane 2014 for further discussion).

Of all the contributors to this volume, Bill Finlayson is especially critical of the continued recourse to ethnographic analogies in hunter-gatherer archaeology, correctly emphasising that there are no modern equivalents for certain conditions of hunting and gathering. This important, one might have thought self-evident, observation is often overlooked or entirely ignored by archaeologists, however. Rather than seeing the lack of suitable analogies for interpreting the material record of HFGs prior to plant and animal domestication as 'a problem' for archaeology, however, a more positive take seems called for which recognises that archaeology is the only source of information about why and how certain things happened in the past. In this sense, a wider conclusion that can be drawn from Finlayson's chapter is that an archaeology freed from imagined ethnographic hunter-gatherers has a lot to tell us, albeit somewhat counterintuitively, about the diverse conditions and situations of *being* hunter-gatherers. Moreover, while the use of analogies is an inescapable part of archaeological interpretation as many have argued previously (e.g. Wylie 1985; Shelley 1999; Lyman & O'Brien 2001; Currie 2016), these do not have to be drawn from ethnography. A case in point being the recent use of agent-based modelling (ABM) to generate fresh insights *inter alia* about HFG mobility (Widlok 2015), social interaction (Barceló *et al.* 2014) and the emergence of HFG diversity (Del Castillo *et al.* 2014). The potential of ABM, is also imaginatively explored in the chapter by Carracedo-Recasens and García-Piquer in a manner that dialectically confronts ethnographic and ethnohistoric data with different theoretical models of HFG settlement behaviour, resource use and social organisation – a process which they term 'experimental archaeology' since it involves repeated testing of hypotheses against known data sets so as to challenge inherent assumptions.

In his chapter, Graeme Warren also offers a critical consideration of the use of ethnographic analogies, tracking the changing history of their use in European Mesolithic archaeology. He notes, in particular, that early use of analogy, especially with the rise of processual approaches, was typically fairly explicit and when invoked the limitations and interpretive constraints imposed were duly noted. In more recent decades, with the growing influence of post-processualist approaches and ideas about agency, symbolism, materiality and dwelling, there seems to have been a decline in explicit consideration of the relevance of particular ethnographic comparisons and the use of analogies has become far more implicit. The main exceptions to this are when new interpretive models which have yet to become part of mainstream archaeological thinking are being proposed, and when interpretive arguments turn to matters of 'belief', 'ideology' or 'cosmology'. From his review of two recent multi-authored works of synthesis, there appears to be a growing assumption that different European Mesolithic HFGs 'fit' one or other of the ethnographically known systems of settlement and landscape dynamics. Warren cautions against such casual assumptions, arguing that the degree of fit always needs to be demonstrated, and critically, also pointing out two important differences between the worlds of the European Mesolithic and those of ethnographically and ethnohistorically documented HFGs. First, European Mesolithic societies would have encountered unfamiliar worlds as they expanded northwards at the end of the last glaciation, having to engage with new environmental conditions and ecological niches that may have required distinctive ways of being that have no ethnographic equivalents. Second, at least until the later phases of the Mesolithic, mainland Europe along with Britain and Ireland would have been a world in which inter-group encounters would have been exclusively between HFGs. Again, with a few notable exceptions, these kinds of encounters and the potentially diverse responses they provoked are virtually unknown in ethnographic and ethnohistoric records.

Most of the other contributors offer equally pertinent critiques of customary uses of ethnographic analogies in hunter-gatherer archaeology, while also offering methodological guidance on how to develop robust relational analogies by setting various boundary conditions. A common thread to many of these chapters concerns the importance of deploying alternative sources for understanding the condition and situation of 'being hunter-gatherers', and how variable this can be and has been. While these studies highlight the value of using multiple sources to interpret the past, they also typically note the common dissonance between different sources and the need to explore and understand these disconnections.

Jana Fortier and Paul Goldstein, for example, discuss the potential of historical linguistics and the spatial and temporal associations between words and things and words and people with reference to proto Sino Tibetan languages, the material culture of modern-day Raute hunter-gatherers who inhabit the subtropical forests of the Nepal Siwaliks mountain zone, and the archaeological traces of earlier HFG inhabitants of this section of the southern Himalayas. As they note, linguistic data can provide valuable insights into more intangible aspects of HFG material culture that have only been rarely studied (e.g. González-Ruibal *et al.* 2011) by ethnographers and ethnoarchaeologists. For example, in the Raute language the term for 'a cape' can also refer to a 'closable bag'. In English, these would be understood as quite distinct objects and treated as belonging to very different classes of object such as 'clothing' and 'containers', respectively. The fact that these terms are conceptually related in Raute and that similar examples also occur, suggests a different ontology of objects perhaps related to an understanding of the particular affordances things offer (in the cape/closable bag case, for instance, both share an ability to be tied/untied) that would not be recognised without these linguistic clues. By tracing the history of these particular object etymologies further back in time through historical linguistic analysis and comparing the evolution of linguistic meanings with the surviving archaeological traces of these same kinds of objects, it is possible to develop more robust 'diachronic analogies' between the ethnographic sources and archaeological subjects of interpretation. This is precisely what these authors do with reference to some common archaeological types such as stone axes and other tools made from worked stone. Fortier and Goldstein argue that these interpretations then need to be placed on a 'continuum of validity' that range from analogies for which direct correlation between the ethnographic present and archaeological past can be demonstrated via those which suggest at least some structural correlation, to those which have only low-level validity and which necessarily should be used with extreme caution and numerous caveats.

Kathryn de Luna's chapter offers another excellent example of the potential for incorporating historical linguistic data into archaeological analyses. More specifically, instead of trying to reconstruct histories of food production and domestication in the conventional manner by tracking the linguistic and cultural distribution of the words for farming and herding, domesticated plants and animals, agricultural tasks and material culture among food producing communities, she highlights the value of looking at this issue by focusing on bushcraft and what this can tell us about the diversity of hunting and gathering, and how these insights can destabilise some of our analytical categories. Using the history of innovations and continuities in the subsistence vocabulary of Botatwe speakers of Central Africa from around 1000 BC to AD 1250, de Luna explains how different subsistence practices became 'tied to the politics of identity and the practices of power'. Intriguingly, and as she notes also counterintuitively, as farming became more established and mainstream among Botatwe speakers, rather than precipitating the demise of hunting, gathering and fishing as socially valued practices, their commitment to cereal agriculture also initiated a 'a regional revolution in the technologies of spear hunting [and] rapid-current fishing' and the invention of 'a new category of landscape, the bush', the mastery of which became a significant source of social distinction. Even more significantly, these data also suggest that the binary between 'food production' and 'food procurement' that 'has been integral to Western intellectual history' for centuries and on which other binaries such as that between the civilised 'us' and the barbarian/savage 'other' have been commonly constructed, does not appear to have been of such significance among Botatwe speakers.

In many ways, Botatwe conceptualisations of different modes of subsistence, such as 'farming' and 'hunting and gathering', challenge dominant Western ideas of the differences between them and whether there is always a necessary re-structuring of human/thing/non-human species relationships during the process of domestication. In his chapter Finlayson, although approaching these issues with different data sets, also encourages us to look at domestication not from the perspective of what it became but from what it was not – namely a change in relations of dependence. He argues that there is an over reliance on modern studies of HFGs for interpreting the archaeological signatures of the Epipalaeolithic and early Neolithic of Southwest Asia which span 'a unique moment in history, characterised by a huge autochthonous shift in lifeways' for which there is no modern analogue. Reviewing the archaeological indicators that are often assembled to suggest that a radical transformation occurred as HFGs also became farmers, Finlayson argues that there is remarkably little evidential support for such claims. He goes on to suggest that the widespread support for a human revolution that wasn't has arisen partly from the imposition of ethnographic models of hunter-gatherer complexity that are still significantly shaped by outmoded, 19th century stadial thinking. Rather than relying on ethnography to explain the origins of the Neolithic, he argues that archaeologists working on these data sets need to think through their data to imagine some other, 'in-between', forms of social and economic practice if they wish to escape the narrow interpretative confines of a farmer–HFG binary. Several of the other papers in this volume offer possible ways to begin to approach this intellectual challenge. These range from the novel approaches to recognising archaeologically different forms of intimate familial sociality and thereby to differentiate Neanderthal ways of being from those of modern humans, to the use of agent based modelling, historical linguistics and archaeological ethnography. Both collectively and individually, the papers assembled here open up new research horizons for understanding and studying HFG diversity in a variety of contexts and from sometimes quite different theoretical perspectives. All of them make the point, nonetheless, that critical engagement with analogy is fundamental to developing new interpretations and understanding of HFGs, both past and present.

Conclusion

As an Africanist archaeologist familiar with the continued presence of HFGs in the contemporary landscapes of Africa, I am often troubled by the archaeological literature, especially that concerning Southwest Asia and Europe, regarding the transition to food production and the origins and spread of 'the Neolithic', and by how quickly hunter-fisher-gatherers disappear from those narratives. If there is one observation to be drawn from the wealth of information concerning the diversity of HFGs around the world, it is that HFGs commonly lived for millennia in what were essentially complex subsistence mosaics involving both food procurement and food production. Reinserting HFGs into the archaeological narratives of post-domestication contexts, to my mind, thus seems essential and long overdue in many regions, and not just Europe and Southwest Asia. Many of the contributions to this volume do precisely this, in a critical, theoretically informed manner that frequently goes against the dominant academic grain, offering more complex and complicating narratives of an HFG presence. As discussed above, other chapters are more concerned with time periods and regional contexts where HFGs lived in a world entirely populated by themselves and other HFGs, highlighting yet another relatively neglected line of enquiry in hunter-gatherer archaeology, namely HFG interactions with other HFGs, especially where significant differences existed between those engaged in such interaction. While the study of HFG diversity is by no means a new topic in either archaeology or in cognate fields such as evolutionary anthropology, ethnography and socio-cultural anthropology, what the chapters in this volume accomplish is to highlight just how diverse and how complex the concept of HFG diversity really is, and hence also just how necessary it is to deconstruct the concept and the taken-for-granted assumptions concerning HFGs on which it is based. In this regard, the chapters presented here offer an excellent, and diverse, selection of ideas and examples of how to address this challenge and thought provoking ideas for further research on these topics.

References

Ambrose, S. H. (1986) Hunter-gatherer adaptations to non-marginal environments: an ecological and archaeological assessment of the Dorobo model. *Sprache und Geschichte in Afrika* 7, 11–42.

Arnold, J. E., Sunell, S., Nigra, B. T., Bishop, K. J., Jones, T. & Bongers, J. (2016) Entrenched disbelief: complex hunter-gatherers and the case for inclusive cultural evolutionary thinking. *Journal of Archaeological Method and Theory* 23, 448–499.

Barnard, A. (2014) Defining hunter-gatherers: enlightenment, romantic, and social evolutionary perspectives. In V. Cummings, P. Jordan & M. Zvelebil (eds), *The Oxford Handbook of the Archaeology and Anthropology of Hunter-Gatherers*, 43–54. Oxford, Oxford University Press.

Barceló, J. A., Bernal, F. D. C., Olmo, R. D., Mameli, L., Quesada, F. M., Poza, D. & Vilà, X. (2014) Social interaction in hunter-gatherer societies simulating the consequences of cooperation and social aggregation. *Social Science Computer Review* 32, 417–436.

Bernsten, J. (1976) The Maasai and their neighbors: variables of interaction. *African Economic History* 2, 1–11.

Blackburn, R. (1974) The Okiek and their history. *Azania* 9, 139–157.

Bettinger, R. L., Garvey, R. & Tushingham, S. (2015) Preface. In Bettinger, R. L., Garvey, R. & Tushingham, S. (eds) *Hunter-Gatherers: Archaeological and Evolutionary Theory,* 2nd edition, v–vi. New York, Springer.

Cannon, A. (ed.) (2014) *Structured Worlds: The Archaeology of Hunter-Gatherer Thought and Action.* Abingdon: Routledge.

Cronk, L. (2004) *From Mukogodo to Maasai: Ethnicity and Cultural Change in Kenya.* Boulder, Westview Press.

Currie, A. (2016) Ethnographic analogy, the comparative method, and archaeological special pleading. *Studies in History and Philosophy of Science Part A,* 55, 84–94.

Dale, D. D., Marshall, F. & Pilgram, T. 2004. Delayed-return hunter-gatherers in Africa? Historic perspectives from the Okiek and archaeological perspectives from the Kansyore. In G. M. Crothers (ed.), *Hunters and Gatherers in Theory and Archaeology,* 340–375. Occasional Paper 31. Carbondale, Southern Illinois University, Center for Archaeological Investigations.

Darwin, C. R. (1839) *Narrative of the Surveying Voyages of His Majesty's Ships Adventure and Beagle Between the Years 1826 and 1836, Describing their Examination of the Southern Shores of South America, and the Beagle's Circumnavigation of the Globe. Journal and remarks. 1832–1836.* London: Henry Colburn. Available online as: Rookmaaker, K. (ed.) (2006) *Darwin's Beagle Diary (1831–1836).* [English Heritage 88202366] (Darwin Online, http://darwin-online.org.uk/).

Del Castillo, F., Barceló, J. A., Mameli, L., Miguel, F. & Vila, X. (2014) Modeling mechanisms of cultural diversity and ethnicity in hunter-gatherers. *Journal of Archaeological Method and Theory* 21, 364–384.

Distefano, J. A. (1990) Hunters or hunted? Towards a history of the Okiek of Kenya. *History in Africa* 17, 41–57.

Domínguez-Rodrigo, M. (2002) Hunting and scavenging by early humans: the state of the debate. *Journal of World Prehistory* 16, 1–54.

Gamble, C. (1992) Uttermost ends of the earth. *Antiquity* 66, 710–711.

González-Ruibal, A., Hernando, A. & Politis, G. (2011) Ontology of the self and material culture: arrow-making among the Awá hunter-gatherers (Brazil). *Journal of Anthropological Archaeology* 30, 1–16.

Fitzhugh, B. 2003. *The Evolution of Complex Hunter-Gatherers: Archaeological Evidence from the North Pacific.* New York, Springer.

Huntingford, G. W. B. (1931) Free hunters, serf-tribes, and submerged classes in East Africa. *Man* 31, 262–266.

Kaare, B. (1995) Coping with state pressure to change: how Akie hunter-gatherers of Tanzania seek to maintain their cultural identity. *Nomadic Peoples* 36/37, 217–225.

Kassam, A. (1986) The Gabbra pastoralist/Waata hunter-gatherer symbiosis: a symbolic interpretation. *Sprache und Geschichte in Afrika* 7, 189–204.

Kratz, C. A. (1980) Are the Okiek really Masai? Or Kipsigis? Or Kikuyu? (Les Okiek sont-ils réellement Masai? ou Kipsigis? ou Kikuyu?). *Cahiers d'études africaines* 79, 355–368.

Kratz, C. A. (1999) The Okiek of Kenya. In R. B. Lee & R. Daly (eds), *The Cambridge Encyclopedia of Hunters and Gatherers,* 220–224. Cambridge, Cambridge University Press.

Kusimba, S. B. (2005) What is a hunter-gatherer? Variation in the archaeological record of eastern and southern Africa. *Journal of Archaeological Research* 13, 337–366.

Lane, P. J. (2014) Hunter-gatherer-fishers, ethnoarchaeology, and analogical reasoning. In V. Cummings, P. Jordan & M. Zvelebil (eds) *The Oxford Handbook of the Archaeology and Anthropology of Hunter-Gatherers,* 104–150. Oxford, Oxford University Press.

Lewis, J. (2000) *The Batwa Pygmies of the Great Lakes Region.* London, Minority Rights Group International 209.

Lyman, R. L. & O'Brien, M. J. (2001) The direct historical approach, analogical reasoning, and theory in Americanist archaeology. *Journal of Archaeological Method and Theory* 8, 303–342.

Mabulla, A. (2007) Hunting and foraging in the Eyasi Basin, northern Tanzania: past, present and future prospects. *African Archaeological Review* 24, 15–33.

Marlowe, F. W. (2002) Why the Hadza are Still Hunter-Gatherers. In S. Kent (ed.), *Ethnicity, Hunter-Gatherers, and the 'Other': Association or Assimilation in Africa,* 247–275. Washington DC, Smithsonian Institution Press.

Marlowe, F. W. (2010) *The Hadza: Hunter-Gatherers of Tanzania*. Berkley, University of California Press.

McCall, G. S. & Widerquist, K. (2015) The evolution of equality: rethinking variability and egalitarianism among modern forager societies. *Ethnoarchaeology* 7, 21–44.

Mutundu, K. 1999 *Ethnohistoric Archaeology of the Mukogodo in North-Central Kenya*. British Archaeological Report S775/Cambridge Monographs in African Archaeology 47. Oxford, Archaeopress.

Newman, J. L. (1970) *The Ecological Basis for Subsistence Change among the Sandawe of Tanzania*. Washington DC, National Academy of Sciences.

Newman, J. L. (1991/1992) Reconfiguring the Sandawe puzzle. *Sprache und Geschichte in Afrika* 12/13, 159–170.

Pluciennik, M. (2004) The meaning of 'hunter-gatherers' and modes of subsistence: a comparative historical perspective. In A. Barnard (ed.), *Hunter-Gatherers in History, Archaeology and Anthropology*, 17–29. Oxford, Berg.

Prentiss, W. C. & Kuijt, I. (eds) (2004) *Complex Hunter Gatherers: Evolution and Organization of Prehistoric Communities Plateau of Northwestern North America*. Salt Lake City, University of Utah Press.

Sassaman, K. E. (2004) Complex hunter-gatherers in evolution and history: a North American perspective. *Journal of Archaeological Research* 12, 227–280.

Shelley, C. (1999) Multiple analogies in archaeology. *Philosophy of Science* 66, 579–605.

Stiles, D. (1981) Hunters of the northern East African coast: origins and historical processes. *Africa* 51, 848–862.

Stiles, D. (1982) A history of the hunting peoples of the northern East Africa coast: ecological and socio-economic considerations. *Paideuma* 165–174.

ten Raa, E. (1969) Sandawe prehistory and the vernacular tradition. *Azania* 4, 91–103.

Walsh, M. (1990) The Degere: forgotten hunter-gatherers of the East African coast. *Cambridge Anthropologist* 14, 68–81.

Widlok, T. (2015) Moving between camps: towards an integrative approach to forager mobility. *Hunter Gatherer Research* 1, 473–494.

Woodburn, J. (1968) An introduction to Hadza ecology. In R. B. Lee & I. DeVore (eds) *Man the Hunter*, 49–55. Chicago, Aldine.

Woodburn, J. (1970). *Hunters and Gatherers: The Material Culture of the Nomadic Hadza*. London, British Museum Press.

Wylie, A. (1985) The reaction against analogy. *Advances in Archaeological Method and Theory* 8, 63–111.

Zwanenburg, R. M. van (1976) Dorobo hunting and gathering: a way of life or a mode of production? *African Economic History* 2, 12–21.